Introduction to
STEEL SHIPBUILDING

ELIJAH BAKER III

Estimator and Surveyor, Newport News Shipbuilding and Dry Dock Company; formerly Professor of Naval Architecture, University of Virginia Newport News Extension Division; Member of Society of Naval Architects and Marine Engineers

SECOND EDITION

McGRAW-HILL BOOK COMPANY

NEW YORK   ST. LOUIS   SAN FRANCISCO   LONDON
TORONTO   SYDNEY   MEXICO   PANAMA

Introduction to
STEEL SHIPBUILDING

PREFACE

This introduction to steel shipbuilding was prepared as a text-book for the shipbuilding classes of the Apprentice School of the Newport News Shipbuilding and Dry Dock Company. The course in shipbuilding at the Apprentice School is designed to give the student an understanding of the ship as a whole, to enable him to understand the relationship of the many shipyard trades to the finished vessel, and to form a basis for his future understanding of the marine industry.

The book stemmed from a series of mimeographed sheets which were distributed to the students for study. After the student studied the material, it was discussed in class, and a written examination was given. From the results of the discussion and the examination, the course content, phraseology, and method of presentation were modified and then tried on the next group. This continued over a period of three years, at the end of which time the entire course was reviewed to determine the following: Was the student receiving the fullest benefit from the time expended, did the manuscript cover the subject matter necessary to prepare the student, or was the subject matter too extensive for our objective, and, finally, was there room for further simplification? It was felt that our objectives had been attained, and it was then decided to put the entire course in print and make it available to the public.

The style is one that may be understood easily by the student with a high school education or the equivalent and may be studied with benefit by those who are not high school graduates.

The mathematical treatment has been reduced to simple arithmetic, except in Chapter XVI where trigonometry is used to explain stability and Chapter XXII where powers and roots are used to explain propeller design. Sufficient background in trigonometry, and powers and roots have been presented at the beginning of each of these chapters to enable the student who has never studied either subject, or who needs a memory refresher, to follow the reasoning. No attempt is made to treat every subject in the chapter outline in an exhaustive manner, since this would require thousands of pages and defeat the purpose of the text. However, each topic is developed to a degree sufficient to explain its relationship to the general subject of shipbuilding. As illustrations of this simplification, the subject of strength of materials is treated in the short span of 26 pages and propeller design in 18 pages. The drawings used throughout the text have been simplified to bare outline sketches. Teaching experience has shown that even the simplest drawings may appear complicated to the student. Therefore, numerous details have been omitted from the drawings to permit the important parts to stand out clearly. To clarify further the relation of the worded descriptions to the drawings, lettered photographs have been used extensively to correlate subject and explanation in the student's mind.

The reception given the first edition far exceeded expectations, as the book was adopted by many apprentice schools, training schools, and colleges and, in addition, the personal purchase by members of shipping concerns, by port engineers, captains, and ships' personnel and others proved gratifying. Very soon after publication, requests were received asking that this book be carried further, or that a new book be written, covering resistance and the powering and propulsion of vessels in the same style and manner as the hull work was covered. After much thought, it was decided that this be undertaken and the same method of clarification of material, that is by trial and error on the students, was begun. After a period of two years, the course content and presentation looked promising and while this additional material may at first appear complicated, the results obtained in classroom work proved satisfactory.

It was found in reviewing the first edition, which was printed in 1943, that the tremendous shipbuilding effort during the war years and the great technological strides in design and technique made since rendered much of the material in the first edition obsolete.

Therefore, it became necessary to rewrite and rephrase over seventy-five per cent of the original wording and make new sketches and photographs of present-day practices.

It is hoped that this second edition will prove useful to ship-builders, ship operators, shippers, ships' personnel, and others who strive for a better basic understanding of sea transportation and its vehicle, the steel ship.

ELIJAH BAKER III

Newport News, Virginia
June, 1953

ACKNOWLEDGMENTS

To the hundreds of students in the Apprentice School of the Newport News Shipbuilding and Dry Dock Company, and the Newport News Extension Division, University of Virginia, who have studied parts or all of this course. Their valuable suggestions and criticisms and the results of their examination papers have been the guiding beacon in the preparation of this book.

To George C. Mason, former Instructor of Apprentices, Hull Drawing Room, who wrote the chapter on "Lines" and aided in the revision of several other chapters. To G. Guy Via, formerly Director of Training, for valuable suggestions as to course content and his careful readings of, and corrections to, the manuscript of the second edition. To John J. Carvil, Instructor in Mechanical Drawing, who previously taught this course for six years, for his suggestions and aid in preparing the index and definitions. To S. A. Vincent, Naval Architect, and John P. Comstock, Assistant Naval Architect, for reading and checking the manuscript and for their many helpful comments. To Mr. John F. Watson, Chief, and other former colleagues of the Hull Technical Division, for their helpful information and aid. To Mr. R. B. Hopkins, Advertising and Publicity Director for the Shipyard; Mr. John S. Lockhead, Librarian, The Mariners Museum; Mr. J. P. Griffith, formerly Photographer, and Mr. B. J. Nixion, Photographer, Newport News Shipbuilding and Dry Dock Company, for the numerous photographs. To Mr. J. D. Smith, formerly Apprentice Instructor, Hull Drawing Room, and Mr. R. A. Dery of the Hull Drawing Room, for preparing with their apprentices all reused and new drawings. To Messrs. Merril Sawyer, J. M. Harrell, and Robert McAmis for preparing the drawings for the first edition. To Mr. W. E. Blewett, Jr., Executive Vice-President, Newport News Shipbuilding and Dry Dock Company, for his permission to publish the material in this text. To Professor Laurens Troost for permission to publish material as noted on powering. To the Goldschmidt Corporation, the Chemical Publishing Company, the Simmons-Boardman Publishing Corporation, and the United States Navy for permission to publish material as noted herein. To Mr. E. F. Hewins, Engineering Technical Division, for writing the chapter on Propeller Design and for checking other chapters on propulsion. To Mr. Harry F. Benford, Assistant Professor of Naval Architecture, University of Michigan, who has used this book for his introductory classes for several years, for checking the manuscript, furnishing valuable material, and making many suggestions on course content. To Mr. Charles W. Spooner,

Associate Professor of Marine Engineering, University of Michigan, for his comments on the chapters on powering and propulsion.   To the staff of the United States Merchant Marine Academy, Kings Point, New York for their many helpful suggestions.   To the many men in the yard who have contributed their ideas and time in formulating much of the material used herein. To Mr. Fairmont R. White, Director of Education, Apprentice School, Newport News Shipbuilding and Dry Dock Company, for suggestion as to contents and presentation.   To the Research Committee of the Newport News Shipbuilding and Dry Dock Company, for reading and checking the manuscript and releasing this material for publication.

                                                ELIJAH BAKER III

Newport News, Virginia
June, 1953

CONTENTS

TO THE STUDENT

Although this textbook is written mainly for the apprentice ship-builder, it is of such a nature that it can be understood readily by those who have other major interests but who also have a desire to learn about ships. It is intended for no particular shipyard trade. Rather, its purpose is to give the apprentices of all trades a *basic understanding of the product they are helping to create.*

Full recognition is taken of the fact that shipbuilding is made up of many trades and that the products of these trades, properly placed in their relation to one another, make up the floating structure known as a ship.

A possible criticism is that the discussion of the ship fitter's art is too extensive. The ship fitter directs the assembly of the steel and his trade is discussed at some length, *but only to give all trades an insight into the make-up of the completed ship.*

Any knowledge that will help the apprentice shipbuilder understand the reasoning behind the construction of the finished product is considered desirable, regardless of the trade he may be mastering.

In order to accomplish our objective, many factors have had to be considered, namely:

1. The new student will probably know nothing about ship-building.

2. The new student will have only a high-school knowledge c/ mathematics, and therefore a complete mathematical treatment of certain phases of our subject is not desirable.

3. The text should be practical rather than theoretical. Enough theory must be presented, however, to explain the practical applications and prevent the course from becoming one of the "dictionary-memory" type.

4. The text should begin in a simple manner and increase in difficulty as it progresses.

5. The content of the course should cover not only the regular "practical shipbuilding" subjects but other subjects, such as launching, stability, powering, propulsion, and propeller design, that will be of interest and use to the student in his later work.

6. The text must be teachable and interesting. These two qualities are correlated and as a consequence are treated together. An effort is made to treat the subject as one that is alive and growing. In many cases, reference has been made to past practice, but only that present practice may better be explained.

7. Riveted as well as welded construction must be considered because riveting as a method of fastening steel together has by no means died out. Also, as a riveted ship usually goes together piece by piece, and a welded ship in large subassemblies, the riveted ship is extremely valuable as a teaching aid because it is easier for the student to visualize the purposes of the component parts and their sequence. This is one major reason that riveted as well as welded construction is presented in this text. Furthermore, riveted ships already built will be plying the seas for a number of years, and these must be repaired and serviced.

With due consideration of the above factors, the text is arranged in the following manner:

A list of symbols and abbreviations used in the text is presented first.

Chapter I is the key chapter. It explains strength of materials in a manner adequate to an understanding of the chapters that follow. Little can be accomplished without a thorough knowledge of this chapter. Furthermore, every trade in a shipyard uses the principles of strength of materials discussed here. Chapter I is therefore of particular importance and should be thoroughly mastered by the student.

Chapters II and III discuss the materials used and the methods of joining them.

Chapters IV to XII describe the parts of a ship by groups and discuss and explain their purpose, using the principles set forth in Chap. I.

Chapters XIII to XVIII border on the field of naval architecture but treat these naval-architectural subjects from the viewpoint of the man in the yard rather than from the viewpoint of the technician.

Chapters XIX through XXI treat of the powering of the vessel and methods of transmitting this power so that the vessel may move.

Chapter XXII presents a simplified method of propeller design based on the latest accepted data. Sufficient mathematics is presented in the chapter to permit the average student to follow the reasoning.

Chapter XXIII describes the trials a ship must pass successfully, and by using the actual trial-trip data taken on the trials of the *S.S. America* as an example, the student is taken on the trial trip. The trial trip of the *S.S. United States* is used to present the Raydist timing device.

Chapter XXIV, the final chapter, is a discussion of Maritime Administration vessels and some of the newer vessels built since the Second World War. This chapter has been added to give the student a chance to compare the characteristics of many of the newer vessels and to obtain an idea of ship production cost. To accomplish the above aim, tables of characteristics and sketched inboard profiles are presented of the more popular vessels constructed during and after the Second World War. A table of costs and selling prices of the more popular vessels is also presented.

There are numerous textbooks on naval architecture, marine engineering, shipfitting, strength of materials, and mechanics which will elaborate on the subjects introduced and correlated in this book.

A list of definitions of shipbuilding terms is presented at the back of the book. These definitions are intended to acquaint the student with general shipyard words and to act as an introduction to the shipbuilder's "language." No attempt is made to cover the expressions that will be used in normal shop practice. The student will acquire the language of his shop as he acquires skill in his particular trade. An inboard profile of a C-2 Cargo vessel with the various parts numbered to correspond to the definition numbers is presented to clarify some of the more difficult definitions.

As the student increases in knowledge, it is hoped that he will be inspired to continue his studies in the higher branches of shipbuilding. In order to aid the student in choosing worth-while books, a list of advanced books with a brief description of their content is given at the end of the volume.

"The Shipbuilder" by John Ruskin (1819–1900) may serve as an inspirational message to the young shipbuilder.

Take it all in all, a ship of the line is the most honorable thing that man, as a gregarious animal, has ever produced. Into that he has put as much of his human patience, common sense, forethought, experimental philosophy, self-control, habits of order and obedience, thoroughly wrought handiwork, defiance of brute elements, careless courage, careful patriotism, and calm expectation of the judgment of God, as can be put into a space 300 feet long and 40 feet broad.

ABBREVIATIONS

A Area of water plane, or of a stressed section

a Pitch ratio

A.B.S. American Bureau of Shipping

AP After perpendicular

B Breadth or beam of ship, or center of buoyancy with ship erect

B' Center of buoyancy, ship inclined

BL Base line

BM Distance from B to M (metacentric radius)

B.M. Bending moment

BP Between perpendiculars

CB Center of buoyancy

CF Center of flotation (CG of water plane)

CG Center of gravity

CL Center line

CI Common interval

D Depth of ship

d Draft of ship; diameter of propeller

Δ (delta) Displacement of ship in tons of 2,240 lb.

DAR Developed area ratio

EHP Effective horsepower

e Propeller efficiency

FP Forward perpendicular

F.S. Factor of safety

G Center of gravity

GM Distance from G to M, or metacentric height

GZ Righting lever

I Moment of inertia of ship's water plane

i Moment of inertia of free surface within ship

K Keel, intersection of center line and base line

KB Distance from K to B, or VCB

KG Distance from K to G, or VCG

xix

KM Distance from K to M

L Length of ship

l Linear ratio

LBP Length between perpendiculars

LOA Length over all

LWL Length on water line or load water line

LCB Longitudinal center of buoyancy

LCF Longitudinal center of flotation (LCG of water plane)

LGM Longitudinal GM, or longitudinal metacentric height

LI Longitudinal interval

L.R. Lloyd's Register

M Metacenter

N Any number

NA Neutral axis

p Pitch of propeller

R Resistance

R_f Resistance, frictional

R_m Resistance, model

R_r Resistance, residual

R_t Resistance, total

RPM Revolutions per minute

SHP Shaft horsepower

SM Simpson's multipliers

S_s Average shear stress

T_a Average tensile stress

T Thrust

t Thrust deduction

V Volume of ship's displacement; ship's speed in knots

V_a Speed of advance of propeller

v Volume of tank

VCB Vertical center of buoyancy

VCG Vertical center of gravity

W Weight

w Wake fraction

WL Water line

WS Wetted surface

Introduction to
STEEL SHIPBUILDING

FIG. 1. *S.S. Old Dominion Mariner* on trial off the Virginia Capes.

CHAPTER I

STRENGTH OF MATERIALS

The majority of the steel items that go into the construction of a steel vessel can be divided into four general groups known as *beams*, *plates*, *columns*, and *shafts*. Each group has its own particular function to perform; in addition, it may also function as a part of and in coordination with any of the other three groups.

As an illustration of this coordination of functions, in a longitudinal-strength calculation we consider that the hull of a vessel acts as a gigantic but rather unusual box-type compound beam or girder made up of thousands of smaller parts, all acting as a unit to give strength to the ship as a whole. Basing the hull-girder strength calculation on this assumption, we proceed to support this compound girder first on a standard trochoidal wave[1] with the crests at the ends of the vessel (Fig. 2) and then on the same type of wave with the crest amidships (Fig. 4). Knowing the type of support and the loads that are to be supported, we can calculate the stresses set up within the girder. Our problem then becomes one of constructing the hull girder in such a manner that it has sufficient strength to resist these stresses. Figures 2 and 4 illustrate the type of support, and Figs. 3 and 5 show the probable method of failure that results from overstressing the vessel when it is supported as indicated.

When we have determined the stresses that the vessel and its parts must withstand when acting as a beam, we can determine the scantlings, or sizes, of the various component parts—beams, plating,

---

[1] The standard trochoidal wave is one whose length from crest to crest is equal to the length of the ship and whose height is one-twentieth of its length. Such a wave is called *trochoidal* because it has the shape of a *trochoid*—the curve described by a point on a wheel that is rolling forward on a flat surface.

1

pillars, etc.—that make up the vessel. The component parts that act with the hull beam, or girder, also must withstand certain local stresses due to concentrated weights such as masts and turbines. These localized weights are compensated for individually by simply making the affected parts of sufficient scantling, or size, to withstand the heavy loads that will be placed on them.

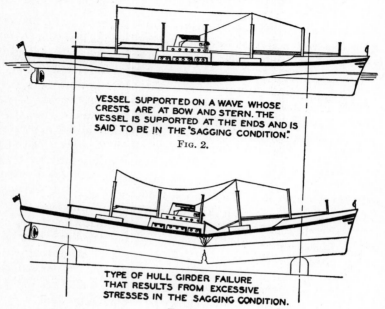

VESSEL SUPPORTED ON A WAVE WHOSE CRESTS ARE AT BOW AND STERN. THE VESSEL IS SUPPORTED AT THE ENDS AND IS SAID TO BE IN THE "SAGGING CONDITION."

FIG. 2.

TYPE OF HULL GIRDER FAILURE THAT RESULTS FROM EXCESSIVE STRESSES IN THE SAGGING CONDITION.

FIG. 3.

The erroneous idea should not be conceived from the above that *a ship's hull is only a beam*, for a ship's hull experiences many stresses that a simple beam never encounters. While we can calculate very simply the required size of beam to carry a certain load in a building, it is much more difficult to apply these calculations to a "beam" that is to drive through heavy seas, rapidly accelerating downward as it pitches along a wave slope, only to have its direction changed and be thrown violently upward by the succeeding wave, and at the same time rolling from side to side, receiving terrific blows from the sea, and being stressed further by internal vibration from its own propulsion machinery and propellers.

To understand completely the structural design of a ship subjected to such complex and often unknown forces would require the use of higher mathematics and an extensive study of strength of materials. We cannot hope to cover this broad field in this text. We can, however, study some of the simpler and more apparent

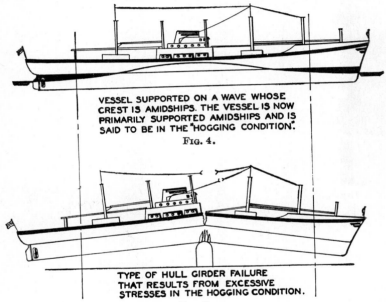

VESSEL SUPPORTED ON A WAVE WHOSE CREST IS AMIDSHIPS. THE VESSEL IS NOW PRIMARILY SUPPORTED AMIDSHIPS AND IS SAID TO BE IN THE "HOGGING CONDITION".

FIG. 4.

TYPE OF HULL GIRDER FAILURE THAT RESULTS FROM EXCESSIVE STRESSES IN THE HOGGING CONDITION.

FIG. 5.

aspects of strength of materials and, by using these as a basis, proceed to discuss intelligently the structure of a ship.

Before we can begin our elementary study, we must become familiar with a few of the terms used in all structural work. The student is strongly advised to familiarize himself thoroughly with these definitions.

Load is the total force acting on a structure and is usually expressed in pounds or tons.

Stress is the force per unit area and is usually expressed in pounds or tons to the square inch.

Strain is the distortion resulting from stress.

There are three types of simple stress as follows:

1. Tensile Stress.   This occurs between two parts of a body when each draws the other toward itself.   Tensile stress can perhaps

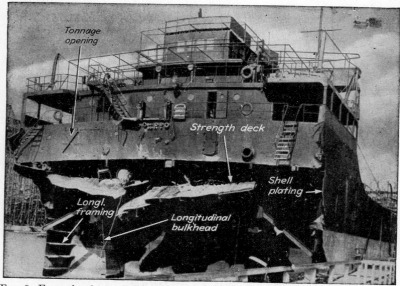

Fig. 6.   Example of a typical hull-girder failure: bow section of the *S.S. E. H. Blum.* The break started in the upper deck and worked downward, tearing the shell, the twin bulkheads, and the supporting longitudinal frames and stiffeners.   The stern of this vessel was later rewelded to the bow and the vessel went back into service.

be best illustrated by means of a tie rod subjected to a steady pull. Assume that the tie rod in Fig. 7 is subjected to a pull of P lb and that its area through section y-y is A sq in.   Then the average tensile stress T_s per square inch would be given by the formula

$$T_s = \frac{\text{pull}}{\text{area}} = \frac{P}{A}$$

Using an actual case as an illustration, let us assume that the rod was supporting a load of 20 tons[1] and the area through y-y is 4 sq in.

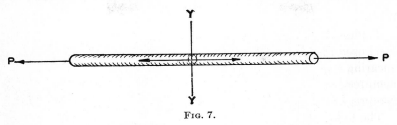

FIG. 7.

Substituting in the formula

$$T_s = \frac{P}{A} = \frac{20 \text{ tons}}{4 \text{ sq in.}} = 5 \text{ tons per sq in.}$$

2. Compressive Stress. This is the reverse of the above. The same formula holds.

$$\text{Compressive stress} = \frac{\text{compressive load}}{\text{area}}$$

3. Shearing Stress. The tendency of one part of a body to slide over another part is known as *shear*. The magnitude of this tendency to slide at any point is termed the *shearing stress* at that point. Consider two pieces of plate tied together with a rivet.

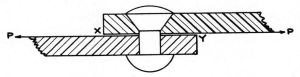

FIG. 8. A rivet in single shear.

If the total shear across the rivet in Fig. 8 at the line x-y is P tons, then the average shearing stress per square inch would be

$$S_s = \frac{\text{pull}}{\text{area of rivet shank}} = \frac{P}{A}$$

[1] All shipbuilding tons are tons of 2,240 lb.

Assume that we have a pull on the plates of 5 tons and that the diameter of the rivet is 1 in. The area of the rivet would be equal to $\pi r^2 = 3.14 \times (0.5 \text{ in.})^2 = 0.785$ sq in. Then

$$\text{Shearing stress} = \frac{5 \text{ tons}}{0.785 \text{ sq in.}} = 6.4 \text{ tons per sq in.}$$

The ultimate tensile strength of mild steel, which is the principal steel used in shipbuilding, is 28 to 32 tons per sq in. The ultimate shearing strength is lower, being only about 22 tons per sq in. No compressive strength is given here, as steel simply flattens out when compressed (at about 18 tons per sq in.).

The following figures may be taken as averages:

	Tons per sq in.
Ultimate tension	30
Ultimate shear	22

Such values are based on the assumption that the material is broken. This is really of little value because the ship's structure should be strong enough to remain unbroken and unimpaired in strength after receiving any stresses that it may have to undergo. The following method is employed to determine how much we can stress a material without distorting it permanently.

DETERMINING THE STRENGTH OF STEEL

A small specimen of the material is placed in a testing machine such as that shown in Fig. 9. The specimen is then pulled by the machine, and a conveniently placed dial shows the amount of tensional load in pounds or tons applied at any one time.

If progressive readings are taken of the amount of tension put on the test piece and at the same time measurements are made of the amount of the corresponding stretch or strain, a set of points will be obtained that can be plotted on a sheet of graph paper. If a curve is drawn through these points, it will look somewhat like Fig. 11 and is known as a *stress-strain diagram.*

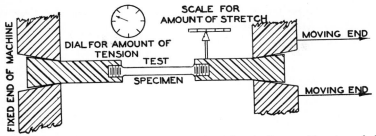

FIG. 9. Diagrammatic sketch of a test specimen in a testing machine, turned side-wise for ease in lettering.

FIG. 10. A testing machine in operation. The test piece being pulled is in the upper left corner. The dials indicate total load and strain.

A study of this curve will answer numerous questions.   Note in the drawing that the strain or amount of stretch up to point *A* is directly proportional to the pull or force applied.   This is indicated by the fact that the line is straight between zero and point *A*.   So up to point *A* we can say that the material follows Hooke's law[1] directly.   If the test specimen is stretched or loaded to any point below *A*, it will contract to its original length when the load is removed.[2]   If the specimen is stretched beyond the point *A*, it will

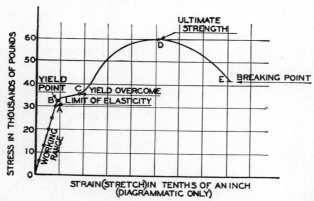

FIG. 11. A typical stress-strain diagram for mild steel.   In this diagram the machine has pacing disks, so no drop-off is noted.

no longer contract to its original length upon removal of the load, and the distortion then becomes a *permanent set*.   Loads that do not stretch the material beyond point *A*, called the *limit of elasticity*, are said to be within the *working range*, for the material is not damaged by the load.   All structures are designed so that stresses resulting from the assumed loads are well within this working range.   If the material is loaded until it stretches beyond point *A*, the material will suddenly yield at point *B* even with little further increase in load and will continue to stretch until it reaches the length indicated by

[1] Hooke's law states that the stretch of an elastic material up to the elastic limit is directly proportional to the stress; that is, if we double the weight attached to the bottom of a spring, we double the elongation of the spring.

[2] See any text on testing materials for further discussion.

point C, where the yield is overcome owing to some hardening in the metal. If the load is further increased slightly, the metal will stretch out of all proportion to the load applied and will continue to elongate past the ultimate strength at point D and fail at the breaking point E. This operation is known as *testing the material to destruction*.

Curves such as these have been plotted for almost every kind of metal and metallic alloy, and therefore we can easily check the strength of any material with which we may have to work. Good structural design becomes then a matter of keeping the stress resulting from the expected loading well within the working range. An attempt is made to do this by means of a factor of safety.

FACTOR OF SAFETY

In order to keep the expected stresses well within the working range and below the yield point of our material, we use what is commonly called a *factor of safety* (F.S.). When we begin to design a structure, we first attempt to determine as accurately as possible the loads that the structure will have to bear. To make the structure just strong enough to carry this calculated load would be extremely dangerous, for it is entirely possible that, owing to some unforeseen circumstance, the structure will be called on to carry two or three times the load anticipated. Furthermore, the structure may rust and corrode, it may become damaged by impact, the workmanship may be poor, or the material may not be up to its standard strength.

In order to allow for these unknown factors, we usually make the structure four times as strong as it need be; *i.e.*, we use a factor of safety of 4, based on the ultimate strength of the material we are using. It would be more sensible to base our safety factor on the yield point rather than the ultimate strength, for the structure would be completely out of shape by the time the ultimate strength was developed by the material. As the yield point for steel is roughly half the ultimate strength, *we are in reality using only a factor of* 2.

It should be noted here that the tie rod shown in Fig. 7 has a tensile stress of 5 tons per sq in.   On page 6, the ultimate tensile stress for mild steel is given as 30 tons per sq in.   The factor of safety for the tie rod based on the ultimate is then

$$F.S. = \frac{30 \text{ tons per sq in.}}{5 \text{ tons per sq in.}} = 6$$

This is more than ample; the size of the tie rod, therefore, could be reduced.

For the rivet shown in Fig. 8 the shear across the shank of the rivet works out to be 6.4 tons per sq in.   The ultimate for mild steel in shear, as given on page 6, is 22 tons per sq in.   Therefore,

$$F.S. = \frac{22 \text{ tons per sq in.}}{6.4 \text{ tons per sq in.}} = 3.44$$

Since this is less than 4, the size of the rivet should be increased.

It is suggested that the student calculate the size of rivet required to give a safety factor of 4 or better in the above case.

STRENGTH OF SHIPS

There are two broad phases of strength.   They are *local strength*, relating to the strength of the individual parts of the ship, and the *hull-girder strength* mentioned previously, relating to the strength of the ship as a whole.

In practice, we must make a weight calculation before we can make the hull-girder calculation, and in order to determine the weight we must first determine the scantlings, or sizes, of the individual members that, taken together, make up the vessel.

CLASSIFICATION SOCIETIES

Actually, for merchant vessels of average length, scantlings (sizes) for most of the parts such as beams, stiffeners, and shell plating are not determined by strength calculations but are regulated by the rules of the classification society that will classify and certify the construction of the vessel.

All maritime nations have their own classification societies that check the strength and seaworthiness of the various merchant ships applying for insurance.   This certified inspection protects the insurance company that actually insures the vessel from great losses, thereby reducing the premiums on maritime insurance. Any vessel can be insured even if it is not built to the rules of a classification society, but the insurance rate will be so high that operation of the vessel may become unprofitable. Also, a vessel not classified may have a very low resale value, for the prospective buyer would be taking a large risk in purchasing an unclassified ship.

In the United States this inspection, protective, and classifying agency is the American Bureau of Shipping; in England, Lloyd's Register; in France, Bureau Véritas; in Italy, Registrano Italiano; and in Germany, Germanischer Lloyd. It should be noted that none of these inspection groups issues insurance or insures a vessel. The insurance is handled by regular insuring individuals or agencies which take the risks based on the findings and reports of these inspection groups. Quite often, a vessel of large size will have twenty or more insurers dividing the total insurance on the vessel. On the other hand, some large corporations take their own risks but keep their vessels in class primarily because it is good business, particularly if they ever expect to sell them.

The rules regulating the construction of ships are fairly fluid; therefore, at intervals a new book of rules is issued. The American Bureau's book of rules costs about $5 and becomes obsolete with the succeeding issue.

These rules apply to most merchant vessels up to 700 ft in length. However, there are numerous scantlings not covered by the rules that must be calculated individually by using the principles of strength of materials.

NAVAL DESIGN

In the design of naval vessels, we have no set of rules as in the design of merchant vessels. This is because of the great and rapid changes that are continually taking place in naval warfare. It would be useless and unprofitable to limit the designers of naval vessels by making them adhere to a detailed set of rules. As a consequence, the warship designer has a more difficult problem than the designer of a merchant vessel, but a more interesting one, for it leaves greater scope for his ideas, inventiveness, and initiative.

The size of every part of a naval vessel must be calculated individually; and as the parts are interdependent, due regard must be taken of all surrounding members in order to harmonize the general construction.

Before we can see how the sizes of these parts are calculated, we must discuss some of the principles of strength of materials. Since the bending moment generally determines the size of a beam, we shall consider this first.

BENDING MOMENTS

A moment of a force about any line is the product of the force times the perpendicular distance to that line.

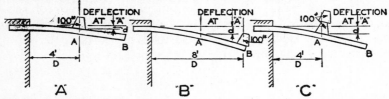

Fig. 12. Bending moments produced by a concentrated load on a cantilever beam.

Figure 12 shows a board built into a wall at one end and loaded by a weight, which produces a force acting downward. The wall is the line of support. In *A* the weight is halfway out on the board, and in *B* all the way out, the weight in both cases remaining unchanged.

It will be noted that, when the weight is on the outer end of the board, the board has more deflection than when the weight is halfway out. This is because of the increased bending moment due to the greater distance of the weight from the point of support, or, mathematically,

$$B.M. = weight \times distance = W \times D$$

In *A*

$$B.M. = 100 \text{ lb} \times 4 \text{ ft} = 400 \text{ ft-lb}$$

In *B*

$$B.M. = 100 \text{ lb} \times 8 \text{ ft} = 800 \text{ ft-lb}$$

At the support, the bending moment (B.M.) illustrated in *B* is twice the bending moment in *A*, and therefore the stress on the board at the support is also twice as great. The bending moment can also be doubled by keeping the distance from the support constant and doubling the weight.

In *C* we have placed another 100-lb weight on top of the original one. The bending moment then becomes

$$\text{B.M.} = 200 \text{ lb} \times 4 \text{ ft} = 800 \text{ ft-lb}$$

We can say, then, that, if we double the distance from the point of support or if we double the weight keeping the distance constant, we double the bending moment.

This is an important rule and should be noted carefully by the student because *the bending moment, rather than the weight supported, determines in large measure the size of the various parts of a vessel.*

If we have a clear picture of these simple bending moments in mind, we can proceed with a discussion of beams.

BEAMS OF RECTANGULAR SECTION[1]

Horizontal strength members loaded vertically are usually referred to as *beams.* Such a member is shown in Fig. 13. As this

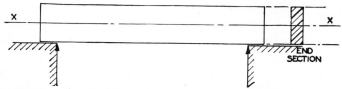

FIG. 13. Side elevation of a rectangular free-ended beam lying across two supports.

beam is of a homogeneous material and rectangular, it is symmetrical about the line drawn through the beam at mid-depth, designated in the figure as the *x-x* axis.

In Fig. 14 we have applied a load directly at the center of the beam and the beam has deflected a certain amount, exaggerated in

[1] All beams discussed in this chapter are considered, for simplicity, to be rectangular in cross section. See any strength-of-materials text for a discussion of beams of other shapes.

the figure for the sake of clarity. This deflection, or bending, caused the upper surface of the beam to shorten and the lower surface to lengthen. This is quite obvious, because the ends of the beam are no longer parallel to each other but are coincident with the radius of the concentric circle, the arc of which is described by the upper and lower surface of the beam. (Actually, a beam loaded at its center does not assume the shape of the arc of a circle; however, for simplicity the arc shape is assumed.)

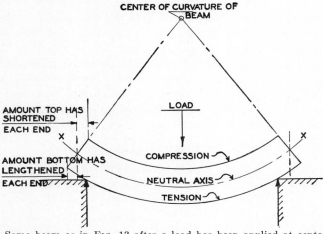

FIG. 14. Same beam as in FIG. 13 after a load has been applied at center (exaggerated).

As the upper section of the beam has been shortened, it must have been compressed, or, in technical language, it is *in compression*. The lower section has been lengthened, and we say that it is *in tension*. As compression and tension are opposite forces, there must be a layer within the beam where these forces become zero and change direction. This layer is found to lie along the locus of the center of gravity of the section, which in our case will be along the *x-x* axis. Note that this refers, not always to the center of the beam, but rather to the *center of gravity* of the beam section. (Lately, *centroid* of cross section has been substituted for *center of gravity* of cross section. For our discussion, either will suffice.)

This line of zero stress can be understood better if we regard the stresses acting within the beam. Consider the beam shown in Fig. 15 as made up of several superposed unconnected layers. When such a beam is loaded and bends, the ends of the various layers remain parallel to each other, each layer simply slipping upon the other so that the ends are no longer in line. In order to create the same internal stress in the beam of Fig. 15 as that created in the beam of Fig. 14, the two upper layers, 1 and 2, would have to be

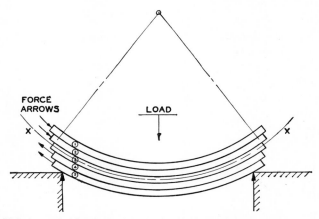

FIG. 15. This beam is identical with the beam shown in FIG. 14 except that it is made of five layers that are free to slide over each other; however, this beam will support only one-fifth as much weight as the beam shown in FIG. 14.

pushed lengthwise and the two lower layers, 4 and 5, pulled lengthwise until they become flush with layer 3. Layer 3 does not require any change. This layer lies along the center of gravity of the beam cross sections and is known as the *neutral layer*. A line along the center of this layer is known as the *neutral axis*, since it is neither in tension nor in compression; *i.e.*, it was neither lengthened nor shortened during the process of bending.

If we wished to keep all the layers in line during bending, we should have to apply some external force in line with the ends of the layers or else glue the layers together before bending (the effect would be the same, for the glue would assume the longitudinal stress).   The external forces required to shorten the upper layers and to lengthen the lower layers are indicated by arrows in the figure.   The direction in which the external force would have to be applied is indicated by the head of the arrow.   By glancing at this figure, we see that it requires more force to bring layer 1 into line than to bring layer 2 into line.   This brings out the important fact that the greater the distance between any particular layer and the neutral axis, the greater the stress on that individual layer.   It also illustrates how the depth of a solid beam controls its resistance to bending, for the farther the layers from the neutral axis, the greater the tension or compression they must assume.   Our original beam (Fig. 14) is of one solid section, *i.e.*, the layers cannot slide over one another, and in this case the force bending the beam must be of equal intensity to the tension and compression set up within the beam.

EFFECT OF DEPTH

The strength of a rectangular beam varies as the square of its depth. Let us compare mathematically the strength of a 2 by 4 set on edge and a 2 by 8 set on edge.   Using the above rule for rectangular beams, call d_1 the depth of the smaller and d_2 the depth of the larger; then

$$\text{Relative strength} = \left(\frac{d_2}{d_1}\right)^2 = \left(\frac{8}{4}\right)^2 = 4$$

That is, the 2 by 8 will support *four* times as much load as the 2 by 4 rectangular beam.   If this reasoning is applied to the five-layered beam shown in Fig. 15, each layer is only $(\frac{1}{5})^2$, or $\frac{1}{25}$, as strong as a solid beam five times the depth of one of the layers, and all layers taken together would be only $\frac{1}{5}$ as strong as a solid beam of the same depth.

All beams, regardless of their shape, may be conceived to be composed of an infinite number of these very thin horizontal layers. When we apply a load to the beam, one surface goes into compression and the other into tension because the infinitely thin layers are restrained from sliding over each other by the web of the beam.

This web is the only thing that resists the longitudinal shearing stress set up in the beam. The layer at the center of gravity, or neutral axis of the beam, is, of course, neither in tension nor in compression, but in shear.

As the tensile and compressive stresses in a beam are very low in the portion along the neutral axis and very high in the portion farthest away from the neutral axis, it is advantageous to move the material from the neutral axis and concentrate it in the flanges.

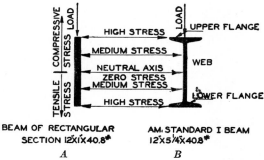

BEAM OF RECTANGULAR SECTION 12"x1"x40.8#

AM. STANDARD I BEAM 12"x5¼"x40.8#

A   B

FIG. 16. Comparison of two beam sections of equal sectional area. Longitudinal shear stress is ignored.

This makes a stronger beam with the same weight or a lighter beam with the same strength. The two beams shown in Fig. 16 have the same depth and same weight; yet beam *B* will carry 84 per cent more load than beam *A*, an effect due entirely to moving the material away from the area of low tensile and compressive stresses (the web) and concentrating this moved material in the area of high stress (the flanges), thus reducing the stress per unit area and strengthening the beam. The flanges also serve to stiffen the beam.

FACTORS AFFECTING THE SIZE OF A BEAM OF RECTANGULAR SECTION

There are five basic factors that affect the size of a beam: (1) the type and amount of load on the beam, (2) the distance between supports, (3) the type and efficiency of end connections, (4) the number of supports, and (5) the material from which the beam is made. We shall discuss the first four of these in order and in a somewhat elementary manner.

1. The Load on a Beam. Beams are loaded in various ways. We shall consider only two, namely, a concentrated load at center and a uniformly distributed load.

a. Concentrated Load. When a beam lying over two supports is loaded as shown in Fig. 17, we say it has a *concentrated load*. The loading shown produces the greatest bending moment at the center of the beam, for the weight is at the maximum distance from

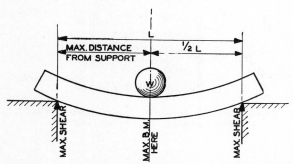

Fɪɢ. 17. A free-ended beam supporting a concentrated load at center.

the points of support, the bending moment in this case being B.M. = $WL/4$; for example, if the weight is 2 tons and the length 10 ft, we should have

$$\text{B.M.} = \frac{2 \text{ tons} \times 10 \text{ ft}}{4} = 5 \text{ ft-tons}$$

where W = total load.

L = distance between supports.

b. Uniformly Distributed Load. A beam with a uniformly distributed load is shown in Fig. 18. This type of loading is uniform along the beam; therefore, certain portions of the load are nearer the points of support than others. These portions, when totaled, produce a smaller bending moment than in the case of the concentrated load. The maximum bending moment for a uniform load is at the center and is given by

$$\text{B.M.} = \frac{WL}{8}$$

Using the same load and distance between supports as in the previous example, we should obtain

$$\text{B.M.} = \frac{2 \text{ tons} \times 10 \text{ ft}}{8} = 2.5 \text{ ft-tons}$$

This is exactly half the bending moment produced by the concentrated load. Other types of loading produce bending moments of different magnitudes.

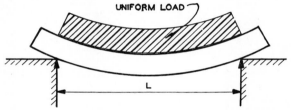

UNIFORM LOAD

L

Fig. 18. A free-ended beam supporting a uniformly distributed load.

The bending, or deflection, of a rectangular beam varies as the bending moment, and the bending moment depends on the load and type of loading. This fact is evident from the formulas above; for when we double the load, we double the bending moment, which also doubles the deflection.

Summarizing, we can say that *in the design of a beam due consideration must be taken of the type as well as the amount of the load.*

2. The Distance between Supports. The distance between supports is usually referred to as the *span*. The span is one of the factors that govern the strength and the deflection of a beam. It affects the beam in two ways.

a. The deflection of a rectangular free-ended beam varies as the cube of the span. Say that the rectangular beam *A* (Fig. 19) supports a certain load over a 10-ft span. On this span the measured deflection is found to be 1 in. How much deflection would the same beam have if the span was increased to 20 ft?   (Assume no change in load.)   Let S_1 = short span; let S_2 = longer span; then

$$\text{Relative deflection} = \left(\frac{S_2}{S_1}\right)^3 = \left(\frac{20 \text{ ft}}{10 \text{ ft}}\right)^3 = 2^3 = 8$$

Deflection on the longer span = 1 in. × 8 = 8 in.

b. The strength of a rectangular free-ended beam varies inversely as the span.   Beam B (Fig. 19) will support only half the load of beam

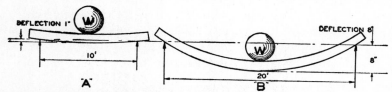

FIG. 19. The deflection of a rectangular free-ended beam varies as the cube of the span; the strength varies inversely as the span.

A, for the span is twice as great.   To illustrate this mathematically, assume that beam *A* will support 10 tons; then

$$\text{Relative strength} = \frac{\text{span } A}{\text{span } B} = \frac{10 \text{ ft}}{20 \text{ ft}} = 0.5$$

and the load that beam *B* will support would be

$$10 \text{ tons} \times 0.5 = 5 \text{ tons}$$

In order to keep our beam sizes and deflections to a minimum, we increase the number of supports, thereby reducing the span.

3. Fixity of the End Connections.   In our previous discussion we have assumed that the beam simply was lying across two end supports and that the ends were free to take the same curvature as the beam.   Now if the ends of the beam are set in concrete, they will be rigidly held.   A beam of this type is shown in Fig. 20.

When the ends of a beam are fixed, the conditions heretofore discussed will be considerably altered.   It will be noted that while the middle section of the beam is curved like a free-ended beam, the ends built into the concrete have taken an opposite curvature.

Fixing the ends of a rectangular beam produces two helpful results.

1. A fixed-ended rectangular beam will support twice as much concentrated load as a free-ended rectangular beam.

2. The deflection of a fixed-ended rectangular beam is only one-fourth as great as the deflection of a free-ended rectangular beam.

As an illustration of the two rules above, compare the relative strength and deflection of beam *B* (Fig. 19) when free-ended and

Fᴵɢ. 20. A fixed-ended rectangular beam with a concentrated load at center.

fixed-ended.   Let us assume that

Free-ended maximum load = 10 tons
Free-ended maximum deflection = 8 in.

Then from (1) the maximum load with the ends fixed would be

$$2 \times 10 \text{ tons} = 20 \text{ tons}$$

and from (2) the maximum deflection with the ends fixed would be

$$\tfrac{1}{4} \times 8 \text{ in.} = 2 \text{ in.}$$

It is very difficult to get complete fixity in the ends of beams in a ship owing to the flexibility of the structure.   However, we can approach a fixity of between 50 and 80 per cent by the use of deep beam brackets and by making the beam continuous over its supports.

Most of the loads on the beams in a ship are uniform, and most of the beams in a ship are partially fixed.   Therefore, it is interesting to note that a fixed-ended beam with uniform load distribution has twice the bending moment at the fixed ends that it has at the middle. If it fails, the fracture will take place at the ends.   This is the reason why brackets are required at the supports of continuous beams.

4. The Effect of the Number of Supports.   When we have a beam with equal spans and symmetrical loading passing over one or more supports, the beam acts as a fixed-ended beam over the support.

In Fig. 21, span *B* is tending to fix span *A* and span *C*. Therefore, over the supports the beam acts as a partially fixed-ended beam, *and failure would take place at that point.*

The greater the number of supports in a given distance, the shorter the span and, as we have already seen, the smaller the bend-

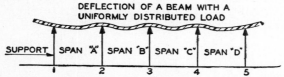

FIG. 21. A beam with a uniform load lying over five supports.

ing moment produced.   This would permit a reduction in the size of the beam.

STEEL SHIPBUILDING PLATES

Flat sheets of steel over $\frac{3}{16}$ in. thick and 48 in. wide or $\frac{1}{4}$ in. thick and 6 in. wide are usually referred to as *plates*.   They are used primarily for the sides, bottom, bulkheads, and decks to make a watertight covering or, in the case of lower decks, to make working

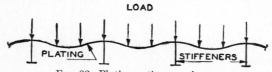

FIG. 22. Plating acting as a beam.

platforms.   When plating is acting to carry a load to its supporting *frames* or *stiffeners* (see Fig. 22), it acts as a series of thin wide beams between the stiffeners.   As explained above, the closer the stiffener spacing, the thinner can the plate be made.

There is, however, a point at which we must cease adding stiffeners in order to reduce plate thickness, for the saving in plating weight, due to the thinner plate, becomes less than the added weight of the stiffeners.   As weight must be kept to a minimum for maximum cargo-carrying ability and speed and as steel is sold by the pound, we must be very careful in our design to see that the ratio of stiffener spacing to plate weight is such that we get the required strength with the least weight. Shell- bulkhead-, and deck-plating design are all based partly on the above principles, as we shall see when we discuss them in detail. Steel plates are also used as webs and flanges in built-up beams and columns.

COLUMNS

When two portions of a ship are so loaded that they tend to come together, we usually insert a prop or a strut between them

ELEVATION   ELEVATION

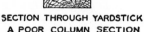

SECTION THROUGH YARDSTICK   SECTION THROUGH DOWEL
A POOR COLUMN SECTION   A GOOD COLUMN SECTION

Fig. 23.

to keep them apart. On a ship, this load ordinarily tends to act vertically, and therefore the prop generally is placed vertically under the load. Such a prop is known among shipbuilders sometimes as a *column* but more often as a *stanchion* or *pillar*.

Just as a beam has the least strength when supported with the thin dimension at right angles to the load, a stanchion likewise is weakest the thin way. As a stanchion is free to bend in any direction, it would naturally bend in its weakest direction. This calls for stanchions to be made from symmetrical sections, the best of which would be circular.

As illustrations of a poor stanchion section and a good one, we can use the typical yardstick and a dowel (Fig. 23), both having the same cross-sectional area. The dowel will support much more weight than the yardstick without collapsing, for it would have no greater tendency to buckle in one direction than in any other direction because it is uniformly strong throughout.

The length-diameter ratio of a ship stanchion is usually small compared with that of an architectural column, and since this ratio is the controlling factor in bending, we very seldom attempt to fix completely the ends of a ship stanchion.

SHAFTS

A shaft subjected to a twisting moment is said to be *in torsion*. This twisting moment is usually called *torque*. A torque will set up a shearing force all along the shaft, as can be illustrated by holding a cigarette firmly at one end and twisting the other.

In addition to torque, a shaft also may be subjected to bending moments. This increases the stress considerably; in the case of propeller shafts, great care must be taken to see that they are in nearly perfect alignment, which reduces the bending moment to a minimum.

The torque in a rotating shaft is given by the following formula:

$$\text{Torque (in lb-ft)} = \frac{\text{horsepower} \times 5{,}252}{\text{rpm}}$$

It can be seen from the above formula that the higher the revolutions per minute (rpm) for a given shaft the less the torque; as a result of this, we can use a smaller shaft for the higher rpm. This explains why a 5,000-hp 80-rpm engine will require a shaft of about the same size as a 20,000-hp 320-rpm engine.

The numerous rotating shafts on a vessel conform to this same principle.

CONTINUITY OF STRENGTH

Since the main forces on the hull of a ship generally vary in a gradual and continuous manner, it follows that the change in the hull strength should be gradual and continuous. No part should be oversized for the load it will have to carry; and, of course, none should be undersized. *Furthermore, any sudden discontinuity or change of shape will cause a concentration of stress at the point of change that may lead to failure of the structure.* Ignoring this fundamental point caused a great loss of ships, material, and men during the Second World War.

This last phenomenon can be illustrated by the simple sketch in Fig. 25, which shows a piece of steel in tension. The fine lines indicate *by their closeness* the intensity of the tensile stress in the piece of steel at any one point, due to the tensile force exerted. It

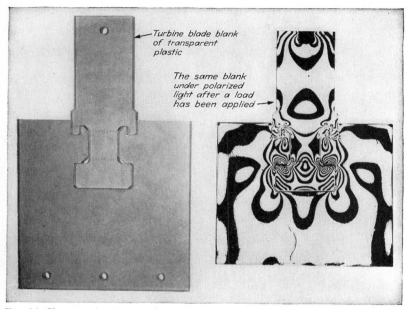

Fig. 24. Unstressed and stressed model of a root of a turbine blade taken through a polarizing lens.

The model is made of plastic and is placed in a machine which exerts tension on the model. By looking at the model through a polarizing lens, or taking a photograph, the lines of stress are shown. As in Fig. 25, which is a sketch only, the greater the stress, the closer the lines. In actual practice, the color of the lines, which does not show in this black and white photo, is also an indication of the stress characteristics. This photo illustrates the point that the greatest stress occurs at the point of abrupt changes of contour.

will be noted that in *A* the lines are parallel, which indicates that the stress intensity is uniform throughout the plate.

In *B* we have welded on the top of the original plate another similar plate of double the width. It might appear, on first thought, that we have considerably strengthened the plate. We now reapply the same load. The stress flow is indicated as before by the fine lines. It will be noted that the stress concentration, shown by the closeness of the lines of stress, has increased at the points *a* and *b* owing to these lines' sweeping out from the smaller plate into the larger plate. If of sufficient intensity, this will cause cracks to start at the corners. These cracks will become progressively larger, causing still greater concentration and finally failure of the plate. The extra material that has been added has actually decreased the strength, entirely because of *the stress concentration that has taken place at the sharp corners.*

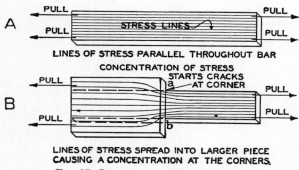

Fig. 25. Stress concentration at corners.

In way of hatches, at the ends of decks that are not continuous, at the ends of deckhouses, and at numerous other points in the structure of a vessel, we find sudden changes in area of metal that may impair the continuity of strength. In Chap. XI we shall discuss in greater detail how we attempt to curb the ill effects of these discontinuities.

Questions and Problems

1. A steel flat bar 4 by 1 in. is subjected to a pull of 20 tons. Calculate the stress. *Ans.* 5 tons per sq in.

2. What is the factor of safety in the above problem? *Ans.* 6.

3. A rivet with a cross-sectional area of 2 sq in. is subjected to a shearing load of 12 tons. Calculate the stress. *Ans.* 6 tons per sq in.

4. Calculate the factor of safety in Prob. 3. If the factor of safety is less than 4, calculate the area of rivet shank required to give a factor of safety of 4. *Ans.* F.S. = 3.66.   Area required = 2.18 sq in.

5. A 2,000 lb weight is supported by a cantilever beam fixed in a concrete wall. The distance from the wall to the weight is 13 ft. Calculate the bending moment at the support. *Ans.* 26,000 ft-lb.

6. If a 2- by 1-in. rectangular beam will barely support 500 lb, how much weight would a similar beam 4 by 1 in. support? Likewise, what would a similar beam 8 by 1 in. support?
Ans. 4-in. beam = 2,000 lb. 8-in. beam = 8,000 lb.

7. A beam lying over two supports has a span of 20 ft. A concentrated load of 3 tons is placed in the center of the beam. Calculate the bending moment produced. *Ans.* 15 ft-tons.

8. A uniformly distributed load of 5 tons is on a beam freely supported between two supports. The span length is 15 ft. A concentrated load of 3 tons is placed on top of the uniform load at the center of the beam. Calculate the combined bending moment. *Ans.* 20.625 ft-tons.

9. A beam with a 3-ton load on a span of 10 ft has a deflection of 2 in. The span is increased to 30 ft. Calculate the deflection. *Ans.* 54 in.

10. A beam on a 20-ft span will barely carry a load of 20 tons. If the span is reduced to 10 ft, what load will the beam carry? *Ans.* 40 tons.

11. If the beam of Prob. 9 with the 30-ft span and 54-in. deflection has the ends completely fixed, calculate the resulting deflection. *Ans.* 13.5 in.

12. If a free-ended beam will carry a load of 10 tons over a certain span, what load will a similar fixed-ended beam carry? *Ans.* 20 tons.

13. Calculate the twisting moment, or torque, in a shaft produced by (*a*) a 30,000-hp turbine at 3,000 rpm and (*b*) a 3,000-hp turbine at 300 rpm.

14. What is meant by a hull-girder failure?

15. What is the difference between weight and load?

16. Define unit stress.

17. What is the average working stress for mild steel in tension?

18. Why is a factor of safety used in engineering calculations?

19. Sketch and label a stress-strain diagram.

20. What relation does the yield point bear to the ultimate tensile strength of mild steel?

21. What is the purpose of a classification society?

22. What is a bending moment?

23. Sketch a simply supported free-ended beam lying across two supports. Indicate and label the neutral axis and the extreme fiber.

24. Why is an I beam stronger than a rectangular beam of the same weight and depth?

25. Why does a concentrated load produce a greater bending moment than a uniform load?

26. What is meant by fixity?

24. Why does an I beam make a poor column?

28. Why is strength continuity important in structural design?

CHAPTER II

MATERIALS USED IN SHIPBUILDING

In the past the hull structure of ships has been made of wood, wrought iron, steel, and concrete. Wood was the first shipbuilding material because the supply was abundant and it was easy to work. There is a limit to the size of a ship that can be constructed from wood, chiefly because of our inability to tie the joints together successfully; as a consequence, the maximum length of such ships has been around 300 ft. Wooden vessels in the 200-ft class have been known to hog, or sag, in a seaway as much as 3 or 4 ft. This caused the seams to work, and dangerous leaks developed as a result. Furthermore, wood is not uniform in strength, is subject to attacks by dry rot, insects, and marine worms (teredos), is combustible, and is heavier than steel of equal strength.

WROUGHT IRON

The first metal to be used in ship construction was wrought iron. The development of the Bessemer and open-hearth (Siemens-Martin) processes of making steel caused the discontinuance of the use of wrought iron, for steel became cheaper and was stronger than wrought iron. It should be noted that wrought iron is strongly resistant to corrosion and that wrought-iron hulls 60 years old are in use today.

STEEL

Mild steel, the type used to the greatest extent in ships, is practically uniform in strength, can be easily worked into shape, and, since the advent of welding, can be joined together with connections developing the full strength of the steel. The main disadvantage of steel is its lack of resistance to corrosion. Careful painting and maintenance tend to overcome this difficulty to a certain extent.

Corrosion-resisting steel (CRS) sometimes is used in parts subjected to excessive corrosive action, but at present its high cost prevents more extensive use.

FIG. 26. Forging the propeller shaft. A 30,000-lb ingot under the 1,200-ton hydraulic press. The ingot was heated to white heat in the furnace at left. The long bar at left, called the porter bar, balances the weight of the ingot. The ingot is rotated by means of the chain which is attached at the center of gravity of the combined bar and ingot.

Armor. Heavy armor steel of the Krupp type is made by a special process whereby the face of the plate is made very hard while the inside remains somewhat soft but exceedingly tough. This steel answers the requirements of armor, for the hard face breaks the head and the tough inner portion absorbs the energy of the projectile, thus reducing penetration.

Special-treatment Steel.   Special-treatment steel (STS) is special-quality nickel-steel alloy.   It has excellent ballistic properties and is used for protective decks and light side armor.   Shields protecting ships' personnel from shell and bomb splinters are also made of STS.

High-tensile Steel.   High-tensile steel (HTS) is now used to a great extent in the main strength members of high-speed warships and large ocean liners.   Its increased tensile strength over mild steel is gained by a reduction in carbon and an increase in manga-

Fig. 27.   Apprentices making wooden patterns.   These wooden patterns will be placed in special casting sand.   After the sand has set, the pattern is removed and molten metal poured into the cavity, thus forming the casting.

nese content.   HTS is roughly about 25 per cent stronger in tension than mild steel.

Forgings.   Forgings are made by heating steel to a white heat and then beating it into the required shape by means of a hammer or press (Fig. 26).   Having great strength and toughness, forgings are used, in general, where these qualities are required.   With the rapid advances made in the techniques of pouring satisfactory steel castings, forgings have been used less and less in shipyards.   They are now used principally for rudderstocks, crankshafts, and propeller shafts because, at present, they are cheaper and tougher than castings.   Certain smaller fittings are still forged by the drop-forging process, *i.e.*, by a single stroke of a steam hammer and the use of forming dies.

Castings. In the manufacture of a casting, a wooden pattern is first made to the exact shape and dimensions of the required finished casting, plus a small allowance for shrinkage and machining. This pattern is placed in special damp casting sand, which forms a shell around it. The pattern is later removed, and molten steel is poured into the hole thus left. Steel castings are quite numerous on a ship and may include the stern frame, stem, stern tubes, rudder frame, propeller struts, spectacle frames, skegs, machinery bed-

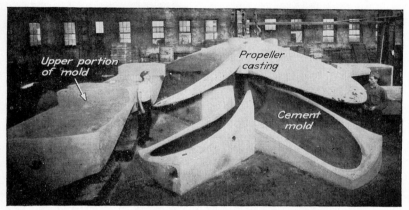

FIG. 28. A propeller casting. The completed propeller casting is being removed from the cement mold. This casting will now be machined and ground to finished dimensions.

plates, anchors, hawsepipes, chain pipes, pipe flanges, and various small hull fittings. Different grades of steel are used, depending on the class of casting that is required. Many other castings are made of brass or similar compositions.

CONCRETE

During both World Wars, a number of ships were built of reinforced concrete (see Fig. 29). The tensile strength was provided by steel rods placed within the concrete. These ships were excessively heavy and were easily injured locally. As a consequence, operation of concrete ships was never commercially successful.

FIG. 29. Photograph of the *S.S. James Aspdin*, a concrete vessel. (See page 31 for particulars.)

PLATES

Plates are sheets of steel rolled to a uniform thickness of ¼ in. or more. Plates less than ¼ in. thick are generally called *sheets*, and their thicknesses are given in gauges. All plate widths are given in inches. The maximum widths for plates to be riveted that can be conveniently handled by most yards are about as follows:

$$
\begin{array}{ll}
\text{8 to 10.2 lb} \ldots \ldots \ldots & \text{75 in. maximum} \\
& \text{63 in. preferable} \\
\text{11 to 15.3 lb} \ldots \ldots \ldots & \text{87 in. maximum} \\
& \text{75 in. preferable} \\
\text{16 to 20.4 lb} \ldots \ldots \ldots & \text{96 in. maximum} \\
& \text{84 in. preferable} \\
\text{Over 20.4 lb} \ldots \ldots \ldots & \text{Up to 110 in.}
\end{array}
$$

The last width is the maximum that can be punched in the average shipyard. The width of plates to be welded *is not limited* by the capacity of yard equipment such as punches and countersinkers.

The inner bottom, bulkheads, deck, shell, trunks, coaming, floors, brackets, girders, built-up sections, and many other structural members are made of plate.

Weights of Plating. The weight of a cubic foot of steel is approximately 490 lb. A plate 1 in. thick weighs, therefore, 40.8 lb per sq ft (see Fig. 30). Plates are specified by weight per square foot. A 20.4-lb plate means one $\frac{1}{2}$ in. in thickness, and a 10.2-lb plate means one $\frac{1}{4}$ in. in thickness. For convenience, the decimal fraction in

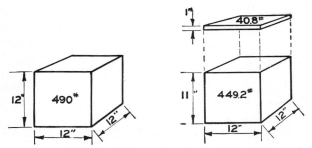

Fig. 30. One square foot of steel 1 in. thick weighs 40.8 lb.

the plate weight is usually dropped. Thus, a 20-lb plate usually refers to one $\frac{1}{2}$ in. thick.

Styles of Plating. The two principal styles of plate used are *plain plates* for work generally throughout the structure, and *checkered nonskid plates* in the machinery spaces and for some decks and platforms. During fabrication, a plate may be drilled, punched, flanged, sheared, planed, beveled, rolled, furnaced, scarfed, countersunk, knuckled, and joggled (see Shipbuilding Definitions).

Plates fall into three classes in regard to curvature. *Flat plates* form the largest portion of the ship's plating, *i.e.*, plates that have little or no curvature and do not have to be bent. *Rolled plates* are those which have a cylindrical curvature in one direction only and which can be shaped while cold. They are usually found at the turn of the bilge in the middle body. Plates having curvature in two directions are heated and hammered out to the required shape;

these are called *furnaced plates*.   If the student will take a sheet of paper, which will represent a steel plate, bend it in any direction to a curve, and while holding this first curve bend it at right angles to the first bend, the paper will crumple and become unfair.   This effect could not be tolerated in a ship's hull plating and is the reason why some plates have to be furnaced (Fig. 81).

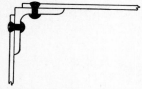

FIG. 31. Riveted corner attachment.

SHAPES

Rolled bars of constant cross section are called *shapes*.   They are usually made of mild steel but may be made of high-tensile steel, aluminum, or almost any other metal that can be passed through the rolls.

1. Plain Angle.   *Plain angles* are used for frames, beams, and hold stringers and, in riveted work, for joining together two pieces of metal that meet approximately at right angles (Fig. 31).

A plain angle and its parts are shown in Fig. 32, sketch 1. Sketch 2 shows a typical riveted attachment of an angle used as a

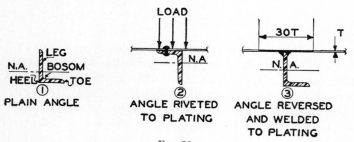

FIG. 32.

plating stiffener.   If the load is as shown, great stress would come on the angle at its toe.   As there is very little material in the toe to resist the stresses set up by the load, this stiffening method is very poor.   Note also that the position of the neutral axis *NA* is close to the bosom of the angle, which also indicates an increase in the stress at the toe.

Sketch 3 shows an *inverted angle* welded to the same plating.   We usually assume that 30 thicknesses[1] of plating act as a top flange for the angle; and we have then, in effect, a channel section.   This gives a fairly symmetrical, or balanced, section that has great strength for its weight.   The method of attachment shown in sketch 3 is over three times as strong as that shown in sketch 2.   With the welded section, we could use an angle of roughly half the size and get the same strength.   This is one illustration of weight saving due to welding.

When the two legs, or flanges, make an angle that is not 90 deg, the angle bar is said to be *beveled* (Fig. 33).   If it is more than

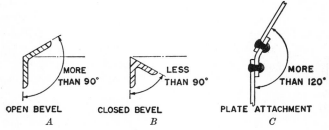

Fig. 33.   Bevels and plate attachment.

90 deg, it is called an *open bevel;* if less than 90 deg, a *closed bevel.* A shut, or closed, bevel is objectionable in several ways.   The beveling work is very difficult; for even when it is done with care, the heel of the bar is seldom in precisely the same plane as the flange, and so when riveted to the shell the contact is imperfect unless the projecting part is removed.   Also, as one flange closes over the other, it may be difficult to punch the rivet holes and to hammer up the rivets.   It is then obvious why all angles should have an obtuse-angle, or open, bevel.   One hundred and twenty degrees is the maximum bevel allowed in an angle.   If more is required, a bent plate is used for the attachment (Fig. 33, sketch *C*).

[1] This is the United States Navy assumption for sections up to 10 in. depth. Sixty thicknesses are permissible on sections deeper than 10 in.   The above assumptions are conservative when compared with actual tests.

2. Bulb Angle.   The *bulb angle* is simply a development of the plain angle in which a small bulb of material has been added to the toe of the angle at the point of highest stress.   This makes the bulb angle considerably stronger than the plain angle when riveted attachments are used (see Fig. 34).

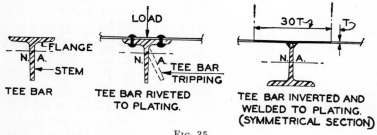

BULB ANGLE   BULB ANGLE SHOWING METHOD OF ATTACHMENT TO PLATING.

Fɪɢ. 34.

Bulb angles are used only in riveted construction.   They were used for frame bars, stringers, bulkhead stiffeners, deck beams, keelsons, etc., but with the advance of welding in shipbuilding their usefulness is rapidly decreasing.

TEE BAR   TEE BAR RIVETED TO PLATING.   TEE BAR INVERTED AND WELDED TO PLATING. (SYMMETRICAL SECTION)

Fɪɢ. 35.

3. T Bar.   A *T bar* (Fig. 35) may be thought of as an angle one leg of which has been centered on the other.   In riveted construction it is used in order to obtain a more symmetrical section and a better connection, for it allows an extra row of rivets to be driven. As a symmetrical section will not fall over or trip as easily as an unsymmetrical one, it is a better section than an angle.   It suffers, however, from the same fault as the angle when riveted to plating as a stiffener, namely, lack of material in the outer fibers.   When used in welded construction, it is inverted and becomes, in combination with 30 thicknesses of plating, a strong and rigid stiffener somewhat akin to an I beam.

4. T Bulb Bar. The *T bulb bar* (Fig. 36) was developed to correct the fault in the T bar, namely, the lack of material in the outer highly stressed fibers. In this case, material was simply added in the form of a bulb at the bottom of the stem.

FIG. 36.

T bulb bars were used primarily for bulkhead stiffeners and deck beams in riveted work, but they are now practically obsolete. They are not used in welded construction.

5. Channel. A rolled shape having two parallel flanges on the same side of the web and at right angles to it is called a *channel*

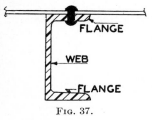

FIG. 37.

(Fig. 37). Channels are very useful for side frames, deck beams, bulkhead stiffeners, and pillars; but as they are not truly symmetrical sections, they have a tendency to trip, or fold over, under load. They are used extensively in riveted shipwork, for the upper flange gives a good rivet connection and the lower highly loaded flange has plentiful material concentration.

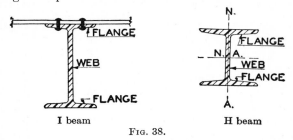

I beam   H beam

FIG. 38.

6. I and H Beams. A rolled shape having a cross section like the letter I is known as an *I beam* (Fig. 38). An I beam may be considered to be a channel with its web centered. This is a truly symmetrical section and for this reason is excellent for deck beams and girders.

When the flanges of an I beam are as wide as the web, it is called an *H beam* and is used extensively as a column or pillar in way of the engine and boiler spaces.   It is not a good section to use as a pillar in the way of cargo holds, for the sharp edges may damage the cargo.

7. Cut Sections.   The use of welding as a connection now permits cutting one flange from a number of shapes previously used intact and thus obtaining lighter sections with no loss in stiffness.   This is due to the fact that the plating to which the stiffener is welded acts in place of the removed flange (Fig. 40).   It is usual to assume that 30 thicknesses of plating act in conjunction with the attached section.

Assume that we have a 4- by 4- by ½-in. angle welded to a piece of ¼-in. plating (see Fig. 39).   The area of a cross section through

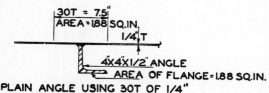

PLAIN ANGLE USING 30T OF 1/4"
PLATING AS THE UPPER FLANGE.

Fig. 39.

this angle is 3.75 sq in.; therefore, the area of the lower flange as welded will be approximately

$$\frac{3.75 \text{ sq in.}}{2} = 1.88 \text{ sq in.}$$

We may now use any number of thicknesses of plating up to 30 in order to make up enough area to balance the lower flange.   In our case it would take, with ¼-in. plating,

$$T \times X = 1.88 \text{ sq in.}$$
$$X = \frac{1.88}{0.25}$$
$$X = 7.52 \text{ sq in. required}$$

Thirty thicknesses of ¼-in. plating = 30 × 0.25 = 7.5 in. of plating, and, as we are within our 30-thickness limit, we can assume that we have a balanced section somewhat similar to a channel but with one flange centered on the web.

8. Built-up Sections. Sections built up entirely of welded plates are now used extensively for both merchant and naval hulls. While they are more expensive than the rolled section, they can be made so that the maximum material will be at the point of greatest

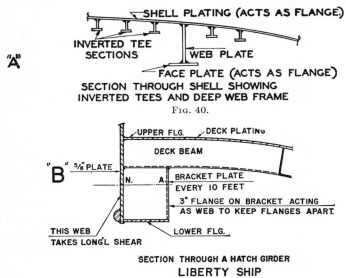

SECTION THROUGH SHELL SHOWING
INVERTED TEES AND DEEP WEB FRAME
Fig. 40.

SECTION THROUGH A HATCH GIRDER
LIBERTY SHIP
Fig. 41.

expected stresses, thus saving weight. Figures 40 and 41 illustrate two of these applications. Many other applications will be noted throughout the text.

OTHER MATERIALS

Other materials used in shipbuilding, but not to the extent of the previously listed material, include the following:

Ferrous Metals and Alloys

1. *Galvanized Iron (Galv.).* Ordinary mild steel dipped in molten zinc. Used extensively by the Navy and, to a lesser extent,

in merchant work to combat corrosion. Expensive to weld owing to poisonous fumes. (Ungalvanized steel is commonly called "black iron" to distinguish it from galvanized iron.)

2. *Corrosion-resisting Steel (CRS).* A variety of stainless steel. Expensive but nearly impossible to burn.

3. *High Elasticity Steel (H.E.S.).* Proposed substitute for mild steel or H.T.S.

	Lb per sq in.
Ultimate stress	72,500
Yield point	50,000

Resistance to corrosion is about twice as high as mild steel.

Nonferrous Metals and Alloys

1. *Bronze.* Used in propellers and miscellaneous cast fittings. Weighs about 550 lb per cu ft.

2. *Brass.* Used in decorative fittings, low-pressure valves, and airport frames. Plated with chromium, it is commonly used for plumbing fixtures. Weighs 527 lb per cu ft.

3. *Copper.* Used in low-pressure piping (deck steam lines in particular), as tubing in evaporators and condensers, and occasionally, as structural material in nonmagnetic areas around the compass. Weighs 550 lb per cu ft.

4. *Lead.* Used as waterproof lining under insulated holds and sometimes in pipes. Weighs 687 lb per cu ft.

5. *Zinc.* Used extensively as electrolytic protection around bronze propellers, in Scotch boilers, condensers, and occasionally, on bilge keels. Known as galvanizing, when coated on other materials. Weighs 449 lb per cu ft.

6. *Monel Metal.* Nickel-copper alloy used in turbine blades, galley dresser tops, sinks, and other places requiring resistance to corrosion or staining. Weighs 551 lb per cu ft.

7. *White Metal.* A lead, tin, antimony, and copper alloy. Used in plumbing fixtures and other miscellaneous castings. Similar to Babbitt metal.

8. *Aluminum.* Used in decorative handrails, machinery castings, and as a structural material to some extent. Its lightness is

somewhat offset by present-day inability to weld it without destroying the heat-treating properties which are necessary for its use in shipbuilding. The entire superstructure of the *S.S. United States* is constructed of aluminum. This aluminum is attached by aluminum special-alloy rivets. In order to drive these alloy rivets satisfactorily, the temperature of the rivets was reduced below freezing by placing them in dry ice in an ordinary ice-cream freezer. The rivets were first dipped in alcohol to prevent condensation from collecting on the cold rivets. When aluminum is used in conjunction with steel, the joints between the two must be insulated from each other to prevent electrolytic action. The alloys used in shipbuilding have a tensile strength of about 42,000 lb per sq in., a yield point of 35,000 lb per sq in., a weight of 129 lb per cu ft, and are highly resistant to corrosion. Present cost is high.

Joiner Material

1. *Wood.* The principal uses of various kinds of wood together with their approximate weights (per cubic foot) are presented below.

PRINCIPAL USES OF WOOD

Member	Kind of wood	Weight, lb per cu ft
Masts and booms...	Norway pine	30.0
	Dense longleaf yellow pine	39.8
Fenders...	White oak	44.3
	Dense longleaf yellow pine	39.8
Outside rails...	Teak	36.3
Grab rails...	Ash	39.8
Ceiling and sparring...	Hemlock	27.0
	Douglas fir	32.0
	Spruce	26.9
Gratings...	Ash	39.8
Insulation...	Balsa	7.5 to 12.5
	Cork	12.9
Tailshaft bearings...	Lignum vitae	78.0
Hatch boards...	Spruce or Oregon pine	26.8
Sole pieces...	Teak	36.3

2. *Wood Substitutes.* These consist largely of the fireproof panel materials which are replacing tongue-and-groove and plywood in partition bulkheads and overhead ceilings in ship accommodations. A typical example is Marinite, composed of a rather tough asbestos-type body sheathed with wood veneer, sheet aluminum, or plain pressed asbestos. Weights run from about 3 to 6 lb per sq ft, depending on the thickness.

3. *Hotel Equipment.* Includes furniture, draperies, rugs, carpets, galley outfit, dishes, silver, etc.

Deck Coverings

1. *Wood.* Used on weather decks. Teak or longleaf pine.

2. *Magnesite.* Used either as a direct wearing surface or as a smooth subsurface under linoleum. A composition applied like Portland cement but lighter and more elastic.

3. *Bitumen.* Similar to street pavement but mixed with coke for lightness. Good wearing qualities.

4. *Cement.* Used as base for ceramic tile, or in laundries and gutters.

5. *Ceramic Tile.* Frequently used in sanitary spaces. It is seldom used on bulkheads owing to its weight. Bulkheads in showers, etc., are either simply painted with a heavy enamel or covered with special waterproof cloth of some sort; however, in special cases it may be used for complete tiling.

6. *Linoleum.* Used as deck covering in crew's quarters. Can be laid directly on a flush steel deck, or, more usually, on a magnesite base. It is normally supplied in plain colors. Now almost abandoned in war vessels due to flammability.

7. *Rubber Tile.* Laid in 9-in. squares or lock joints and glued to a cement or magnesite base. Takes heavy wear and keeps its appearance since the design is carried all the way through the material. Slippery when wet.

8. *Asphalt Tile.* Similar to rubber tile but less slippery.

9. *Brick Tile.* Used in galleys. Contains abrasives and is formed with nonskid surface.

10. *Vinyl Tile.* Looks somewhat like rubber tile, but has longer lasting qualities.

Insulating Materials

1. *Wood Decks.* See above.
2. *Magnesia.* Used in blocks or mixed and applied in a dough-like cement. Used around boilers, turbine casings, steam lines, etc. Held in place with sheet iron in the case of boilers and turbines, and with canvas, spun glass, or asbestos cloth around pipes and valves.
3. *Hair Felt.* Used principally around cold-water lines to prevent sweating as well as for keeping water cool. Enclosed in a canvas jacket.
4. *Cork.* Similar in use to hair felt.
5. *Boilerbrick.* Refractory material used inside boilers to prevent tubes from overheating.
6. *Cork Paint.* Granulated cork and paint applied to steel to prevent sweating.
7. *Sound Insulation.* More properly classified as a joiner material. Usually consists of rather soft perforated joiner panels.

Protective Materials

1. *Filler Materials for Inaccessible Pockets and Corners.*
   a. *Cement.* Either plain or mixed with coke to save weight.
   b. *Pine tar and shellac.* Frequently used as armor-backing compound.
   c. *Red lead.* Pumped behind doublers, etc.
   d. *Balsa.* Used to fill hollow rudders, bilge keels, etc. Usually dipped in hot tar prior to installation.
   e. *Proprietary filling materials.* Sold by various paint and petroleum companies. Frequently used in hollow rudders and other inaccessible places.
2. *Protective Coating Materials.*
   a. *Paint*
   Primer. Red lead or zinc chromate.
   A.C. (anticorrosive). Resists rusting.

A.F. (antifouling). Generally contains copper or mercury or both.

Boottop. Special paint for area between light load line and deep load line. Must stand being alternately wet and dry.

Antigalvanic. Used around bronze wheels, also inside valves and pumps.

Topside paint. A composition which tends to keep its appearance despite salt spray and smokestack gases.

Plastic and vinyl-base bottom paints. Require sandblasting of hull in preparation. Best types sprayed on hot. Need as many as 6 coats, 6 mils in thickness.

Interior paints. Innumerable varieties. Enamels and gloss paints easiest to keep clean. Enamel paint presents greater fire hazard.

b. *Bitumastic-type coatings (asphalt or coal-tar pitch).* Applied either hot or cold, depending on variety. Used in chain lockers, sea chests, inside foundations, and other out-of-sight areas.

c. *Cement wash.* Used as a protective coating in fresh-water tanks. Better (more flexible) proprietary substitutes are available.

The student will encounter numerous other materials not mentioned here which are used exclusively by certain companies on their ships because of the personal preferences or experience of the company management. The student will do well to make a note of these materials and, as the ship ages, watch their behavior, thus obtaining firsthand knowledge of their value. It is largely by this type of observation, and by borrowing from the experience of others, that the industry progresses.

Questions and Problems

1. Give four reasons why wood makes a poor construction material for large vessels.

2. What is Krupp-type armor?

3. For what purposes is STS used?

4. Why are concrete vessels usually unsuccessful?

5. What parts of a vessel are usually forged?

6. List the three main steps in producing a casting.

7. What is the difference between a steel plate and a piece of sheet metal?

8. Give the thickness in inches of plates: (*a*) 30 lb; (*b*) 120 lb; (*c*) 5 lb; (*d*) 15 lb.

9. Why is a furnaced plate expensive?

10. Make a simple sketch and label the parts of the six shapes used to the greatest extent in the hull of a ship.

CHAPTER III

RIVETING AND WELDING

RIVETING

Although the joining of steel plates by rivets is giving way to welding, riveting is still important in ship construction. As an illustration of its continuing importance, all the seams amidships of the *S.S. United States* are riveted and the butts are welded. This riveting was done as a safety feature, because when a plate begins to tear in a completely welded structure, the fracture crosses the welding line and into the next plate, acting as if all the plating were

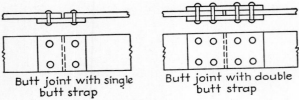

Butt joint with single   Butt joint with double
butt strap   butt strap

FIG. 42.

a solid sheet. Where the plating is discontinuous, as in the way of a riveted lap, the plate tears to the lap, and because of the discontinuity, usually stops. It is for that reason that all welded Liberty ships must have crack arresters fitted throughout the midship length (USCG regulation). The sheer strake is split by cutting a ⅛-in. wide slot for a distance of about 200 ft on each side, and a plate is riveted over the slot for the entire length. The theory here is that any crack developing would run to the slot and stop. All welded T-2 tankers are now strapped with either four or eight straps. Most newly constructed vessels have either a riveted seam or a strap for the same reason.

46

There are two standard types of riveted joint used in shipbuilding to connect plates. They are the *strap joint* (Fig. 42) and the *lap joint* (Fig. 43).

When riveted joints occur at the ends of plating, they are called *butts*. When they occur at the sides of the plating, they are called *seams*.

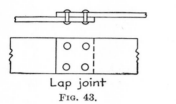

Lap joint

Fig. 43.

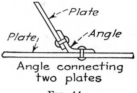

Angle connecting two plates

Fig. 44.

Where plates meet at right angles, or nearly so, they are connected by an angle or some other suitable shape, as in Fig. 44.

Figure 45 shows the connection of a riveted stiffener to a plate. The shape and size of the stiffener will depend upon the strength required.

Riveted joints usually receive all primary stresses: tension, compression, and shear (Fig. 46). Except for a slight secondary bending due to the attachments yielding under load, rivets are not subject to bending.

The amount of compression that a rivet will withstand is usually called its *bearing value,* and so compression on a rivet is usually referred to as *bearing.*

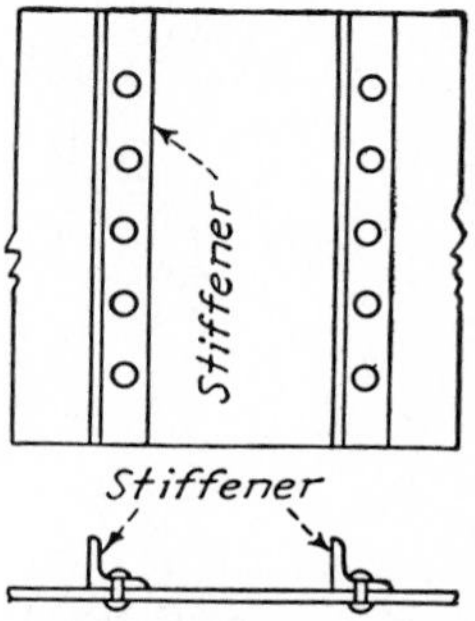

There are four methods of failure of a riveted joint (see Fig. 47).

1. *All rivets may be sheared.*

2. *The plate may tear between rivets.*

3. *The rivet may pull through the plate or the rivet may fail in tension.*

4. *Rivets may tear through plate longitudinally, owing either to insufficient bearing area or to insufficient edge distance.*

Stiffeners riveted to plate

Fig. 45.

These modes of failure may be eliminated, in general, by the following methods, each applicable to the correspondingly numbered failure:

1. Increase the size of the rivet or the number of rows of rivets.
2. Increase the distance between rivets.

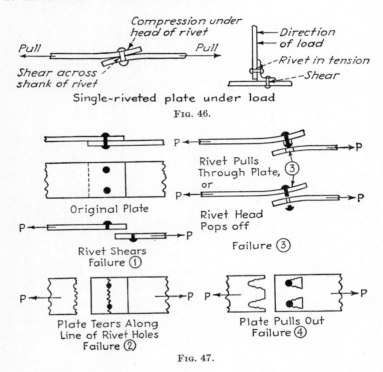

Single-riveted plate under load

Fig. 46.

Fig. 47.

3. Make the thickness of the plate and the size of the head sufficiently large so that this type of failure will not occur before the rivet fails in shear.

4. First, make the plate thick enough in proportion to the rivet diameter to make the bearing value on the rivet equal to the shear on the rivet, and, secondly, make the "edge distance" sufficient. If the distance from the center of the rivet hole to the edge of the

plate is made 1½ times the diameter of the rivet, this method of failure will be eliminated.

Fulfilling the above requirements leads us to multiple rows of rivets. Multiple-row joints sometimes fail by combining methods 1 and 2 as in Fig. 48.

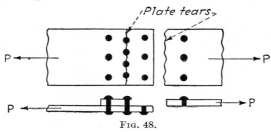

Fig. 48.

In designing a riveted joint, each possible method of failure must be calculated. The strength of the weakest divided by the strength of the solid plate is the efficiency of the joint. Maximum efficiency is not desired for riveted joints in shipwork, for the entire ship's plating is weakened to about 85 per cent (7 diameters) by riveting the shell to the frames (Fig. 49).

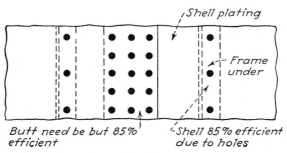

Fig. 49.

In watertight or oiltight work, the rivet spacing is limited to that spacing which will prevent bulging of the caulked edge between the rivets. This rivet spacing is in general 3½ diameters for oiltight work and 4 or 4½ diameters for watertight work.

We cannot obtain absolute tightness by close spacing of rivets. Caulking is usually required, together with close rivet spacing. If the rivets are spaced too far apart, caulking the seam will cause the plate to distort between the rivets.

The procedure used in edge and butt caulking is shown in Fig. 50. It should be noted that, if the distance between the caulked edge and the first row of rivets is greater than twice the diameter of

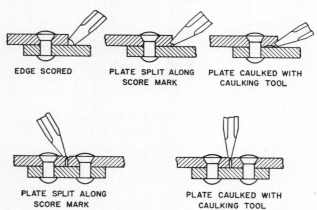

EDGE SCORED   PLATE SPLIT ALONG   PLATE CAULKED WITH
                        SCORE MARK   CAULKING TOOL

PLATE SPLIT ALONG   PLATE CAULKED WITH
   SCORE MARK   CAULKING TOOL

Fig. 50. Methods of splitting and caulking a riveted joint.

the rivets, leaks will probably develop, owing to the long span between the caulked edge and the rivets.

WELDING

Welding is the art of uniting two pieces of metal, at or near, the melting point, without using another metal having a lower melting point to make the joint. Soldering and brazing differ from welding in that they make the joint with a softer metal. A soldered or brazed joint has a strength no greater than that of the softer metal employed, but a properly designed and executed weld will equal or surpass in strength the metals joined.

If the union is made by heating the metal to or above the melting point, it is called a *fusion weld*. If the union is made by heating the metal to just below the melting point and applying pressure, it is called a *pressure weld*.

Forge Welding. The forge welding of iron and steel by hammering the parts together after heating them to a plastic condition in a blacksmith's forge has been practiced in shipyards for many years as a means of making joints in a forging. The use of welding to replace riveting as a connection between the members of a ship's structure is comparatively recent, and this sort of welding is the subject of this chapter.

Ship Welding. The welding of hulls on the shipways has been made possible by the development of welding processes for uniting metals through the application of fusing heat without compression, or hammering, and of appliances for doing this welding while the parts to be connected are in place on the structure. All these processes involve *fusion welding*.

The welding of a light structure is also done in the shipyard shops by machines using a combination of pressure with less than fusion heat. This is known as *resistance welding*.

Fusion Welding. The method of fusion welding consists essentially in depositing molten metal in a joint at a heat that is sufficiently high to fuse together the deposited metal and the adjoining pieces.

We can generate this necessary heat in any one of the following three ways.

1. By the use of an electric arc, known as *arc welding*.

2. By *gas combustion*, such as is used in oxyacetylene welding.

3. By a chemical reaction, such as *Thermit welding*.

1. *Arc Welding.* Arc welding may be subdivided into two types, *metallic arc welding* and *carbon arc welding*.

a. Metallic arc welding. In metallic arc welding, a metallic electrode is used to strike an arc at the joint to be welded in order to provide heat for welding. To do this, the operator brings the end of the electrode in contact with the metal to be welded. The electrode is then withdrawn about $\frac{1}{8}$ in. Electrons (negative electric charges) will flow across this $\frac{1}{8}$-in. space and bombard the base metal. Owing to this bombardment, the temperature of the base metal in way of the arc rises to about 2300°C (4172°F), and a crater is formed in the base metal. The electrode melts, and particles of the electrode are projected along the electron stream into the crater. This is finally filled, and the weld is thus formed. Metallic arc welding is done with either a bare metal electrode or a covered one.

Experience has shown that some refractory oxides, such as titanium and calcium oxide, will increase the electron-emission rate. Therefore, these or similar oxides are used as fluxes to coat covered electrodes.

If bare electrodes (uncovered) are used, the metallic particles on their way from the electrode to the base metal are exposed to the atmosphere. This exposure is undesirable in that the weld metal is both oxidized and nitrogenized. Oxygen converts the carbon, silicon, and manganese in the weld metal into oxides, which float to the surface as slag, thus changing the properties of the weld metal. The nitrogen is absorbed in the weld metal, making the weld brittle.

The use of covered electrodes reduces the oxidation of the alloying elements as well as the absorption of nitrogen. These results are made possible partly by the action of the flux on the electrode, but primarily by the air-excluding action of the gaseous envelope created by the burning of the electrode covering. Welds produced by covered electrodes are better in tension and have greater resistance to impact than those produced by the uncovered type.

b. Carbon arc welding. In carbon arc welding, an arc is struck with a carbon electrode, and the end of a rod of metal is placed in the arc to supply the material for the weld. Carbon arc welding is used principally in the brazing of cast iron. The disadvantages of this method of connection are overcome by the use of a brazing metal of which the tensile strength equals or exceeds the low tensile strength of the iron casting. Further strength is secured from the carbonizing effect of the arc, from which carbon is absorbed by the cast-iron base metal, thus increasing its tensile strength.

2. Gas Welding. Gas welding is the art of welding by means of a torch. In this method, heat for welding is provided by a torch through which streams of gas and oxygen are united, producing a flame of high temperature. This flame is directed at the joint to be welded, and the end of a metal rod is placed in the flame to supply material for the weld. The gases most commonly combined with oxygen in gas welding are acetylene and propane.

3. *Thermit Welding.* Thermit welding is the process of welding by means of a chemical heat produced by the combination of the elements making up what is known as *Thermit.* This is a mixture of finely divided aluminum with an oxide of iron and alloys. On being heated by a priming of magnesium powder, the aluminum combines violently with the oxygen of the metallic oxide, producing a fluid slag and great heat. Thermit welding is essentially a casting process, as a fire-clay mold must be built around the joint to confine the molten metal. The excess is chipped off after the weld has cooled.

Thermit welding is chiefly used to repair large hull forgings or castings without their removal from the ship and is usually performed while the ship is in dry dock. The phenomenon on which the process is based is also responsible for the development of the incendiary bombs used in the Second World War.

Resistance Welding. In resistance welding, the pieces to be joined are clamped together and an electric current is passed through the joint until the heat produced by the resistance of the metal makes it plastic at the weld. Pressure is then applied to bring the surfaces to be united into close contact and also to exclude air so as to prevent oxidation. This method is used principally for joining sheet metal in the shops. Resistance welding may be subdivided into three main types, *butt, spot,* and *seam.* In resistance butt welding, the pieces are brought together edgewise. In resistance spot welding, the material is overlapped and the welding is done in spots made in an intermittent line down the middle of the lap. In resistance seam welding, the material is also overlapped, but the spots are so close together that actually they form a continuous line.

Types of Welds. There are two basic fusion welds, of which all other such welds are simply a variation. These basic welds are the *fillet* and the *butt* and are shown in Fig. 51.

Design of a Welded Joint. The design of a weld is based on the assumption of a uniform direct stress across the throat. This assumption is not correct, for the stress distribution is very uncertain; the throat is not always perpendicular to the direct stress, penetration increases the actual width of the throat, and there are locked-up stresses[1] in the weld. The above effects are ignored in the design and are taken care of by using suitable working stresses obtained experimentally.

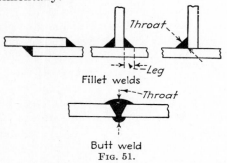

Fillet welds

Butt weld
Fig. 51.

Design stresses for welds (merchant-ship practice) are as follows:

	Lb per sq in.
Shear	7,950
Tension	15,000
Compression	15,000

Example: To illustrate the design of a weld, assume that we have a ½-in. weld all along both sides of the flat bar shown in Fig. 52. How much would the bar have to be overlapped to support a straight pull of 40,000 lb on the bar?

Solution: The ratio of the throat width to the leg of a right-angled isosceles triangle is 0.707, and so our throat width will be

$$0.707 \times 0.5 \text{ in.} = 0.3535 \text{ in.}$$

---

[1] These locked-up stresses are due to the shrinkage that takes place during the cooling period of the weld metal. If a proper welding sequence is not used, these locked-up stresses may become great enough to break the weld or tear the plate. Also, weather and poor welding technique are factors tending to produce locked-up stresses.

The area required will be

$$\frac{\text{Total load to be supported}}{\text{Allowable stress per sq in.}} = \frac{40,000 \text{ lb}}{7,950 \text{ lb per sq in.}} = 5.03 \text{ sq in.}$$

The length of weld required to give 5.03 sq in. of weld metal would be

$$\frac{\text{Sq in. required}}{\text{Throat width}} = \frac{5.03 \text{ sq in.}}{0.3535 \text{ in.}} = 14.22 \text{ in.}$$

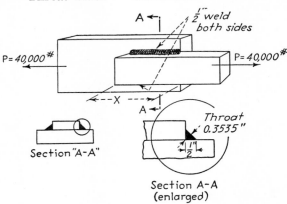

Fig. 52.

The overlap required would be half the above as we are welding on both sides. Therefore,

$$\frac{14.22}{2} = 7.11 \text{ in. overlap required}$$

Attachments 100 per cent efficient are impossible with riveted connections, but are possible to obtain in welding.

There is much more to learn about riveting and welding. The serious student is referred to Rossell's "Riveting and Arc Welding"[1] and to Navy pamphlets for further discussions.

Questions and Problems

1. Sketch a plate that has failed by a combination of tearing through the center row of rivet holes and shearing the outer row of rivets.

[1] Simmons-Boardman Publishing Corporation, New York.

2. What is the difference between a seam lap and a butt lap?

3. To what type of stresses are riveted joints subjected?

4. How can you eliminate failure of a joint due to the rivets' shearing?

5. What is the difference between oiltight and watertight rivet spacing?

6. Explain the action of the refractory oxide used as the covering of a welding rod.

7. Differentiate between forge and fusion welding.

8. Give a brief description of carbon arc welding.

9. How is a Thermit weld made?

10. Calculate the strength in a tension of a ½-in. butt weld 10 in. long.

Ans. 75,000 lb.

CHAPTER IV

KEELS

In the past a vessel's keel was thought of as the "backbone" of the hull. It is still a member of importance, for it ties the transverse bottom members together and distributes the imposed loads fairly evenly over a large area. Some of the newer, larger vessels have dispensed with the traditional keel. Eliminating the keel increases the difficulties of dry-docking, for special blocks must be placed to support the vessel; therefore, this practice is not recommended. In twin-bulkhead tankers (Fig. 139), the keel could be dispensed with if it were not for the difficulty of dry-docking. Most merchant vessels are dry-docked with the keel resting directly on the keelblocks and carrying most of the weight of the vessel, the bilge blocks bearing only a small proportion. As the keel assembly is usually a massive structure, it absorbs a large proportion of the stresses produced by hull-girder action when the vessel is in a seaway.

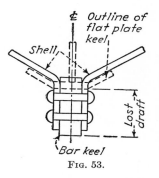

Fig. 53.

Bar Keel. The *hanging keel*, or bar keel, was used to a great extent in former days (Fig. 53). Its stiffness protected the shell plating somewhat if the vessel grounded on a hard or stony bottom. It also reduced the rolling of the vessel when in a seaway by acting similarly to a bilge keel. Its chief disadvantage was that it increased the draft of the vessel without increasing the displacement. This is an important consideration, for some vessels are designed for trades in which the draft is at a premium.

Tons per Inch. The average 400-ft cargo vessel has a *tons per inch of immersion* of about 50; *i.e.*, the vessel will sink 1 in. for every

50 tons added to its load.   If a ship had to cross a bar at the mouth
of a certain harbor and the increase in draft due to the bar keel was
8 in., then the loss in cargo that could be carried (assuming that the
vessel without the bar keel could just skim over the bar) would be

$$8 \text{ in. } \times 50 \text{ tons per in. } = 400 \text{ tons}$$

which would be a considerable loss from the owner's point of view.
This type of keel is almost obsolete, but it still may be found in
yachts and smaller boats, for which increased draft is not
objectionable.

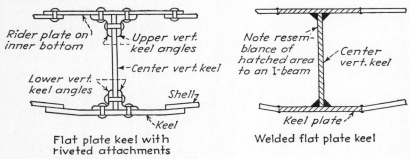

Flat plate keel with
riveted attachments

Welded flat plate keel

Fig. 54.

Flat-plate Keel.   In order to reduce the draft, the *flat-plate keel*
was adopted.   The flat-plate keel is in reality just one of the shell
plates increased in thickness to withstand docking and grounding
loads.   The flat plate extends from the stem to the stern frame.   If
riveted, it is usually lapped over the garboard (adjoining) strake.
If welded, the seam is simply butted directly to the garboard strake
(Fig. 54).

The flat-plate keel itself bears only a comparatively small portion
of the total keel stresses.   However, in conjunction with the center
vertical keel and the rider plate, it forms a rigid and powerful I
beam.

Figure 54 shows both the riveted and the welded type of flat-plate
keel assembly.   If riveted, the flat keel plate is attached to the
center vertical keel by the lower vertical-keel angles, and the center

vertical keel is attached to the rider plate, the center strake of the tank-top plating, by the upper vertical-keel angles. This assembly is rigid, massive, and strong. If of welded construction, the angles and laps are omitted, with a corresponding saving in weight.

Before the advent of welding, either the keel was made intercostal and the floors continuous, as in small single-bottom ships, or the keel was continuous and the floors were cut at the keel and riveted to it by angle clips. The severance of the floors in way of the vertical keel reduced the strength of the bottom of the hull so that the thickness of the vertical keel was increased to compensate for this weakness.

As the longitudinal bending moment is greatest amidships, the keel scantlings are greatest in way of this maximum moment.

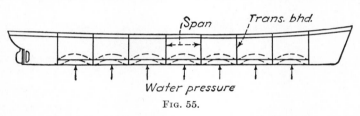

Fig. 55.

They may be decreased toward the ends of the ship because of the decreasing bending moment. The transverse bulkheads assist in supporting the keel and bottom as shown in Fig. 55. These supports transform the keel from a long flexible girder to a series of rigid girders of short span.

Special care should be taken in designing the riveted connections of the floors to the center vertical keel. The size of the angle clips should be consistent with the size of the plates connected, and a sufficient number of rivets should be used to give a good strong attachment. If the stresses are excessive, two angles should be used. The use of two angles, properly designed, will nearly double the strength of the joint.

In double bottoms of the cellular type, the keel always runs continuously. The floors are connected through the reverse frames to the tank-top plating and through the frames to the bottom shell.

When thus connected, the entire structure forms a double bottom composed of numerous rectangular compartments bounded by the floors, longitudinals, and keel. The boxlike girders formed by this

Fig. 56.

cellular construction give great strength and rigidity to the vessel's bottom.

If the cellular double bottom is all welded, the above remarks relating to the continuous keel do not apply, for all connections are considered 100 per cent effective, if properly welded, and the keel may be either continuous or discontinuous and still develop

100 per cent of the plate strength. Subassembling large sections of the double bottom has been made possible by the use of welding. This subassembly work is usually done with the assembly inverted, which eliminates the difficult overhead welding of the floor tops to the tank-top plating (see Fig. 59). The assembly thus formed is

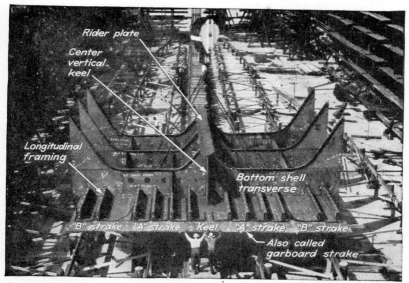

Fig. 57. Laying the keel (welded construction). Here the flat keel is being guided into position, but notice the difference. The entire subassembly shown here not only contains the flat keel but the center vertical keel, the rider plate, the deep webs, the longitudinal frames, and *A* and *B* strakes port and starboard.

then turned over and placed in the vessel in sections weighing from 50 to 150 tons each. Of course subassembling is not limited to double-bottom structure as many other parts are subassembled on the platens, such as bows (Fig. 78), stems, bulkheads, and even 10- to 20-ft cross sections of large tankers, complete with keel, longitudinals, and framing. The main limiting factor as to the size of subassemblies which may be constructed is the lifting capacity of the cranes in a particular yard.

Another advantage of subassembling is that this work may be done at points distant from the vessel under construction, and under cover if necessary, thus eliminating crowding and the resultant increase in cost and time needed to complete the vessel.

Attached to the underside of the flat-plate keel of many vessels is a rubbing strip, consisting of a flat bar about 3 in. thick and 6 in. wide, whose purpose is to protect the flat-plate keel from being

FIG. 58. An 87-ton subassembly of a bow section for the *S.S. United States.* This section was built upside down on the skids to facilitate welding. It is being installed in one piece and welding will be mostly down. The size of subassemblies is limited only by crane facilities.

damaged if the boat should run aground. It also protects the keel plate during dry-docking, but it damages the dry dock's keelblocks considerably.

Bilge Keel. *Bilge keels* are fitted to most large ships to reduce the rolling of the vessel when in a seaway. They are finlike pieces of steel plate fitted to the vessel in the vicinity of the turn of the bilge. They are fitted only in the midship length of the vessel, for this is the portion subjected to the greatest action of the water when

FIG. 59. Subassembly of an entire double-bottom structure. This photograph shows an entire double-bottom structure, including floors, longitudinals, and center vertical keel welded to the tank-top plating. The forward section has been skidded aside to be inverted and placed in the ship as a unit. All overhead welding has been eliminated.

the vessel is rolling. Bilge keels reduce violent rolling but have no effect on the vessel's stability.

Bilge keels commonly consist of two general types, the flat-plate type and the filled double-plate type. The flat-plate type, shown in Fig. 61, usually consists of a T bar riveted to the shell, with a bulb plate, or other extender, riveted to the outboard edge of the T. It is now common practice to weld a steel plate directly to the shell leaving notches in way of the shell butts to prevent stress concentration at that point. The filled double-plate type is used on the

FIG. 60. Center vertical keel, riveted construction. Some of the bottom shell has been laid and riveted. The bottom angles to the center vertical keel have been laid and riveted, and the center vertical keel in the amidship portion has been riveted. This gives a good picture of a part of the ship's backbone.

larger vessels. It consists of two plates either attached to the shell by angle bars or welded directly to the shell. Balsa or some other easily worked wood is used as a filler to give rigidity to the plates. Pitch is usually gunned into the bilge keel to fill up any empty

KEELS

KEELS

space where water might collect and corrode the inside of the bilge keel. This precaution is necessary, for the inside of the bilge keel is inaccessible after it is in place on the ship.

Pressure on the Bottom of a Vessel, Due to Dry-Docking. When a ship is completely water-borne, the upward pressure from the supporting water is distributed fairly evenly over the watertight envelope or hull of the ship. When a vessel is dry-docked, however, the situation changes radically, for the total weight of the vessel may have to be borne by small portions of the ship's bottom.

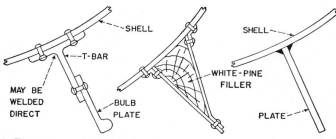

Fig. 61. Three types of bilge keels. In the center sketch above, if the section is welded, the filler is usually omitted. If the type at the right is used, the bilge keel should be cut where it crosses a butt in the plating. This is known as serrating and is a USCG requirement.

The keel takes most of this load. Bilge blocks, which are pulled under the bilges in order to keep the vessel upright when the water is pumped out of the dock, take but a fraction of the total load. War vessels usually have great masses of concentrated weights, such as armor and turrets, which are well distributed as regards support when the ship is afloat but which would become dangerously concentrated on a few bulkheads and bottom longitudinals if it were attempted to dry-dock them in the same manner as merchant vessels. In order to distribute this weight concentration more evenly over the bottom and thus prevent bottom damage, docking keels, paralleling the center vertical keel, used to be (and in some cases still are) fitted in most large warships. Figure 62 shows a typical docking keel.

At present, before dry-docking some naval vessels, we build a cradle in the bottom of the dry dock, so arranged that the longitudinal and transverse bulkheads, acting with the keel, bear on it and assume the support of the weights above them.

When it becomes necessary, as it sometimes does, to dry-dock a merchant vessel with a full or part cargo, special cribs are placed at strategic locations, such as under longitudinals and under transverse

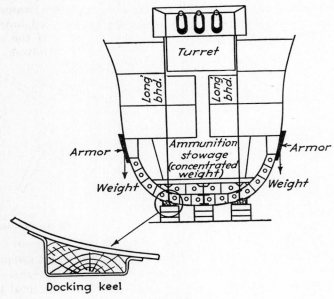

FIG. 62.

bulkheads to take the load; however, most insurance companies will not permit the dockmaster to load the blocking over 15 tons to the square foot of supporting material. As dry-docking charges are based on gross tonnage, it should be noted that, in the case of partially or fully loaded ships, the repair yard *adds* the cargo tonnage to the gross tonnage of the vessel to obtain the total tonnage, for the dry-docking charge. This partially covers the cost of the extra cribbing.

Questions

1. What is the disadvantage of the bar keel?

2. Sketch and label a riveted-keel assembly.

3. Does a bilge keel increase the stability of a ship?

4. What is the purpose of the rubbing strip?

5. Why are cradles built to dry-dock a naval vessel when this is not required for a merchant vessel with no cargo?

6. What is the main objection to deleting the keel of a twin-bulkhead tanker.

7. What are some of the advantages of subassembling?

8. What limits the size of subassemblies?

CHAPTER V

FLOORS AND DOUBLE BOTTOMS

In the design of a ship the bottom structure is of great importance, for it acts as the lower flange of the box girder formed by the hull. In conjunction with the keel the bottom must resist the longitudinal stresses produced by the uneven support of the hull girder by the crests and hollows of actual waves at sea. Like the keel itself, the entire bottom must be stiff enough to withstand the concentrated pressures due to docking and grounding and strong enough to support the weight of the cargo.

The additional strength and stiffness thus required are obtained by deepening the transverse framing across the bottom of the hull to form what are known as *floors*. A ship's floors, therefore, are not horizontal as in a building but are vertical transverse structures extending across the ship, from bilge to bilge, and usually placed on every frame.

FLOORS

The floors in a single-bottom ship are generally of plate, tapering in width from the center line out to the bilge, around which they are usually carried. If riveted, the floor plate is fitted between the frame and reverse frame, with its lower edge connected to the bottom shell plating by the frame bar and its upper edge stiffened by the reverse frame, which is extended along it for that purpose. In welded construction, the frame is omitted in way of the floor, and the reverse frame may be replaced by a flange or faceplate.

Most of the floors in a double-bottom ship are of plate, but intermediate floors under the holds may be of open construction so as to reduce weight. These open floors are built up out of structural shapes, forming frame and reverse frame, which are connected by a flanged plate bracket at each end of the floor and by angle struts and stiffeners in between. The plate floors are called *solid floors*, to distinguish them from those of open type. About one-quarter of the weight of a solid floor is saved by replacing it with an open floor (see Figs. 64*A* and *B*.) Calling a floor solid does not mean that it

Fig. 63. The double bottom partially completed. Note the solid floor at the forward end with lightning holes; however, the tank top and bottom shell is connected by a flat steel plate for all purposes.

is watertight, for a solid floor has lightening, limber, and air holes cut into it.

As in all structural design, the effectiveness of the structure (in this case the floors) depends upon its being held up to its work by auxiliary structural members. The auxiliary structure consists of widely spaced longitudinal girders (usually called *bottom longitudinals*) that keep the floors from tripping, or folding over, in a fore-and-aft direction. In a single-bottom ship the girders include a center keelson and one or more side keelsons on each side, consisting of rider bars of angle or channel along the top of the floors, riveted to intercostal plates clipped to the floors and shell. In a double-bottom ship, the center vertical keel is supplemented by similar full-depth side longitudinal girders.

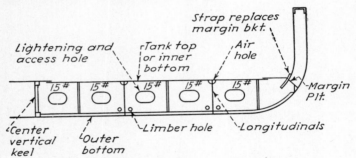

FIG. 64A. Solid floor as used on C-3 type vessels.

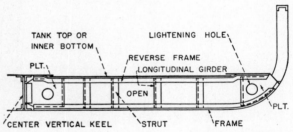

FIG. 64B. An open floor. This type of floor is approximately 25 per cent lighter than a solid floor. In colliers or ore carriers that are unloaded by buckets weighing as much as 5 tons, this type of floor should never be used, as the pounding quickly destroys the structure.

In small vessels, the floors may be short enough to be fitted in one piece, with the vertical keel intercostal, but in most ships the floors are cut at the center line and fitted in two pieces. In large double-bottom ships it is the usual practice to stop the floors at the continuous vertical keel, to which they are connected by angle clips if riveted or directly connected if welded. The side longitudinal girders were usually fitted intercostally between solid plate floors but were not cut at open floors; however, in modern welded construction the side girders are usually continuous.

To avoid buckling of the floor plates between the auxiliary longitudinal girders, the former must be made of sufficient depth and

FIG. 65. Double bottom showing open floors. Except at the outboard and inboard edges, the tank top and shell supports are connected by struts.

thickness. Much weight is saved by cutting lightening holes along the neutral axis of nonwatertight solid floors. These holes are indispensable for access in the construction and maintenance of the double bottom. Their size must be limited, or they will reduce the stiffness of the bottom. A thick floor plate, however, lightened properly, is stiffer and more durable against rust than a thinner plate without any lightening holes.

Extra strength and rigidity in the ship's bottom are required under the machinery space because of the concentrated loads found there. This is further necessary on account of the heavy stress and vibration set up by the engines and the increased liability to corrosion due to the heat and moisture in these compartments. The thickness of the floors is therefore increased throughout the machinery space, and open floors are not permitted.

DOUBLE BOTTOMS

From the earliest times it has been recognized that an empty ship, riding high out of water with its center of gravity well above the water line, is top-heavy and unstable. Therefore, it is subject to serious damage due to pounding and is likely to capsize in a storm. It has been found that a vessel in a light condition is difficult to steer and is likely to be driven off its course in rough weather. For these reasons, it has always been the practice to bring an unloaded ship farther down into the water by placing some heavy material, known as ballast, in the bottom of its hold.

For many years this ballast consisted of dirt, sand, gravel, or stone, taken from the shores of the harbor where the ship unloaded its cargo. This practice involved a serious delay at both ends of the route, for the ballast could not be put in until after the cargo had been completely taken out and had to be removed before a return cargo could be loaded. It was also undesirable from the standpoint of expense, for wages had to be paid for handling ballast, and no freight was paid for carrying it.

About 1885 the carriage of water ballast in iron and steel ships was made possible through the introduction of the *McIntyre tank*. This tank was formed in the bottom of the ship by a watertight plate built above the floors of a single-bottom ship and supported by fore-and-aft girders riding on the tops of the floors. Into the space thus provided, water ballast could be pumped to give the vessel sufficient draft when light (see Fig. 66). At first glance, one would think that at this time they could have simply plated over the floors, but this was not possible for their shallowness prevented access (see Fig. 66 for depth of single-bottom floors). Also, the increased depth of double bottom needed for access with the old-type floor resulted in solid floors being overly strong, hence the development of the open- or bracket-type floors and later the lightened solid floor.

Since this water could be handled by the ship's own pumps and pumped out or in without waiting for the ship to be loaded or unloaded, the delay and expense associated with the use of other types of ballast were obviated by the adoption of water ballast.

Tankers and colliers, owing to the nature of the trade they are in, carry cargo only in one direction and once discharged must

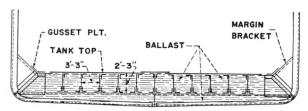

Fig. 66. The McIntyre system of ballast tank. This was the forerunner of our present cellular double-bottom system.

proceed from the discharging point to the loading point in ballast. In order to ballast and deballast rapidly, the coal colliers have special large ballast pumps installed. Tankers may use their cargo pumps as well as the special pumps installed in some tankers.

The McIntyre tanks, as first constructed, had two disadvantages. (1) The tank top, being raised about 18 in. above the floors on which the cargo had formerly been supported by means of dunnage planks, reduced the ship's cubic capacity for carrying cargo. (2) Although well adapted for carrying ballast, they contributed very little to the longitudinal strength of the hull.

The last-named defect was overcome in later ships by extending the floors up to the tank top and the fore-and-aft girders down to the shell, producing the modern type of cellular double bottom. The additional cubic capacity of the cargo holds required when a double bottom is fitted can be easily provided during the design of a new vessel.

I: was soon realized that a double bottom possesses a high safety value, in addition to its usefulness for carrying ballast. This safety value lies in the fact that the tank top forms an inner bottom, or second skin, which might save the ship from sinking if it strikes a sunken obstruction or runs aground. Even though the outer bottom is torn open, the watertight inner bottom will limit the flooding to the double-bottom space and protect the cargo from damage by water.

The depth of the double bottom and floors is determined by the depth adopted for the center vertical keel but should be sufficient

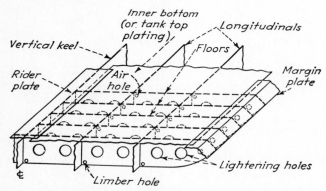

Fig. 67. Modern cellular double-bottom structure.

for ready access to all parts of the double-bottom space so as to allow proper construction and maintenance. In ships carrying heavy bulk cargoes, such as iron ore, the double bottom may be made much deeper than is required for strength and access, in order to raise the center of gravity of the loaded ship and thereby produce a more comfortable period of roll (see page 212).

A further advantage of the double bottom lies in its availability for carrying fuel oil and water. Thus the cargo space is saved that was once wasted by the large bunkers and tanks formerly required for carrying coal and fresh water.

Figure 67 shows a modern cellular double bottom sketched in isometric projection. The term "cellular" is derived from the fact that the double-bottom space is divided into rectangular cells by the floors and longitudinals. These members act as deep web frames that resist and distribute the upward push of the water on the ship's bottom.

INNER-BOTTOM PLATING

The inner bottom is generally fitted in rectangular plates and extends from the centerline strake, called the *tank-top rider plate*, to the outer strake on each side, called the *margin plate*. In riveted construction, the inner-bottom plating is usually arranged in fore-and-aft strakes, having their adjacent butts shifted, or placed in different frame spaces, so as to avoid lines of weakness due to the inefficiency of the riveted joints.

In welded work, the inner bottom is often plated transversely between the fore-and-aft centerline strake and the margin, and a shift of butts is not necessary, for no line of weakness is produced by the welded connections.

The rider plate is made heavier than the rest of the inner bottom and forms the top flange of the centerline keel girder. In riveted work, the margin plate is usually knuckled down to meet the shell at right angles, unless the depth of the double bottom exceeds the bilge radius, in which case the margin plate is carried straight out without knuckling. In welded ships it is quite usual to carry it straight to the shell. The inner-bottom plating is lighter than the bottom shell but is increased in thickness in the engine and boiler rooms to allow for corrosion and the weight of machinery.

The terms *double bottom* and *inner bottom* are not synonymous or interchangeable, for each applies to a different part of the ship's structure. The double bottom is the compartment between the inner and outer bottoms. The inner bottom is merely the plating forming the top of this compartment or tank; it is also called the *tank top*.

Questions

1. What are the requirements of the bottom structure?
2. Sketch a typical open and solid floor.
3. Is it permissible to cut lightening holes in solid floors?

4. What is the purpose of bottom longitudinals?
5. Why are open floors not permitted under machinery spaces?
6. What were the objections to the McIntyre ballast tanks?
7. What is a cellular double bottom?
8. Is it possible for a man to "go down into" the inner bottom?
9. Except for lightening, why are holes cut in a solid floor?
10. Differentiate between a limber hole and an air hole.

CHAPTER VI

FRAMES AND FRAMING SYSTEMS

In the transverse system of framing, the closely spaced principal frames run transversely inside the shell. These transverse frames are further supported by side stringers, bottom longitudinals, and other widely spaced auxiliary longitudinal framing.

The longitudinal system of framing differs from the above in that the shell and bottom plating is supported by closely spaced frames

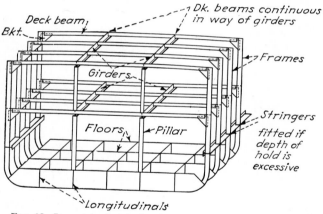

FIG. 68. Isometric sketch showing transverse framing system.

running fore and aft. These longitudinal frames are then reinforced by widely spaced deep transverse frames.

Transverse Frames. The frame spacing is the distance measured on the center line between the frames. It is usually 2 to 3 ft on merchant ships and 4 ft on naval vessels. This spacing is reduced at the bow and stern because the actual span of the shell lying over the frames is greater than is shown by measuring the distance on the center line (Fig. 69). Also, the bow and stern plating is subjected to direct blows from the sea and to panting stresses resulting from the violent pitching of the vessel in a seaway, both of which require additional support behind the shell.

The marked frame spacing is always 4 ft in naval vessels. This is a help to the shipbuilder, for he is enabled to locate the distances of any point in a fore-and-aft direction by noting the frame numbers

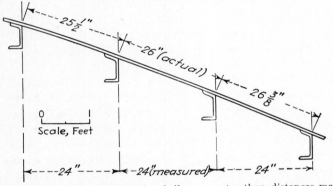

Fig. 69. Distances measured along the shell are greater than distances measured along the center line.

and multiplying by 4. This is not possible in some parts of a merchant vessel, owing to the varying frame spacing. Where extra shell support is needed in a naval vessel, half frames are introduced; thus, successive frames would be numbered 21½, 22, 22½, 23, etc.

Of course, the wider the frame spacing, the greater the span of the shell plating. If we increase this span, we must increase the thickness. Also, the larger the vessel, the greater the load on the shell and framing. This requires the fitting of heavier plating and frames on a large vessel than on a small one, and the plating being heavier permits a wider span between shell frames. As an illustration, the American Bureau requires frames spaced 27 in. apart on a ship 400 ft long and 32 in. on a ship 600 ft long. (These figures are general and are dependent on the span of the frames and other factors enumerated in the rules.)   On an all-welded hull 400 ft or longer, it probably would be cheaper and better to space the frames 36 in. apart and increase the shell thickness 0.01 in. for each inch by which the frame spacing exceeds the rule spacing.   (This would be an addition of $0.01 \times (36 - 32 \text{ in.}) = 0.04$ in. for the 600-ft ship above.)   This will add to the weight of the shell but will reduce the number of frames and the amount of welding required.

If the framing is riveted, the forward frames toe aft and the after frames toe forward.   This is done to avoid acute angles, or closed bevels, between the flanges of the frame, which would render proper riveting difficult.   Consideration of which way to toe the frames is not necessary with welded construction, for the simpler section used for frames usually permits ready accessibility.

Longitudinal Frames.   In a longitudinally framed ship the principal fore-and-aft frames (Figs. 70 and 71) are about 30 to 60 in. apart vertically.   The heavy transverse webs that support these smaller longitudinal frames are placed about 10 to 16 ft apart, and the span of the longitudinal frames is thus shortened.   This lessening of the span gives rigidity to the shell and framing system.

Figure 71 shows a ship of the *Isherwood type*, so called because this type of construction was reintroduced and patented by the British naval architect, Sir Joseph Isherwood.   The figure also illustrates the *bracketless system* of construction.   In this particular type of longitudinal framing, the brackets at the ends of the longitudinal frames are omitted, and the shell is heavied in way of this omission.

With longitudinal framing, the frames may, under certain conditions, contribute to the longitudinal strength of the ship and thereby effect a saving in steel weight.   This system is not much used in freighters, however, since the decks in a freighter are closer together than the bulkheads.   This means that longitudinal frames must either be made excessively heavy, owing to the great unsupported span, or, more commonly, additional supports must be furnished in the form of heavy transverse web frames spaced at intervals of

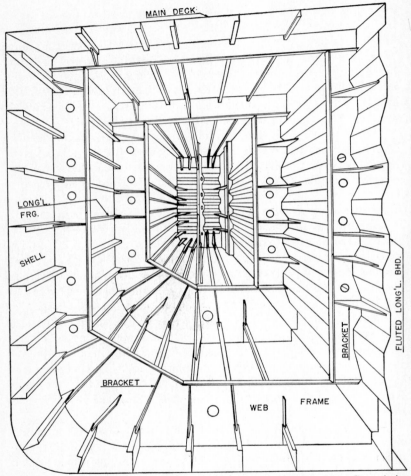

FIG. 70. Perspective showing the interior of a wing tank on a Maritime Commission T-2 tanker with longitudinal bracketed framing. See Fig. 250 for a general arrangement. Looking aft in this tank you see the two deep webs and the longitudinal framing supporting the shell. On the right we see the fluted bulkheads which are unstiffened because the flutes, or creases, serve in place of the stiffeners. Two webs on the right support the fluted bulkheads. Two deep deck beams support the longitudinal deck beams which in turn support the deck plating.

perhaps 8 to 12 ft. These webs protrude into the holds and seriously hamper the stowage of cargo. The advantages of the longitudinal framing system are very effectively used in tankers, for there are no 'tween decks, and the distance between bulkheads is about the same as the distance from bottom shell to deck. The web frames are, of course, not objectionable in the stowage of bulk liquids, coal, and ore.

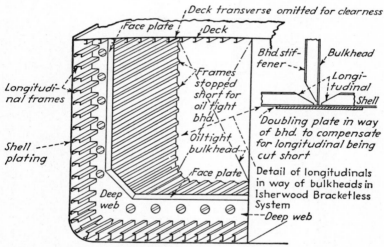

Fig. 71. Sketch showing the longitudinal bracketless system of framing.

Ships are frequently built with longitudinal framing in the decks and bottom shell, where their continuity acts most effectively, being at a maximum distance from the neutral axis, and are built with transverse framing on the side shell to take advantage of the close supports afforded by the decks. Transverse framing of the side shell is more effective in preventing damage from piers.

Types of Frame Section. Small vessels, if transversely framed and riveted, sometimes use angle bars for frames. These are beveled and attached to the shell in such a manner that the leg of the angle is at right angles to the center line of the ship. The toe

FIG. 72. Shell framing. Riveted construction. The frames are being erected Note the shape of the frames lying on the tank-top plating.

Fig. 73. Welded construction. The framing already attached to the shell is placed in the vessel as a unit. Both longitudinal and web frames are shown.

of the angle is parallel to the shell, as shown in Fig. 74. This type of construction is not suitable for large vessels because the neutral axis is close to the shell and there is not much material in the toe of the angle, all of which results in too much flexibility and weakness. For larger riveted vessels the plain angle is sometimes used in combination with a reverse frame, as shown in Fig. 76. The reverse frame adds material to the toe and tends to center the neutral axis. The stiffness is greatly increased by this condition. Channels and bulb angles, when used for frames, will accomplish a similar result with a reduction in the amount of riveting. This was the object in mind when these sections were designed.

For riveted work, bulb angles and channels are the usual frame sections (Fig. 74). Channels are used for the main framing, and

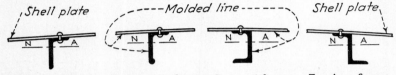

Plain angle frame   Bulb angle frame   Channel frame   Zee bar frame

Rolled sections

FIG. 74. Types of frames used in riveted construction.

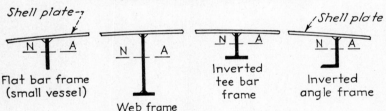

Flat bar frame (small vessel)   Web frame   Inverted tee bar frame   Inverted angle frame

FIG. 75. Types of frames in welded construction.

bulb angles are used in the peak tanks. Depth for depth, the channel is more effective than the bulb angle, and therefore channels are used in way of cargo spaces, for they decrease the cargo capacity less than the bulb angle. The bulb angle is used in the peak tanks because there the frame depth required to make the two sections equal in strength is not a factor. Most foreign shipbuilders prefer bulb angles for the frames of their ships if of riveted construction.

All the above frame types *are becoming obsolete* owing to the advent of welding. Figure 75 shows some of the welded types now

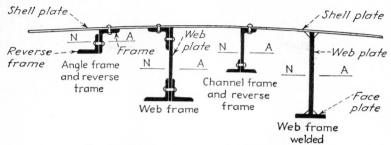

FIG. 76. Riveted and welded built-up frames.

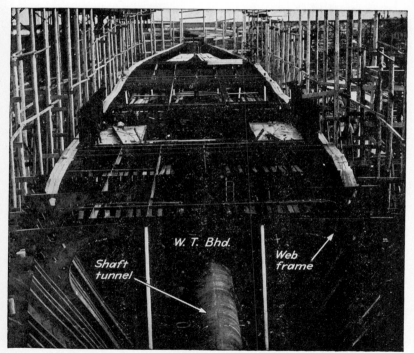

FIG. 77. Web frames. The shell frames have been placed in their proper location. Four of the deep web frames are now in place. This is a picture of a deep hold near the stern where many web frames are fitted because of the great span and vibration likely to be encountered.

in use. The welded designs are simpler, stronger for their weight, and usually cheaper to construct and fit.

Web Frames. Web frames *are massive, deep, built-up members fitted into the hull to add strength and rigidity at points of special stress* and to support the side stringers, which, in turn, support the transverse frames. The main member is a deep web of plate and usually

FIG. 78. Deep web frames and stiffeners subassembled to their plating in the building dock. Typical welded construction. Note the almost complete stem upended and about ready to be lifted into position.

is lightened by cutting holes along the neutral axis. If riveted, an angle attaches it to the shell, and usually two angles form the inboard flange of the frame. If of welded construction, it is attached directly to the shell by welding, and a flat bar, usually called a *faceplate*, is welded along the inboard edge. Web frames extend from the turn of the bilge to the deck above. They make a belt of great rigidity around the ship in line with their position. Stringers are fitted behind the web frames and over the smaller transverse frames so that the stiffness furnished by the web may be utilized by the plating.

The size of web frames and their spacing are dependent on their span and depth below the lowest deck. Webs were formerly used in conjunction with small transverse frames, about every sixth transverse frame being dropped and a deep web taking its place (Fig. 68). This construction, in combination with a stringer, permitted a reduction in the size of the regular frames. This practice has fallen into disuse.

Sometimes web frames were fitted at the ends of hatchways to take the loads imposed upon the sides of the vessel by the deep

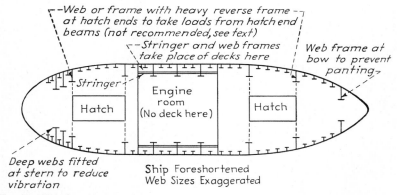

FIG. 79. Sketch showing location and purpose of deep web frames. Webs at hatch ends are typical only when centerline stanchions are fitted. With two rows of stanchions, the webs would be omitted.

hatch end beams. These webs are now eliminated by stiffening the regular frame in way of the hatch end beams.

Web frames are useful in absorbing the vibration resulting from the propellers and engines and are fitted for this purpose around the stern section of high-powered vessels. They are useful also in counteracting panting stresses in the bow sections.

Deep webs are fitted in way of the engine and boiler spaces to support the shell. This is usually necessary owing to the fact that the decks do not run through these spaces and the great span calls for extra stiffening. A heavy stringer is run behind the web at deck level to transfer web stiffness to the intermediate frames (Fig. 79).

Questions

1. What is the essential difference between transverse and longitudinal framing?

2. Why are most merchant cargo ships transversely framed and most tankers longitudinally framed?

3. On a naval vessel how far aft of the forward perpendicular is frame 137?

4. Give two reasons for the close spacing of frames in the bow and stern of a transversely framed ship.

5. In a riveted ship in what direction does the toe of the frame point? Why?

6. Give three reasons why deep web frames are used.

7. Where would you expect to find web frames located in the hull of a ship?

CHAPTER VII

SHELL PLATING

The shell plating is the outer watertight covering of the hull. The frames help to stiffen and support this outer covering. When the outer portion of a pipelike structure takes most of the load, it is called a *monocoque* type of structure. The hull plating, which includes the shell plating and the plating of the "strength"[1] deck

FIG. 80. The shell not only acts as a watertight envelope, it is also a main strength member.

of a transversely framed merchant ship, takes about 90 per cent of the total stress resulting from hull-girder strains and is almost a true monocoque type. The hull plating of most tankers and naval vessels is supported by longitudinal framing, and this framing takes

[1] In most merchant vessels, the strength deck is the upper deck. In all cases, it is the deck used as the upper flange of the hull girder in the longitudinal-strength calculation (see *S.S. Blum*, Fig. 6).

some of the load resulting from the longitudinal bending strains, the remainder being taken by the shell.

As shipbuilding changed from the age of wood to the age of iron, the tendency was to make the plating thick and to space the frames closely together, according to the previous practice in wooden construction. With steel replacing iron, the present tendency is to space the frames farther apart and to accept much thinner shell plating. This change is based on past experience as well as mathematical consideration. As in all engineering practice, past experience is invaluable in new design, and the trial-and-error method has been the basis of our present practice relating to shell plating.

In general, merchant vessels have shell plating that is much heavier than that used on naval vessels of the same size (except in way of certain armored spaces). This is because the merchant vessel is subjected to rougher treatment and less care than the naval vessel. The merchant cargo vessel may be thought of as a heavy-duty truck specially designed for water usage where repair stations are few and far apart. If the student keeps this idea in mind, he will better understand the reason for the massiveness of some of the parts on the average merchant ship.

The shell is composed of steel plates, most of which are rectangular in shape. They are arranged in a longitudinal manner on the ship and, when in place one after the other, are known as a *course*, or *strake*, of plating.

The thickness of these plates varies according to the size of the ship and the location of the plate. It is now common practice to run the plating vertically in way of the anchor so that the anchor will have a smooth surface to slide upon as it comes up to the hawsepipe. The thickness of the shell plating varies between $\frac{1}{4}$ and $1\frac{1}{4}$ in.

TYPES OF SHELL PLATE

In general, there are three types of plate fitted on the hull. They are called, according to their fitted shape, *flat*, *rolled*, or *furnaced* *plates*. Fortunately, the great majority of plates are flat and do not have to be worked into shape. Rolled plates have cylindrical curvature in one direction only and are usually found at the turn of the bilge amidships. These can be rolled cold by a machine. Furnaced plates have curvature in two directions and must be heated and hammered to shape over a specially prepared and shaped steel form, or cradle (see Fig. 81). They are necessary at

FIG. 81. Forming a furnaced plate. The plate to be shaped is placed on the special steel form. Wooden boards are placed on the heated plate, which has been moved out of the furnace in the background, so that the weight of the ingot, when lowered, will not dent the plate but be distributed. The flames are from the burning boards. By raising and lowering the ingot, the plate is forced to the shape of the form.

some points of the bow and stern; but as they are expensive, they should be avoided whenever possible.

Layout of the Shell Strakes. Owing to the greater girth (distance around a body) of a ship amidships than at the ends, it is obvious that, if we place sufficient plating amidships and then run the courses parallel to each other, we shall have too much plating at the ends. To obviate this difficulty, certain strakes are dropped as they approach the bow and stern. These *drop strakes* are shown in Fig. 83. The other strakes run through in a continuous line from stem to stern and are known as *through strakes*.

So that the end of the drop strakes may be attached into the through strakes, a plate of about double width is fitted into the through strake below the drop strake, as shown in Fig. 83. This plate is known as a *stealer*.

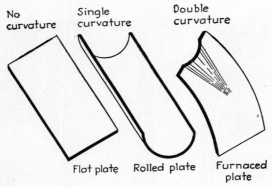

FIG. 82. Three types of shell plates.

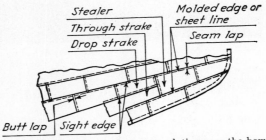

FIG. 83. Method of deleting excess plating near the bow.

Other plates with special names are *dished plates*, the *boss plate*, and the *oxter plate*. The boss plate is a furnaced plate fitted at the swelled-out portion in way of the stern frame and is shown in Fig. 85. An oxter plate, the use of which is fast disappearing, is a furnaced plate fitted at the point where the stern frame joins the counter (Fig. 85). Dished plates are U-shaped plates and are usually formed on a flanging machine.

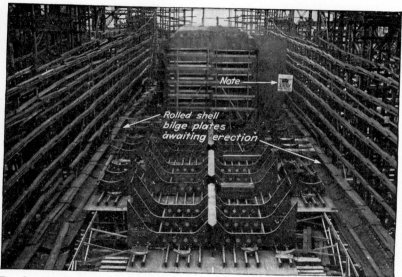

FIG. 84. Note the bottom shell in position and the rolled bilge plates laid out, port and starboard, ready to be erected. The X-ray machine is in the background to make X-rays of primary welds. Primary welds are welds made where the plating changes from a continuous line, that is, the structure takes a change in shape; or to use a more embracing, if confusing, expression, at any discontinuity.

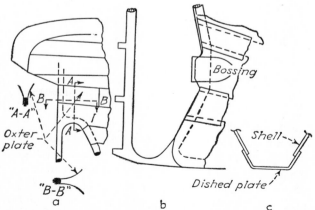

FIG. 85. Old type stern assembly showing the oxter plate.

Transverse joints at the plate ends are called *butts*, and the longitudinal joints are called *seams*. The *sight edge* is the edge of the plating visible from outside the hull. The edge visible from inside is called the *molded edge* or *sheet line* (Fig. 83).

Identifying the Shell Strakes. There are four strakes of shell plating that have names, but all the strakes except the keel are

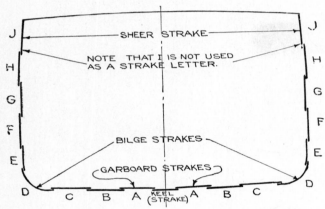

FIG. 86. Names and letters designating the shell strakes.

designated by letters of the alphabet, beginning next to the keel with A. The named strakes are

1. The keel, at the very bottom center.
2. The garboard, at each side of the keel.
3. The bilge strake, at the turn of the bilge.
4. The sheer strake (the upper course of the main hull plating), located just under the sheer line.

The location of these strakes is shown in Fig. 86.

Compensation for Holes Cut in the Shell. There are American Bureau rules that must be complied with in designing merchant ships if the vessel is to be classed with this society. These rules specify certain dimensions for the thickness of the shell amidships, at the ends, along the sides at the sheer strake, and under the bottom forward. They also specify that compensation must be

made, either by an increase in the thickness of the plate or by a
doubler around openings in the side of the ship, for cargo ports,
gangways, and other ports. This requirement for increasing
plating thickness at hull discontinuities is due to the stress concentration that takes place at these points (see page 24 for a
further discussion of this subject). Doublers are fitted around

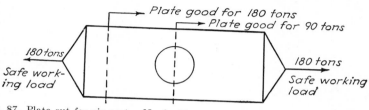

FIG. 87. Plate cut for air port. No doublers are fitted; 50 per cent of strength is lost.

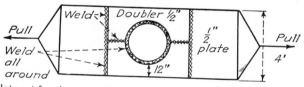

FIG. 88. Plate cut for air port. Compensating doublers are fitted; no strength is lost.

openings to make up for lost area as well as to alleviate the stress
concentration around the opening.

Consider the flat hull plate shown in Fig. 87. Assume that this
plate is ½ in. thick and 4 ft 0 in. wide. The metal area would be
0.5 in. × 48 in. = 24 sq in. Assuming the steel to be good for 30
tons per sq in., the plate would reach its ultimate strength at a load
of 24 sq in. × 30 tons = 720 tons. Using a factor of safety of 4,
the working load" would be

$$\frac{720 \text{ tons}}{4} = 180 \text{ tons}$$

Now, if a 24-in. air port is placed in the center of the plate, half
the area of the plate is lost and the plate is good for a working load
of 90 tons only. In order to compensate for this loss of strength, we

may add a doubling plate (Fig. 88) of say ½ in. thickness and 1 ft in width on each side of the hole, giving

$$(0.5 \text{ in.} \times 12 \text{ in.}) + (0.5 \text{ in.} \times 12 \text{ in.}) = 12 \text{ sq in. of metal area}$$

which would exactly make up the area lost due to the air port and would thus restore the strength of the plate.

The American Bureau specifies that any hole cut in the shell of a riveted ship which reduces the effective sectional area of the individual plate by more than 20 per cent must have sufficient compensation by means of doublers or collars to bring the area back to 80 per cent. In an all-welded ship, 100 per cent compensation is

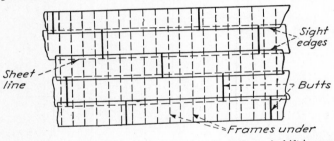

FIG. 89. Method of shifting the butts of riveted shell plating. A shift is necessary to stagger the line of weakness where the plates are butted. This is not required in a welded shell.

demanded by the American Bureau. Each individual hole cut in a naval vessel is considered on its own merits.

The reason only 80 per cent compensation for holes is demanded in a riveted ship is because the holes punched in the plate, to take the riveting of the plate to the frame, have already reduced the strength of the plate about 20 per cent.

Amidships the shell plating is usually of uniform thickness. It may be reduced toward the ends, for the bending moment and the loads are less. This reduction amounts to about 20 per cent.

The Sheer Strake. The sheer strake forms a portion of the upper flange of the hull girder. This calls for a general thickening of this course of plating. If the sheer strake has to be heavied, it is good practice to increase the thickness of one or two strakes below the sheer strake; for it has been found that, although the sheer strake may remain unimpaired owing to its large sectional area, the strakes below show signs of weakness. Some naval vessels and some other vessels of high speed use high-tensile steel (HTS) in the sheer strake to save weight.

There are numerous systems of arranging the seams of shell plating for riveted work. None of these systems is necessary in welded construction, for a welded joint is 100 per cent effective. In general, in riveted work, it is best practice to shift the butts so that there are at least two frame spaces between butts in adjacent strakes and at least five passing strakes between any two butts in the same frame space. If butts are shifted in this way, the shell will have a general effectiveness of about 80 per cent. Figure 89 shows this shift of butts.

METHODS OF PLATING THE HULL

The shell plating may be arranged in any one of several ways. Sometimes a combination of the following ways are used. All methods listed below apply to riveted construction except the one shown in Fig. 90, sketch *D*. It should be noted that these several arrangements were devised in order to get the most satisfactory attachments at the least cost. In a modern yard, riveted shell plating for ships up to 500 ft long is becoming an oddity. The *S.S. United States* is riveted on the seams for half length amidships and welded on the ends. The systems listed below are, however, still in use in some yards, and as there are thousands of ships afloat that have riveted shell plating a discussion of these systems is considered warranted.

1. In-and-out System (Fig. 90, sketch *A*). This is sometimes known as the *sunken-and-raised system*. In this system the inner plate is against the frame and the outer plate laps over the inner plate and is not joggled, or offset. As a consequence, a space is left between the two plates equal to the thickness of the inner plate. This space is filled by a steel liner with a breadth not less than $3\frac{1}{2}$ times the diameter of the connecting rivets.

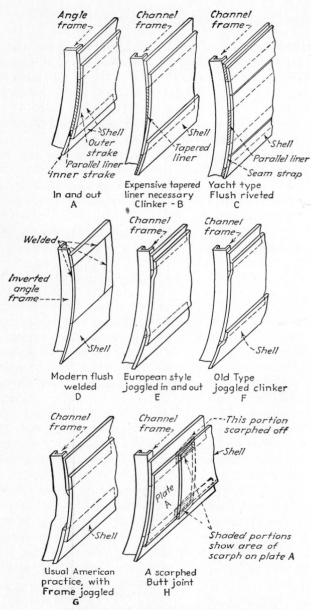

FIG. 90. Methods of plating the hull.

98

2. Clinker System (Fig. 90, sketch *B*). This system is somewhat similar to the weatherboarding used on a house. It is more expensive than the in-and-out system, for twice as many frame liners are required and each one must be tapered and fitted. Also, the connecting rivets must be of varying length. This system is therefore generally unsatisfactory. Sometimes, if there is an odd number of strakes, one of the strakes is still applied clinker fashion.

3. Flush System (Fig. 90, sketch *C*). This system is sometimes used on yachts for appearance's sake. Even on yachts it is used only above the water line. It is extremely expensive, for it requires seam straps as well as liners. These seam straps are usually continuous, and the liners are fitted between them. Fitting these curved plates accurately, edge to edge, requires considerable care and much time. This system has fallen into disuse.

4. Flush Welding (Fig. 90, sketch *D*). Numerous vessels are being built that have the seams riveted and the butts welded. Many others have plating that has both butts and seams welded and the plating welded directly to the frames. This gives a plating that is flush and obviates liners, seam straps, and joggling. If the shell plating is thin and is welded to the frames, an unslightly ridge is apparent along the line of the frame owing to the welding. Also, *difficulty has been experienced with shrinkage of plates welded all around the edge*. These two difficulties will perhaps be overcome in the future, and in this case the other systems of plating mentioned here will fall into disuse.

5. Joggled Systems. The three joggled plating systems listed below are in general use in foreign yards. Joggling relieves us of the necessity of fitting liners, and all the plating is in direct contact with the frames. Either the plating may be joggled on one edge or both edges, or the frame may be joggled. If the plating is joggled, or offset, the longitudinal stiffness of the plate will be increased.

a. Joggled In-and-out System (Fig. 90, sketch *E*). The inner plate is fitted as in the in-and-out system. The outer plate is joggled on both edges. This joggle, or offset, is, of course, equal to the thickness of the inner plate. This system is very popular in Europe.

b. Joggled Clinker System (Fig. 90, sketch *F*).   In this system only the upper edge of each plate is joggled.

c. Joggled Frame (Fig. 90, sketch *G*).   The joggled frame is the system used extensively in this country for riveted construction. This enables the plates to bear flat on the frame.   The joggling is done by machine and is relatively cheap, compared with plate joggling.

Vessels designed to operate in icy seas sometimes have the plating doubled in way of the water line near the bow, for about one-twentieth the length of the ship abaft the stem.

NOTE: The term "doubled" does not necessarily mean that the plating is increased exactly 100 per cent.   It means that the plating is thickened, or more material is added, in proportion to the amount of load to be carried or in proportion to the size of hole cut in the plate.

From the ship repairer's viewpoint, it is much cheaper to renew a plate that has welded seams and butts and is riveted to the frames than to renew an all-welded plate.   In the first case the rivets are simply burned out and the new plates reriveted, whereas the plate that is welded to the frames must be chipped lose, which is an expensive process.

Questions

1. What is a monocoque-type structure?
2. Why is the shell plating of merchant vessels thicker than that usually fitted on naval vessels?
3. Why are drop strakes necessary?
4. What is a stealer plate?
5. Define sight edge, sheet line, and seam.
6. Where is the garboard strake located?
7. In a riveted shell plate 40 in. wide it is desired to cut an 8-in. hole.   Would doubling be required?
8. Why is the sheer strake thicker than the strake below?
9. Make a simple sketch of the five methods of plating a riveted ship.

CHAPTER VIII

DECK BEAMS

A deck beam in a vessel has three primary functions, (1) to act as a beam to support vertical deck loads, (2) to act as a tie or as a strut to keep the sides of the ship in place, and (3) to act as a web under the deck plating to prevent plate wrinkling due to the twisting action on the vessel from gunfire or from the ship's sailing at angles to a heavy sea.

Beam Brackets. Deck beams run athwartship from side to side of a vessel and are fastened to the frames by beam brackets.

Brackets are fitted to the ends of beams where they connect with the supporting frame. Brackets tend to fix the ends of the beams and are necessary in order that the beam may develop its full strength at the connection. Deck beam brackets are a decided nuisance in a refrigerated or passenger vessel, and in this class of ship they are often omitted. However, the beam-end connections must be made strong enough to develop the strength required by the classification societies. Deck beams are subjected to end-on compressive forces when acting as a strut and to tensional forces when acting as a tie to keep the sides from springing apart when the vessel is in the sagging condition. A bracketed beam tends to check the racking and the twisting of the hull when the vessel is in a seaway. The usual depth of the beam bracket is $2\frac{1}{2}$ times the depth of the beam. Figure 93 shows typical welded and riveted beam brackets.

Function of a Beam. It is the function of the beam to take the deck load and transfer it to the frames. The frames in this case act as pillars and carry the load downward, where it is distributed over the bottom by the floors. Water pressure under the bottom

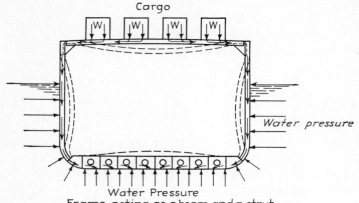

Cargo

Water pressure

Water Pressure
Frame acting as a beam and a strut

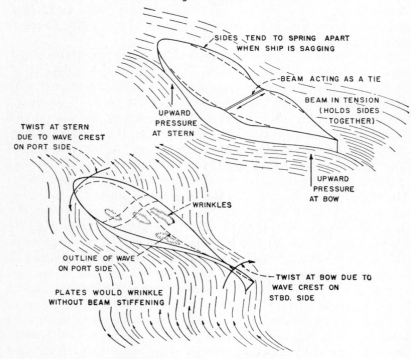

SIDES TEND TO SPRING APART
WHEN SHIP IS SAGGING

BEAM ACTING AS A TIE

BEAM IN TENSION
(HOLDS SIDES
TOGETHER)

UPWARD
PRESSURE
AT STERN

UPWARD
PRESSURE
AT BOW

TWIST AT STERN
DUE TO WAVE CREST
ON PORT SIDE

WRINKLES

OUTLINE OF WAVE
ON PORT SIDE

TWIST AT BOW DUE TO
WAVE CREST ON
STBD. SIDE

PLATES WOULD WRINKLE
WITHOUT BEAM STIFFENING

BEAMS ACTING AS A WEB FOR DECK
PLATING (SHIP IN QUARTERING SEA)

Fig. 91. Some actions of ships' beams and frames.

of the vessel, transmitted through the floors, frames, and deck beams, supports the load on the deck of the vessel (see Fig. 94).

The beams support the decks or platforms with their permanent or temporary loads.   Besides their primary function of supporting

Fɪɢ. 92. This shows the deck beams almost completed.   Note how the beams are cut in way of the hatches and the cut ends supported on headers, or carlins.

a deck or platform, they assist in maintaining the relative positions of the opposite sides when the vessel is subjected to longitudinal bending forces or the forces due to the water pressure upon the immersed surface that tend to crush in the sides of the vessel (see pressure-gradient curve, Fig. 94).

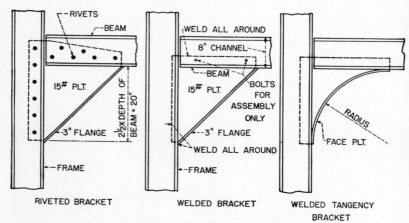

FIG. 93. Typical riveted and welded brackets.

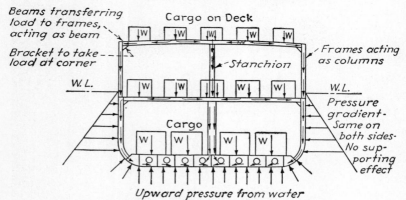

FIG. 94. Distribution of the loads from the cargo.

Sections Used for Beams. Deck beams used in riveted construction are bulb angles, bulb tees, or channels. Plain angles are suitable only for very small ships.

If of the welded type, inverted plain angles, inverted T bars, or plates with welded faceplates as the lower flanges make good sections. Large T bars, suitable for welded beams, are now produced by splitting I beams down the center of the web. If the cut is

alternately offset in opposite directions at short intervals, two 7-in.
T bars, suitable for intermittently welded connections, can be
obtained from one 12-in. I beam. This operation is performed by
an automatic burning device, which will cut this joggled offset in
four to six plates or beams simultaneously. The resulting beams
are called serrated sections (Fig. 95).

Fig. 95. Cutting two 7-in. stiffeners out of a 12-in. plate. The four burning torches
travel along a template at the center which joggles the line of the torch at stated
intervals 2 in. each way. The stiffeners are installed with the joggled edge welded
to the bulkhead where it touches. This saves welding, steel, and weight.

Beam Sizes. Beam sizes depend upon the spacing of the beams,
the number of supporting pillars and girders under the beams, the
thickness of the deck plating, and the height between decks.

'Tween-deck beams are designed to support a load resulting from
an assumed basic cargo of a certain density (weight per cubic foot)
completely filling the 'tween-deck space. This explains why the
deck height determines, in a manner, the size and spacing of the
beams.

Beams are usually fitted on every frame under decks that are
unsheathed. It is usually more satisfactory to fit the extra beams
than to increase the thickness of the deck plating. These extra
beams also help prevent buckling of the plating due to compressive

loads resulting from hull-girder action. Fitting beams on every frame allows us to decrease the depth of the beams and thus increase the headroom by that amount.

As the weather deck is subjected to excess loads resulting from heavy seas breaking over the vessel, the beams under these decks are made heavier than would be normally required. There are cases on record where the entire forward exposed deck has been "stove in" owing to the weight of water piled on the deck by an excessively large wave (see Fig. 213).

If a deck beam with a single top flange is used, such as a channel, less riveting is required. The deck plating acting with the beam flange tends to prevent the beam from tripping, or folding over. For welded beams, antitripping brackets are sometimes used to prevent this folding action.

T bars make fair beam sections when riveted, for their symmetry discourages tripping and the double upper flange gives a good connection, although it increases the required number of rivets. They form excellent sections when inverted and welded.

Deck beams, whether fitted on every frame or only on every other frame, are always fitted in line with the side frames. When fitted in this manner they form, in conjunction with the side frames and the double bottom, a continuous belt around the inside of the hull. This ringlike belt enables the relatively thin side, bottom, and deck plating to assume great compressive loads without buckling.

Deck Camber and Sheer. Camber is put in a deck so that water falling on the deck will run down to the scuppers and drain overboard. The beams and plating are arched upward, and this arching is known as *camber*, or *round of beam*. Camber is usually measured in inches per foot of breadth of ship. For example, a deck may have a camber of 12 in. in 50 ft. This means that on a ship 50 ft wide the deck at center amidships would be 12 in. higher than at the side.

Camber is measured at the center line of the ship. The amount of camber on a particular ship varies. A ship with much camber in the freeboard deck is permitted by the Freeboard Regulations to load to a greater draft than a vessel with less camber.

The camber of the longest beam in the ship is similar to the camber of the shortest one. To obtain the camber of a beam that is shorter than the longest beam, place the shorter beam on the camber curve of the longest, with their centerline spots coinciding. It will be noted that the ends of the shorter beam will be above the ends of the longer. This will mean that the deck at the side will have to rise to meet the ends of the shorter beams. Thus a cambered deck that is parallel to the base line at the center line will have sheer at the sides (see Fig. 96).

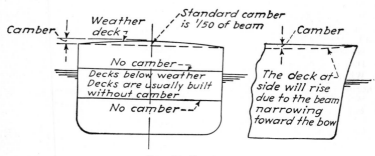

Fig. 96. Camber.

During the First World War the ships built at Hog Island[1] were designed for simplicity of construction with no sheer or camber. Aside from the fact that they looked as if the ends were drooping, they were very serviceable ships. The *S.S. Normandie* had decks that were practically flat, but a clever manipulation of the paint line near the deck made her appear to have a beautiful sheer. Camber does not add to the strength of a deck, for the sides of the ship are too flexible to offer enough support to get the arch effect.

In most ships today, the lower two or three decks are flat decks, but the weather deck has sheer. The Freeboard Regulations allow a deeper draft to be assigned to a vessel with sheer than to one without sheer, for the sheer enables the former to ride the waves with a drier deck. Standard sheer is made up of a parabolic curve

[1] A great shipyard built near Philadelphia in 1917 for the mass production of ships. There were 50 building ways at this one yard.

forward with a height at the bow of 0.2 times the length of the vessel plus 20 in. and a parabolic curve aft with half that height at the stern. Thus a 400-ft vessel with a 55-ft beam, if her sheer and camber were standard, would have

$$\text{Sheer} = (0.2L + 20) = (0.2 \times 400 + 20) = 100 \text{ in. at bow}$$

$$\frac{100}{2} = 50 \text{ in. at stern}$$

$$\text{Camber} = 0.02 \times \text{beam} = 0.02 \times 55 \text{ ft} = 1.1 \text{ ft or } 13\frac{1}{4} \text{ in.}$$

amidships

The above is standard; however, almost any sheer or camber may be used by the designer.

Questions and Problems

1. Give the three primary functions of a deck.

2. Why are beam brackets necessary?

3. Upon what four factors does the size of a beam depend (based on A.B.S. rules)?

4. What would be standard camber for a boat 75 ft wide?

5. How much sheer would a ship 800 ft long have if her sheer were standard?

6. Why are weather-deck beams usually heavier than required to support the normal deck loads?

7. What is the advantage of fitting deck beams on every frame?

8. Is a cambered deck stronger than a flat deck?

CHAPTER IX

PILLARS AND GIRDERS

The numerous "posts" fitted throughout a vessel are known to shipbuilders as *pillars, stanchions,* or *columns.* They are used to give vertical support to girders, deck beams, and heavy concentrated loads. The pillar assumes the load and transmits it downward toward the bottom of the hull, where it is distributed over a large area.

PILLARS

Use of Pillars. When a pillar is placed under a beam or girder, it not only reduces the deflection of the beam but also relieves the

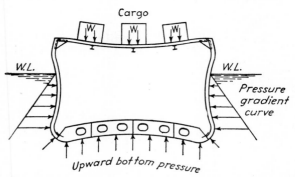

Fig. 97. Exaggerated shape of an unpillared vessel with a deck load.

beam brackets and the frames at the side of the hull. If the beams had no pillars for support, they would behave as shown in an exaggerated manner in Fig. 97. The load from the cargo is deflecting the beam. This deflection produces a rotation at the top of the frame due to the rigid bracket connection. (NOTE: The actual rigidity of the bracket connection would not be great enough to cause any such rotation as shown in the figure. This exaggeration

109

is considered permissible for educational purposes.) The load would then be taken by the frame down to the turn of the bilge. The upward pressure of the water would cause a deflection in the double bottom that in connection with the load from the frames would cause a depression of the bilges. Figure 98 shows a vessel that has been properly pillared. This pillaring has greatly relieved the conditions mentioned above.

Besides acting as compression members keeping the decks apart, pillars also act as tension members tying the decks together. Thus,

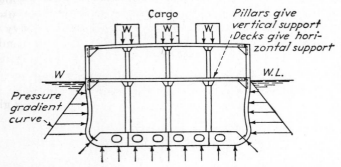

Fig. 98. Same vessel as in Fig. 97, pillared. Beam-end connections are relieved. Note the effect of adding a deck on the sides.

if a lower 'tween decks is loaded with cargo, the upper 'tween decks is forced, through the tension action of the pillar on the deck, to support a portion of this load. The line of pillars thus forces all decks to act together as a unit.

Pillars should be placed under heavy weights of a permanent nature carried on deck. Under windlasses, cranes, winches, and other hoisting machinery pillars become particularly important, for they force the decks below to assume a part of the straining action resulting from the loads placed on the machinery. The rigidity of this support also reduces the intense vibration accompanying the machinery's operation. Pillars may be used to advantage under the forward part of the weather decks of high-speed vessels to help the beams assume the load thrown upon them by great masses of water coming aboard in a heavy sea.

Partial Bulkheads. Where the load to be supported is particularly great, partial bulkheads usually take the place of pillars. A partial bulkhead may be thought of as a continuous row of pillars placed so close together that they touch. Partial bulkheads are more efficient supports than pillars but are at times undesirable in that they block access.

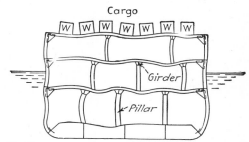

FIG. 99. Exaggerated effect of having the pillars out of line.

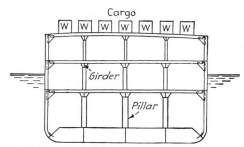

FIG. 100. Same vessel as in FIG. 99 with the pillars in line.

Arrangement of Pillars. The naval architect should be careful to place pillars *vertically in line* with each other. If this is not done, bending moments will be induced in the pillars that will greatly reduce their efficiency, and severe vibration may be set up throughout the vessel (see Fig. 99).

Size of a Pillar. The size of a pillar depends upon the *load* it has to support, the *location*, and the *length* of the pillar. Where pillars support, say, only passenger spaces, they may be comparatively small.   However, if the location is toward the bottom of the vessel, the pillar must support not only the load from the deck directly above but also the loads brought down by pillars several decks higher.   This calls for heavier pillars in the holds than in the 'tween decks (Fig. 100).

Pillars in Relation to Internal Arrangement.   Shipyards sometimes receive a set of contract plans, one of which shows an excellent arrangement for cabins, public spaces, etc., while another shows an excellent layout of pillars and girders.   When these plans are superposed for a check, it is sometimes found that a pillar will run through a main stairway or down an elevator shaft or even appear in the middle of a bathtub.   In any such case, it may be necessary to rearrange the pillar and girder plan or alter the arrangement of the vessel, in order to bring the location of the pillars and girders into agreement with the desired arrangement plan.   Had these plans been worked out together properly by the owner's naval architect so as to secure their agreement in the first place, this difficulty would have been avoided, endless correspondence would have been saved, and the ship's owner would have been satisfied instead of being disgruntled because of a comparatively poorly arranged vessel.

Types of Pillars.   Numerous types of pillars are used, some of the most commonly employed being shown in section in Fig. 101.   As mentioned in Chap. I, the hollow-pipe or hollow-plate circular-type pillar gives the greatest strength for the least weight.   H beams are used to a great extent for engine-room columns primarily because of the ease of attaching the flat sides to the structure above and below.   They are usually objectionable as hold pillars owing to their sharp corners, which have a tendency to damage cargo.   The octagonal pillar, as shown in Fig. 101, is a cheaper pillar section to produce than the circular-plate pillar.   The circular-plate pillar is cheaper than the pipe pillar.   The octagonal pillar has therefore become very popular as a pillar section in both merchant and naval work.

Other Considerations.   Acceleration factors have a great effect on the size of pillar required.   As the vessel pitches, rolls, and heaves, the dead loads are forced to move with the vessel.   This accelerating and decelerating effect becomes serious near the bow and stern of a vessel; in some cases, the dynamic load will be double the static weight. (That is, a 1,000-lb weight near the bow may produce a load of 2,000 lb owing to the rapid deceleration that takes place when the bow of the vessel pitches into a large wave.)

Care should be taken to protect pillars as much as possible from damage by cargo. If a pillar is bent out of the vertical, its strength

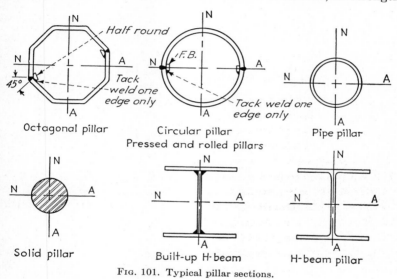

Fig. 101. Typical pillar sections.

as a support practically disappears. Pillar connections should be designed to be equal in strength to the unbent column. The head-plate, or cap plate, (top connection) and spring plate, or sole plate, (bottom connection) should be designed properly to distribute their loads above and below.

GIRDERS

Girders are heavy fore-and-aft beams placed under the transverse deck beams and along the top of a row of pillars. In newer construction the girders are slotted and the beams pass through the upper portion of the girder as shown in Fig. 102. Without this

girder under the beams, the beam over the pillar would be amply
supported but the beams in between would have only the negligible
support afforded by the deck plating (Fig. 103).

I beams, T bars, channels, and built-up sections are used as
girders. Two typical deep built-up girders are shown in Fig. 104*A*.
Both are of welded construction.

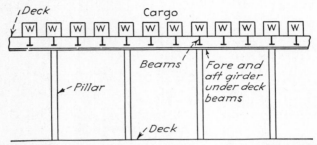

Fig. 102. Section through centerline girder under deck beams. This girder reduces
the span of the beams passing over it.

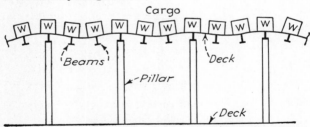

Fig. 103. No girder under deck beams. Pillar supports only the beam directly
overhead.

Pillars and partial bulkheads are excellent structural members,
but they are a great hindrance to the stevedore in stowing cargo.
They also limit, in some cases, the types of cargo that may be
carried. Sometimes pillars are made so that they may be removed
during the loading process and then replaced after the cargo is in
position.

The cargo is usually wedged between the pillars, bulkheads, and
shell so that it is unable to shift when the vessel is rolling in a seaway.

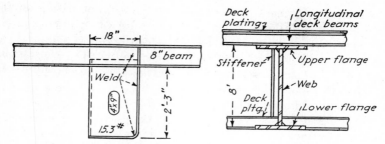

"Built up" hatch end beam   Deep "built up" girder

Fig. 104A. Typical deep "built-up" beams and girder.

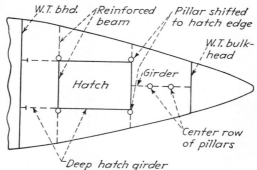

Fig. 104B. Pillars shifted in way of hatch.

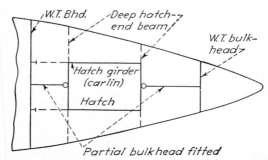

Fig. 104C. Partial bulkheads and deep-hatch end beams sometimes take the place of pillars.

A good arrangement of pillars lessens their interference with the loading process. Two arrangements are shown in Figs. 104*B* and *C*. The upper sketch shows a hold that has a center row of pillars. The line of the center row is shifted to the hatch edge in way of the opening. The lower sketch shows a partial bulkhead fitted on the center line. The hatch is supported in this case by the centerline partial bulkheads and the deep hatch end beams. No hatch corner pillars are fitted. Of course, if the girders are made sufficiently deep and massive, the pillars may be eliminated altogether.

As the beam, or width, of a ship increases, the number of pillars or partial bulkheads fitted must be increased in order to keep down the span of the deck beams and thus reduce their size (see page 105). Care should be taken to work out the proper ratio between the size of pillars, the size of girders, and the size of deck beams required in order to give the lightest and best total structure.

Questions

1. What is a stanchion?
2. Why should pillars always be fitted in a vertical line?
3. Why is a pillar fitted under the windlass?
4. Give the advantage and the disadvantage of fitting a partial bulkhead.
5. Upon what three things does the size of a pillar depend?
6. Sketch three typical pillar sections.
7. How does acceleration affect the size of a pillar?
8. What is the purpose of deck girders?
9. Why should pillars be well protected when cargo is being loaded and unloaded?

CHAPTER X

DECKS

A ship's deck is a horizontal platform extending across the hull at various heights above the inner bottom. It resembles, structurally, the floor in a house.

Some decks have longitudinal sheer and athwartship camber, while others are entirely flat. A deck is bounded by the shell and connected to the beams and to the trunk and hatch openings.

Method of Support. The deck plating, or planking, is supported at regular intervals by the deck beams, just as the shell plating is supported by the frames. The beams are supported at their outboard ends by the frames, to which they are usually attached by beam knees or beam brackets. They are further supported at intermediate points by pillars (stanchions), girders, and bulkheads.

Purpose of Decks. Decks are useful in several ways, depending on their location in the ship. The upper deck increases the ship's seaworthiness by forming the watertight top of the hull and also contributes strength by acting as the upper flange of the hull girder. The lower decks act as working platforms for the operation of machinery and the loading of cargo and also provide living space for passengers and crew.

An important function of the deck is to serve as a horizontal diaphragm, keeping the ship in shape longitudinally as the bulkheads do transversely. On small vessels, decks may be of wood planking laid over steel beams and tie plates, but on large ships all decks are usually of steel throughout, so as to contribute more strength to the hull structure.

While the upper exposed decks may be covered with wood sheathing either of teak or of pine, the lower decks in living spaces are usually covered with a patented mixture similar to cement, but of more elastic nature, which gives a smooth deck. Quite often,

especially in the newer vessels, they are simply painted. Some of
the decks of naval vessels were covered with heavy linoleum; now a
less combustible substitute is used. Sheathing a steel deck with
wood adds little to its ability to withstand longitudinal stress but
stiffens it so as to increase its resistance to heavy seas that may be

Fig. 105. Deck plating. The plating here is welded over deck beams riveted at the
ends. Note the heavy stringer plates, which are the outboard plates. This construction occurred during the transition period between welding and riveting.

shipped during stormy weather. Sheathing a steel deck adds to the
comfort of passengers by

1. Insulating the space below. Wood decking has a low heat-
transmission value.

2. Keeping the open deck from becoming so hot that the passengers are unable to walk on it. This is particularly important in
the tropics.

3. Preventing sweating underneath the deck.   Sweating is due to large and rapid temperature changes.   Wood decking resists this tendency.

4. Adding to the appearance of the ship.   This is important in passenger vessels only.

Deck Plating.   The deck plating, like the shell, is usually fitted in wide fore-and-aft strakes, the plates being rectangular in form amidships and tapering at the ends of the vessel to conform to the

Fig. 106. All-welded deck plating.   Note the X-ray machine (its use has been explained previously).   The gunwale bar is still riveted in order to arrest any cracks that start in the welded structure.

curvature of the sides.   In riveted ships, generally, the deck seams (the longitudinal side joints of the plating) are single-riveted and the deck butts (the transverse end joints) are double-riveted.   The connection of the deck plating to the beams is generally single-riveted.   In welded construction the weld is carried all around the plate, and in some cases the weld metal is ground flush with the upper surface of the plating.

In riveted construction the different strakes of deck plating may be lapped in either clinker or in-and-out fashion.   With a wood

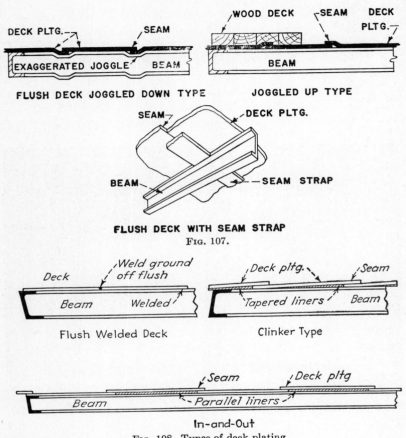

FLUSH DECK JOGGLED DOWN TYPE   JOGGLED UP TYPE

FLUSH DECK WITH SEAM STRAP
Fig. 107.

Flush Welded Deck   Clinker Type

In-and-Out
Fig. 108. Types of deck plating.

deck laid over riveted plating, both of the above arrangements are
objectionable, since the planks must be of a varying thickness above
the high and low surfaces of the plating and liners have to be fitted
under the plating in way of the deck beams. By joggling the laps
of the plating, these liners may be eliminated; and if the laps are
joggled down and the top flanges of the beams offset to suit, a flush
surface is obtained. This flush surface allows the wood planking or

composition decking to be of uniform thickness.   Heavy plating is
sometimes made flush on top by the use of riveted seam straps underneath (see Fig. 107).   If the decks are welded, all planking can be
of the same thickness, since the plating is flush.   Figures 107 and
108 show examples of the above types of deck plating.

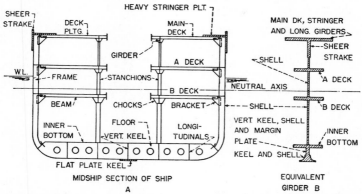

Fig. 109. A midship section and its equivalent girder.   Note that the plating has
been omitted in way of the hatch cuts.   This has been done since there is no plating
in the cuts and the plating between the hatches does not add strength to the vessel.

Stringer Plate.   We had previously discussed the fact that, in
investigating the strength of the ship as a whole, the vessel may be
considered to be a gigantic beam supported over a wave crest at its
center, in one condition, and between wave crests located at the
bow and stern, in another (see page 3, as a memory refresher).
Heretofore the student has been asked to assume that this is true.
With our knowledge of the action of beams (pages 101 to 106) and
strength of materials firmly in mind, let us carefully investigate this
assumption.

Equivalent Girder.   Figure 109 shows a typical midship section
and a sketch of a girder equivalent, in the amount of steel contained
and its distribution, to the midship section.   This girder is called an
equivalent girder.   As a rule, in actual practice, we do not make up
an equivalent girder; it is shown here merely as an illustration.

Consider Fig. 109, and think of it as the cross section of a beam.

For the upper flange of our beam, we have the deck plating and the longitudinal girders under the deck.   The deck plating at the center of the deck is usually cut by the hatches and engine casings.   In order to keep a strong continuous uncut row of steel plating in the upper flange of the hull girder we fit *stringer plates* along both sides of the deck, running from the stem to the stern.   This row of plating is heavier than the regular deck plating.

If we calculate the area of the stringer plates, the deck plating inboard of the stringer plates, to the hatchway cut, and the continuous longitudinal girders and bunch them together, we obtain an equivalent upper flange as shown in sketch *B*.   As there is no deck plating in a hatch and the plating between the hatches is discontinuous because of these openings, the plating in way of the hatches is ignored in the longitudinal strength calculation.

If we do the same to *A* and *B* decks, we obtain the two horizontal lines shown as *A* and *B* on the equivalent girder.   We now bunch the areas of the tank-top plating, the longitudinals in the double bottom, the center vertical keel, the flat keel plate, and the bottom plating to the turn of the bilge, which gives us the equivalent mass of steel that forms the bottom flange of the girder.   If we now calculate the area of both sides of the shell plating from the top of the sheer strake down to the turn of the bilge and combine them, we obtain the web of the girder.   The upper and lower flange of the girder, which are the highest stressed portions, will then be made up of the main strength deck and its supporting structure and the bottom shell and its surrounding structure.   As the portions of *A* deck and *B* deck are near the neutral axis, they will be stressed very little and, therefore, are not particularly important as strength members (see page 14).   This makes it important that the strength deck and the bottom structure be made sufficiently strong to withstand any usual loading without failure.

A striking example of a failure of the upper deck occurred on the *S.S. Majestic* in the summer of 1924 and resulted in such serious damage that she had to be laid up for repairs from December, 1924, to May, 1925.   This case illustrates not only the importance of continuity of strength and avoidance of stress concentrations around hatchways and deck openings but also the importance of the upper deck as the top flange of the hull girder (see page 121).

The *S.S. Majestic* was the German-designed and -built *S.S. Bismarck.* The vessel was constructed with two outboard uptakes, which pierced the deck somewhat toward the sides.   The plating between the uptakes was only ⅝ in. thick, and it was not thought that it would assume any load.   The main strength members were the stringer plates, which were 2 in. thick, and the two strakes running inboard of the stringer, which were 1½ in. thick.

It was discovered in the summer of 1924 that the thin ⅝-in. plating between the uptakes had fractured.   This received very little attention at the time, for this plating was not designed to take any load.   The stringer plates were covered on top with wood decking and below with joiner work; and as it was the rush season, their inspection and repair were deferred until later.   The vessel continued her trips until December, at which time she ran into heavy weather.   During the storm a loud "cannon-like report" was heard; investigation showed that the deck had cracked all the way across and that the port stringer plate had also parted.   The crack ran down the side of the vessel and stopped in a porthole.

The vessel made its way into Southampton, and all trips were canceled.   New stringer plates were installed and doubling plates were added around all openings, which compensated somewhat for the stress concentration at the sharp corners.   A complete description of this near catastrophe can be found in an article by naval constructor E. Ellsberg in *Marine Engineering*,[1] from which the above was taken.

The *S.S. Leviathan* (the former German *S.S. Vaterland*) showed the same defects, and considerable reinforcement was necessary in way of openings in the deck.

These two instances establish two facts, namely, that the strength deck should have sufficient steel to resist the stresses imposed by longitudinal bending and that sufficient steel alone will not be enough to keep the ship from breaking (both ships had sufficient steel area) if we do nothing to relieve the stress concentration in way

[1] August, 1925.

Fig. 110. A model of a hatch opening and proposed reinforcements. This is a plastic model made to be placed in polarized light to study the stresses in the sharp corners. As mentioned in this chapter, a square cut in a strength member tends to concentrate stress at its corners and, as a result, cracks start. In a welded ship this may be disastrous since the plating may crack until the vessel is torn in half. Plastic models are made with every conceivable reinforcement possible and then the best is chosen. Model testing is cheap compared with ship testing.

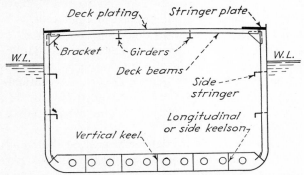

Fig. 111. The fore-and-aft girders in a transversely framed ship.

of deck openings. Therefore, *all cuts in the main ship structure should be doubled and the corners should be well rounded* (see Fig. 110).

The stringer plate should not be confused with the side stringers, which are girders. There are three sets of fore-and-aft girders in a ship, namely, longitudinals and keelsons in the double bottom, stringers in the sides along the frames, and girders located under the decks (see Fig. 111). The word "stringer" is sometimes applied to all three groups, but it should be used only for the side girders.

Questions

1. How is the deck plating supported?
2. What is the purpose of wood sheathing?
3. What is the difference in the riveting of a deck seam and a deck butt?
4. Why is the clinker-type of deck plating objectionable?
5. What is the purpose of the stringer plate?
6. Sketch a typical equivalent girder, and indicate and label the equivalent parts.
7. Why should the corners of all holes cut into the strength deck be rounded, doubled, or both?
8. Differentiate between side stringer, girder, and longitudinal.

CHAPTER XI

BULKHEADS AND FLOODING

A ship is divided into compartments and tanks by transverse or longitudinal bulkheads. Bulkheads are important for the following reasons:

1. If watertight, they prevent water from passing from one compartment to the other and in case of a shell puncture may save the ship.

2. They act as fire checks by providing fire-resistant boundaries.

3. After all other means have failed, they permit the flooding of a hold and thus allow the extinguishing of fires.[1]

4. They act as structural diaphragms and resist the transverse deformation of the hull caused by racking stresses.

The numerous rules (American Bureau, Coast Guard, Senate Report 184, Load Line Regulations, International Convention for the Safety of Life at Sea, etc.) relating to bulkhead spacing will undoubtedly seem confusing and conflicting to the student. However, if we space the bulkheads in such a manner that they satisfy the subdivision requirements of the Convention for the Safety of Life at Sea, the other rules will automatically be complied with.

SUBDIVISION RULES RELATING TO BULKHEAD SPACING

It long has been recognized that a ship should be able to suffer a shell puncture and still survive. It has also long been recognized that a vessel primarily carrying passengers should be made relatively

---

[1] Flooding a hold should be done only as a last resort. It will undoubtedly quench the fire, but it also may cause the ship to capsize owing to the attendant loss of stability (see page 214). If there is any doubt as to the ability of a particular ship to remain upright with a certain number of her holds flooded, it is better to let her burn herself out, for an upright ship even though burned out is usually less of a liability than one that is capsized.

safer than a ship primarily carrying cargo. It is possible to make a vessel practically nonsinkable by constructing the compartments within her of such minute size that a great number of holes may be punctured in the side without flooding more than a small space.

Fig. 112. The transverse watertight bulkheads are being erected.

This minute subdivision is common practice in naval work but is not economically feasible in merchant cargo-ship construction. The owners want the distance between bulkheads to be as great as possible so that the vessel can carry almost any type of cargo. The humanitarians interested in the crew's welfare, the underwriters interested in the ship's safety, and the men responsible for wartime transport service, interested in transporting troops, all want the bulkheads as close as possible to prevent the ship's sinking in case the shell is punctured by collision or war damage.

It would not be good sense, economically, for one nation to set up standards of subdivision that would penalize its own ships. Shortening the holds in a merchant vessel increases her chance for survival if the shell is punctured but also increases the difficulty of loading and decreases the number of types of cargo that can be

Fig. 113. Watertight bulkheads in position.

carried. In order that no nation should be penalized for making its ships safer, the International Conference for the Safety of Life at Sea was called and met in London in 1949. All the principal maritime countries were represented, and they all signed the agreements that were reached at the conference. This convention not only stabilized bulkhead spacing but also was concerned with safety devices such as lifeboats, life rafts, radio, watertight doors, etc.

As we are interested only in bulkheads in this chapter, we shall discuss only the portion of the rules of the convention that relates to bulkheads.

Ocean-going ships were graded at the conference according to their general character, with the pure cargo vessel, carrying only 13 passengers[1] at one end of the scale and a luxury passenger liner like the *S.S. United States* carrying practically no cargo, at the other end of the scale. The signers of the convention all agreed that the safety of the ship should be commensurate with the nature of the trade in which she engaged. In the discussion below, a one-compartment vessel is one that will remain afloat with one compartment flooded; a two-compartment ship is one that will remain afloat with two adjacent compartments flooded; etc.

The result of this convention, simplified for clarity, is that every ship carrying more than 12 passengers and engaged in international voyages must be at least a one-compartment vessel. As the character of ship approaches that of the luxury liner, *i.e.*, as her length and the number of her passengers increases, the spacing of the main bulkheads in proportion to the length of the ship gradually decreases. As a result, a small vessel, say, 400 ft long, with relatively few passengers such as a USMC "C" type will be a one-compartment vessel; an intermediate type of ship, 500 or 600 ft long, with, say, 200 or 300 passengers, will be a two-compartment vessel; and a ship 800 ft long, with 1,000 passengers or more, may be a three-compartment vessel. The *S.S. America* is a three-compartment ship, and the *S.S. United States* four or more.

The manner in which bulkheads act to prevent foundering is illustrated in Fig. 114. These sketches show a two-compartment merchant vessel with holes progressively longer torn in her side. Sketch *A* shows the vessel floating at her normal load water line. In sketch *B* the shell of the vessel has been punctured between bulkheads so that one compartment is flooded. The ship will sink downward and trim forward until the buoyancy lost in way of the flooded space is made up by the buoyancy regained in the process of the ship *sinking deeper into the water*. When the buoyancy regained by deeper immersion is exactly equal to the buoyancy lost, the vessel will cease to sink and will again be floating in equilibrium.

[1] Cargo vessels carrying 12 passengers or less do not come under the rules of the convention; however, they must adhere to the Coast Guard regulations.

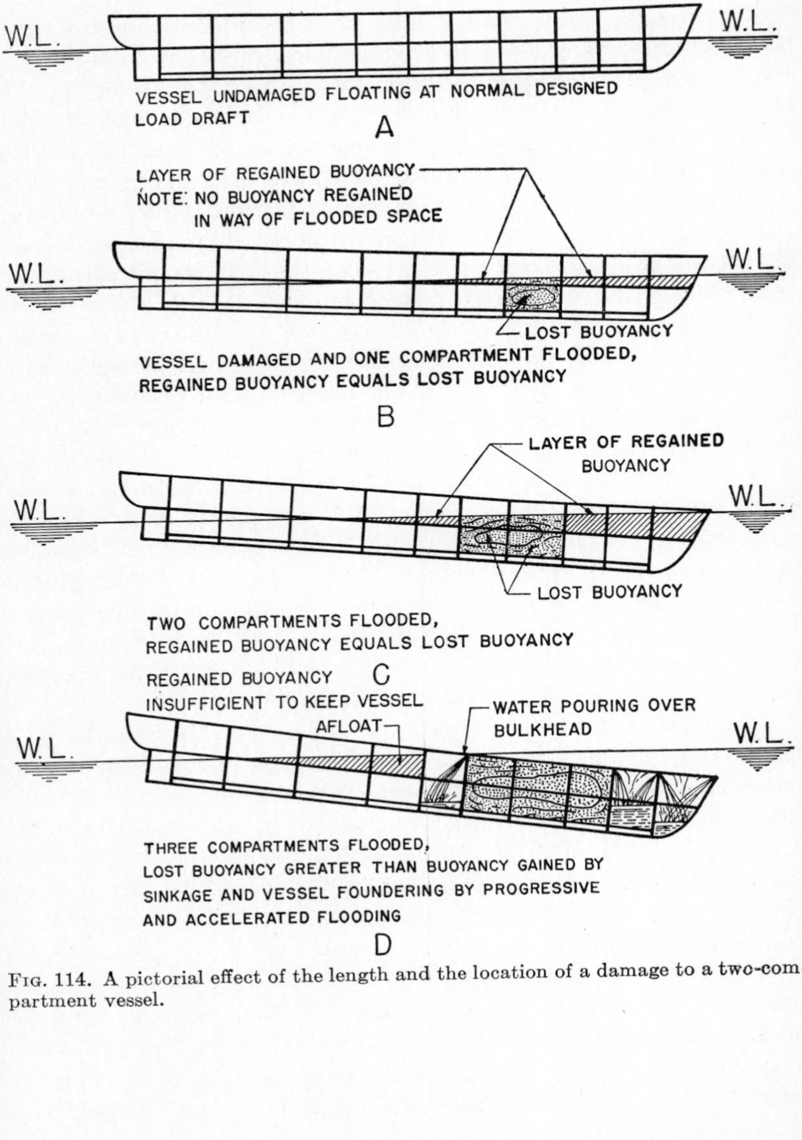
W.L.
W.L.
VESSEL UNDAMAGED FLOATING AT NORMAL DESIGNED LOAD DRAFT
A
LAYER OF REGAINED BUOYANCY
NOTE: NO BUOYANCY REGAINED IN WAY OF FLOODED SPACE
W.L.
W.L.
LOST BUOYANCY
VESSEL DAMAGED AND ONE COMPARTMENT FLOODED, REGAINED BUOYANCY EQUALS LOST BUOYANCY
B
LAYER OF REGAINED BUOYANCY
W.L.
W.L.
LOST BUOYANCY
TWO COMPARTMENTS FLOODED, REGAINED BUOYANCY EQUALS LOST BUOYANCY
C
REGAINED BUOYANCY INSUFFICIENT TO KEEP VESSEL AFLOAT
WATER POURING OVER BULKHEAD
W.L.
W.L.
THREE COMPARTMENTS FLOODED, LOST BUOYANCY GREATER THAN BUOYANCY GAINED BY SINKAGE AND VESSEL FOUNDERING BY PROGRESSIVE AND ACCELERATED FLOODING
D

FIG. 114. A pictorial effect of the length and the location of a damage to a two-compartment vessel.

In sketch *C* the damage has extended across a bulkhead, and consequently two compartments have been flooded. The vessel must sink and trim more than in sketch *B* in order to regain the lost buoyancy, for more buoyancy has been lost. As she has sufficient freeboard to make up the lost buoyancy, *the ship will still float, but at a deeper water line.*

In sketch *D* two bulkheads have been crossed, and three compartments have been flooded. As before, the ship starts sinking deeper in the water so as to regain the lost buoyancy; but in the process the upper deck goes under the surface of the water, and the water pours into undamaged compartments. The foundering then becomes accelerated and progressive, *and the entire ship sinks below the water.* The particular vessel shown in the figure cannot remain afloat with more than two compartments flooded and is therefore a two-compartment ship. If her bulkheads had been spaced closer, she might have remained afloat with three compartments flooded; in that case, she would have been a three-compartment vessel.

All the above discussion is based on the assumption that the vessel remains upright during the flooding process and simply fills and goes down. We shall see later that this is very seldom the case. Flooding a vessel usually reduces stability (as in the case of the *S.S. Normandie*), and the vessel might capsize with only one compartment filled, even though she would have sufficient buoyancy to float upright with two compartments filled. If this were the case, her two-compartment floodability would be fictitious. The stability of a flooded ship will be discussed in Chap. XVI.

BULKHEADS REQUIRED BY THE AMERICAN BUREAU

Besides the regular intermediate watertight bulkheads required by the convention, there are four bulkheads required by the American Bureau of Shipping as follows:

1. Collision Bulkhead. This bulkhead is required as a safety provision. Should the ship have the bow broken open by ramming or other means, this bulkhead would serve as an auxiliary bow. Very little change in trim would take place, for little water would enter the ship. If the forepeak tank were already filled with salt water, no excess water would enter. The American Bureau requires that this bulkhead be placed not less than one-twentieth the length of the vessel abaft the stem (measured on the load line).

2. Afterpeak Bulkhead. This bulkhead is required to be fitted in all screw vessels and to be arranged so as to enclose the shaft tubes in a watertight compartment. This is a logical requirement, for a broken shaft tube might allow water to enter into the afterpart of the ship. A watertight afterpeak bulkhead prevents this.

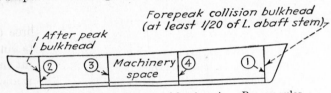

FIG. 115. Bulkheads required by American Bureau rules.

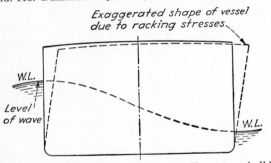

FIG. 116. Deformation caused by a racking stress. Transverse bulkheads relieve this tendency.

3 and 4. Machinery-space Bulkheads. Machinery spaces must be enclosed by watertight bulkheads. The American Bureau also has other requirements for bulkhead spacing, but if the subdivision rules are satisfied it will be found that the rules of the bureau also will be satisfied.

BULKHEAD PLATING

Bulkheads usually are plated horizontally. Therefore, the thickness of the plating must be increased gradually toward the bottom of the ship to allow for the increased water pressure encountered there (Fig. 117).   As the lowest strake of plating has to support the greatest head (pressure) of water, this strake must be the heaviest. The water pressure on a bulkhead at various levels is shown by the water-pressure curve of Fig. 117.

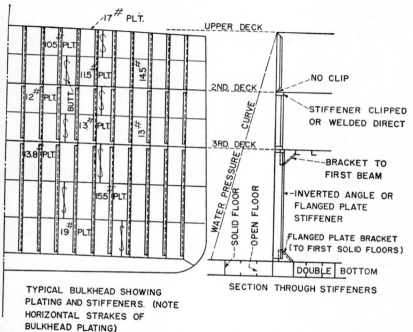

TYPICAL BULKHEAD SHOWING PLATING AND STIFFENERS. (NOTE HORIZONTAL STRAKES OF BULKHEAD PLATING)

SECTION THROUGH STIFFENERS

Fig. 117. A typical merchant-ship watertight bulkhead.   Note that the plating decreases in thickness as the head, or height, decreases, and that the stiffeners decrease in the same proportion.   The top stiffeners are sniped, as the plating in shear will amply contain the head pressure.

BULKHEAD STIFFENERS

Bulkhead stiffeners usually run vertically since the vertical span (*i.e.*, the distance from deck to deck) is usually less than the horizontal span (the distance from shell to shell).   As the water pressure and, consequently, the load become less and less as we approach the upper deck, the size of the stiffeners may also become less and less. It will be noted in Fig. 117 that the lower stiffener is bracketed to the tank-top plating and to the underside of the third deck. Between the third and second deck the stiffener is simply clipped to the deck by a riveted angle or is welded directly. The upper stiffener depends solely on the plating for its upper and lower attachment. This system of plating stiffeners and attachments is typical only of merchant work.

Sometimes a combination of vertical and horizontal stiffeners can be used to advantage. Typical riveted bulkhead-stiffener sections

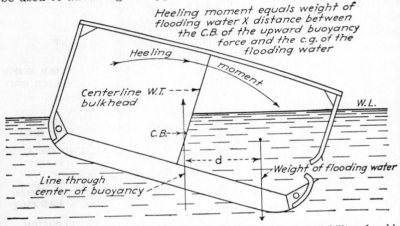

Heeling moment equals weight of flooding water X distance between the C.B. of the upward buoyancy force and the c.g. of the flooding water

Heeling

moment

Centerline W.T. bulkhead

W.L.

C.B.

d

Weight of flooding water

Line through center of buoyancy

Fig. 118. Effect of unsymmetrical flooding on the transverse stability of a ship. Equalizing pipes or valves in the centerline bulkhead would alleviate this condition.

are T bars, channels, flanged plates, T bulb bars, and bulb angles. Typical welded stiffener sections are inverted tees, inverted angles, and inverted flanged plates.

LONGITUDINAL BULKHEADS

Watertight longitudinal centerline bulkheads are a real source of danger to the normal merchant vessel and, as a consequence, are no longer fitted unless some method is adopted that will permit any flooding water to pass through the bulkhead and thus equalize the water level on both sides.

The danger of unsymmetrical flooding was brought to the attention of naval architects when the *S.S. Empress of Ireland* capsized, with the loss of 1,000 lives, owing to the flooding of one engine room after she was in a collision. Having one side of a vessel flooded and the other side intact sets up a heeling moment that, if greater than the vessel's righting moment, causes the ship to capsize as shown in Fig. 118. It is common practice to fit transverse bulkheads in way of the boiler spaces of high-powered vessels. This is done in the hope that the vessel will be able to operate in case one of the boiler rooms is flooded. The statements above in regard to longitudinal bulkheads do not apply to naval vessels except in a very restricted way, for their subdivision is so minute that any heeling moments produced by unsymmetrical flooding are relatively small. Also, any heel that is produced may be rapidly corrected in most cases by counterflooding (see page 220).

COFFERDAMS

Cofferdams are usually formed by placing two bulkheads a few feet apart. The purpose of a cofferdam is to prevent leakage of oil from a bunker or cargo tank into an adjoining space where the presence of oil would be dangerous or otherwise undesirable. Cofferdams are commonly fitted between oil tanks and adjacent boiler rooms, pump rooms, water tanks, holds, etc. The principle behind the use of cofferdams is based on the fact that the first of the closely spaced bulkheads, under pressure of the full head of oil in the tank, may happen to spring a leak, but in this case only a small amount of oil will seep through; therefore, little pressure will be experienced by the second cofferdam bulkhead. Also, the space between the cofferdams permits visual inspection of both bulkheads and ready access for quick repair if a leak should occur.

As a well-made welded joint is watertight and oiltight, cofferdams are not required, in so far as watertightness is concerned, in welded ships but are usually fitted.

Questions

1. What three functions do bulkheads perform?

2. Why was it necessary for the International Conference for the Safety of Life at Sea to be "international"?

3. What is a two-compartment ship?

4. Why are bulkheads plated more heavily at the bottom than at the top?

5. Why are cofferdams constructed between oil tanks and fresh-water tanks in riveted ships?

6. What ships come under the rules of the International Convention for the Safety of Life at Sea?

7. Who regulates vessels not coming under the convention?

8. What four bulkheads are required by the American Bureau?

CHAPTER XII

STEM, STERN FRAME, AND RUDDER

The stem, stern frame, and rudder, all being large heavy fittings at the ends of a ship, are usually considered together.

The stem is the main frame connecting the two sides of the shell plating at the bow. It is strongly fastened at the bottom to the forward end of the keel.

The stern frame performs a similar function at the stern. In addition, it furnishes support to the rudder and in single-screw and triple-screw ships to the propeller shaft.

STEM, STERN FRAME, & RUDDER.

Fig. 119. Location of the stem, stern frame, and rudder.

The rudder is important as the means of steering the ship. It is a broad streamline fitting, hinged at its forward edge to the stern frame, and is controlled by a vertical shaft (the rudderstock) attached to it at the top and extending upward into the hull, where it is connected to the steering gear.

Figure 119 shows the location of the three parts mentioned above. Discussing these parts in detail, we shall begin with the stem.

STEM

The stem may be regarded as a more or less vertical extension of the forward end of the keel. Its functions are therefore similar to those of the keel. The stem must give strength and rigidity to the hull structure along the center line of the bow and furnish an effec-

tive connection between the two sides of the shell plating.   Since
the bow is the part of the ship that first encounters the pounding of
heavy seas and the impact of obstructions in the ship's course, just
as the keel is the first part to meet the bottom in grounding or docking, the strength and massiveness of the stem must be comparable
with those of the keel.   As in all other parts of the ship's structure,
the stem's ability to give strength and rigidity to the entire bow
depends largely on the effectiveness of the support given by auxiliary
structure within the hull, such as the decks, breasthooks, stringers,
and bow framing generally.

One of the simplest types of stem consists of a heavy flat bar of
mild steel to which the shell plating is flanged and riveted, as it is to

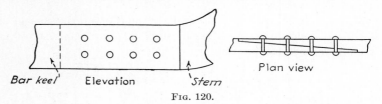

Bar keel   Elevation   Stem

Plan view

F*ɪɢ*. 120.

a bar keel.   Sometimes the stem bar is a forging, often having its
sides rabbeted to receive the shell plating in a flush-riveted joint.

With a flat-plate keel the after end of the stem is gradually
reduced in height and increased in width for connection to the
forward ends of the flat and vertical keels.   With a bar keel the
stem is usually a bar of the same cross section as the keel and is
joined to it by a scarf joint no thicker than the bars connected, as
shown in Fig. 120.

In another design of bar stem the upper part is a forging or rolled
flat bar and the lower part is a steel casting, the two sections being
scarfed together at a point just above the round of the forefoot.
Figure 121*a* shows the connections of the vertical keel and shell
plating to this casting on a riveted ship.

1. The Soft-nosed Stem.   On most of the recent ships, a stem
built up out of welded plate has been fitted in connection with a
casting at the bottom.   The stem plate is furnaced to a large radius
at the top, becoming narrower toward the bottom, and is reinforced

inside by welded-plate chocks to which decks and breasthooks may
be attached. A section of this type of stem is also shown in Fig.
121*b*. The advantage of the use of welded plate instead of a heavy
bar is that it forms a "soft-nosed" stem, which is less apt to cause
serious damage in collisions than the old-style bar stem. This is
due to the fact that a bar stem is relatively sharp and, in case of a
collision, would knife through the plating of another vessel. The
soft-nosed stem would crumple and offer a broad surface by virtue

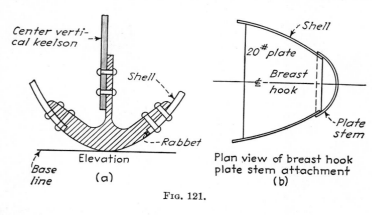

Fig. 121.

of which, if it did penetrate the shell of another vessel, the penetration would be kept to a minimum. A combination of soft-nosed
vessels and ample subdivision would prevent many sea disasters.
It would seem to be the best practice to fit a rigid stem up to a
point above the water line and then above this fit a soft-nosed
rounded clipper bow, since any damage done by ramming would
probably be above the water line of both vessels. Figure 122 shows
the plating attachment and structural backing of a modern plated
stem.

2. Bow Types. There are three types of bows in general use, the
plumb-stem bow, the clipper bow, and the raised-forefoot, or spoon,
bow.

The *plumb-stem bow* is illustrated by Fig. 123, sketch *A*. This has
been the usual merchant bow, but it is generally given a slight for-

ward rake to avoid the appearance of leaning backward. This type usually has very little flare to the sides; as a consequence, the vessel cuts through rather than rides over the waves. Difficulties are encountered with this type of bow when the anchor is raised; for the

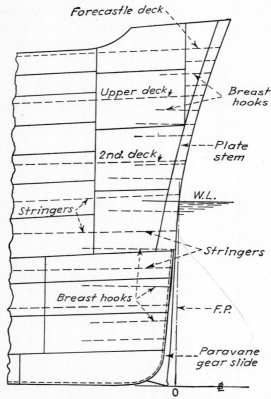

Fig. 122. A modern semisoft-nosed plated stem.

latter has to slide along the shell plating up to the hawsepipe, and this may cause damage to the shell.

The *clipper-type bow* carries the flare of the sides forward of the forefoot (Fig. 123, sketch *B*), which enables the anchor to come up

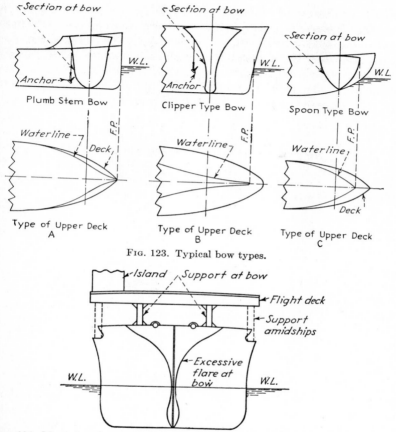

Fig. 123. Typical bow types.

Fig. 124. Most aircraft carriers have excessive flare forward to take the flight-deck supports.

into the hawsepipes without fouling the shell plating. This also gives a longer and wider forecastle deck; more room is thus provided for deck machinery, and the deck remains drier in rough weather, for the flare throws the water aside. Most aircraft carriers are built with great flare forward; this gives a wider base for supporting the forward end of the flight deck, as shown in Fig. 124.

The *spoon-type bow* (Fig. 123, sketch *C*), is used extensively on sailing yachts and icebreakers and also on a large number of merchant ships. A vessel with this type of bow will rise to the waves, which increases its seaworthiness. When a vessel with a spoon bow is in waves of its own length or longer (which in large vessels is very seldom), model tests have shown that it has less resistance and therefore is easier to drive than the clipper or plumb type.

STERN FRAME

The stern frame is similar to the stem in being a vertical extension of the keel and has the same function of connecting rigidly the two

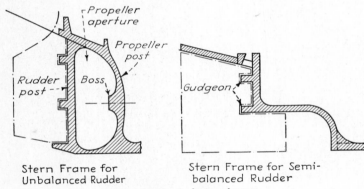

Stern Frame for
Unbalanced Rudder

Stern Frame for Semi-
balanced Rudder

Fig. 125. Typical stern frames.

sides of the shell plating. In addition, it must support the rudder and, in single-screw or triple-screw ships, the propeller shaft. In most ships the stern frame must also furnish a solid foundation for the transom frame to which the overhanging stern, or fantail, is attached. For these reasons, the design of the stern frame is necessarily more complex than that of the stem.

As shown in Fig. 125, the stern frame on a single-screw ship is composed of two posts called the *rudderpost* and *propeller post*, enclosing a space for the propeller called the *propeller aperture*. The after post is the rudderpost and furnishes support to the rudder by means of projecting lugs called *gudgeons*. These lugs do not take the weight of the rudder but act as bearings for the vertical hinge pins, or pintles, on which the rudder swings. The pintles are bolted into similar projections on the forward edge of the rudder called *rudder lugs.*

The forward post of the single-screw stern frame is the propeller post. It is bossed, or swelled out, to receive the after end of the stern tube, through which the propeller shaft passes out of the hull, and thus supports the propeller itself. The design of a stern frame

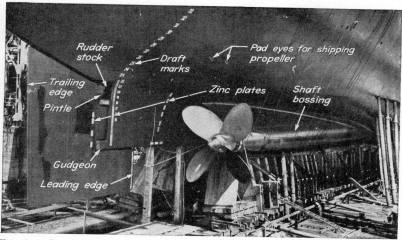

Fig. 126. Semibalanced partially underhung rudder as fitted on the *S.S. America.* The rudder is of hydrofoil shape. The balancing portion forward of the rudder stock is about 25 per cent of the total area.

for a triple-screw ship is generally similar to that for a single-screw vessel, since in both cases one of the screws is on the center line.

In twin- or quadruple-screw ships none of the shafts passes out of the hull on the center line; hence, there is ordinarily no forward post in the stern frame. In such ships the propeller aperture is commonly omitted and the shell plating is carried aft to the rudderpost, which, in this case, is often called the *stern post.* On some large vessels of this type an aperture is sometimes provided forward of the rudder to ensure a better flow of water to the propellers and to obviate vibration set up by the tips of the blades passing too close to the shell plating (Fig. 125). This vibration can usually be reduced by making this tip clearance not less than one-sixth the diameter of the propeller.

On ships having a bar keel the stern frame is commonly forged out of heavy flat bar tapered at the forward end to the same section as the keel, to which it is connected by a scarf joint, as in the case of the stem. When a flat keel is used, the forward end of the stern frame is flattened and widened for connection to the after end of the vertical-keel bars and flat keel and is usually rabbeted to receive the last keel plate. The top of the stern frame is generally extended up into the hull and attached to the transom frame.

RUDDER

In its simplest form a rudder consists of a wide flat blade and a vertical shaft, or stock, by which this blade is turned so as to steer the ship. The flat-blade rudder is found only on older ships and small boats. The newer type rudders are of streamlined section.

Rudders may be of the semibalanced or unbalanced type. A semibalanced rudder has part of the blade extended forward of the rudderstock, while an unbalanced rudder has all of its effective area aft of the stock. Semibalanced rudders are of several types, the most important of which are shown in Fig. 127.[1]

From this figure it is evident that a semibalanced type of rudder requires a smaller steering engine, for the water pressure on the forward edge tends to throw the after edge over. About 25 per cent of the total area of the rudder is placed in the forward balancing section. Semibalanced rudders are in general used on warships and large merchant ships, for they give maximum maneuvering ability without requiring excessively powerful steering gear.

On most ships, the shaft that turns the rudder is made in two sections that are bolted together just below the counter with a scarfed or flanged coupling to facilitate the unshipping of the rudder. The lower section of the shaft to which the blade is

---

[1] Quite often the expression "balanced rudder" is used for "semibalanced rudder." The term "semibalanced" is used in this text, for no rudder is "balanced" throughout the entire turning angle.

attached is called the *main piece;* the upper section, which extends upward into the hull, is called the *rudderstock.* The stock is generally a forging, which is usually cheaper and also superior to present-day castings in its resistance to torsional stress.

The weight of the rudder is borne by a rudder bearing within the hull, usually placed above the top of the sternpost on the cant floors. The stock is enclosed within a watertight trunk below this point.

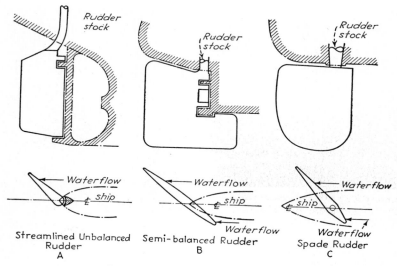

Fig. 127. Some typical rudder shapes.

The inside of the rudder bearing is cylindrical and forms the top bearing for the rudderstock. The upper surface of the bearing is flat or conical and supports a rudder carrier keyed and bolted to the head of the rudderstock. A projecting shoulder is turned on the rudderstock above and below the carrier to keep it from slipping up or down the stock. All rudder-bearing surfaces are lined with non-friction metal or micarta and thoroughly lubricated.

1. Single- and Double-plate Rudders. Rudders are constructed in many different ways according to the type and size of ship and the service for which it is intended. One of the simplest types is the single-plate rudder. This is formed from a heavy steel plate, cut to the designed shape and fastened to the main piece by heavy arms which are placed on alternate sides and between which the rudder plate is riveted. The arms may be either steel forgings or castings and are separate pieces shrunk and keyed onto the main piece, which is generally a forging. As a hydrofoil, this type of rudder is very inefficient. Since the stress in a rudder decreases from the top to

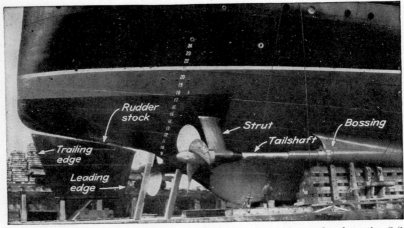

FIG. 128. Completely underhung semibalanced spade rudder as fitted on the *S.S. Acadia.* The stern is of the cruiser type. The rudder is supported entirely by the rudderstock. No pintles or gudgeons are fitted.

the bottom and from the stock to the after edge, both the main piece and rudder arms are tapered to a smaller size at the bottom and after end, respectively.

The arms are extended forward of the main piece to take the pintles and are therefore spaced to suit the gudgeons on the stern frame. The rudder stock is bolted and keyed to the top of the main piece by means of a flanged coupling placed either vertically or horizontally. A single-plate unbalanced rudder is illustrated in Fig. 129.

An alternative form of the single-plate rudder has the blade, arms, and main piece combined into a single steel casting. Very large

rudders of this type have been successfully installed; but their high
cost, excessive weight, liability to warp during production, and
poor hydrofoil section have kept them from general use.

Most large modern rudders are of double-plate design, having a
central frame on each side of which a plate is riveted or welded. At
one time this frame was usually a steel forging or casting made in

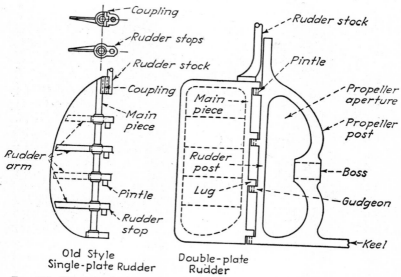

Old Style
Single-plate Rudder

Double-plate
Rudder

Fig. 129. Old-style single-plate and the modern hydrofoil unbalanced rudder.

one piece with arms and a main piece. In later designs the arms
have been replaced by stiffening webs of plate. A double-plate
rudder of this type is shown in Fig. 129.

Many modern rudders are of completely welded construction, the
side plates being welded together or to a heavy forged or cast bar at
the outer edges and stiffened internally by welded plate webs.
Since the reduction in stress toward the after edge of a rudder makes
it possible to taper the blade in thickness, such rudders are of a
streamlined hydrofoil form, the leading edge being comparatively
wide and rounded and the after, or trailing, edge pulled out to a

thin line.   Streamlining the rudder has, in some cases, reduced the over-all resistance of a vessel as much as 5 per cent.   A welded rudder of this type is shown in Fig. 130.

In the past the hollow interior of double-plate rudders was filled with some light wood and coated with red lead to prevent corrosion. A more recent practice is to leave the interior hollow and paint it with bituminous enamel.   The larger rudders have access manholes in the side plating for inspection and maintenance.   This method of construction in some cases gives the rudder enough buoyancy to float itself, thus reducing the load on the rudder bearing.

2. Goldschmidt Contraguide Rudder. Another type of rudder, which is being used extensively on the Maritime Commission C-3 type vessels, is known as the *Goldschmidt contraguide rudder.*   This rudder is offset in opposite directions at the level of the propeller hub in such a manner that the propeller blade in passing by the rudder throws its stream of water, or "race," against the offset face of the rudder (see Fig. 132), thus giving a forward thrust, or push, to the ship.

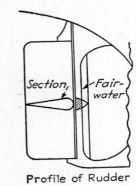

Profile of Rudder

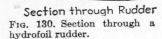

Section through Rudder

FIG. 130. Section through a hydrofoil rudder.

It has been found by experiment that the maximum efficient rudder angle is between 30 and 35 deg from the center line of the ship.   To turn a rudder to a greater angle decreases the speed of the ship but does not decrease the turning radius.   As a consequence, rudder stops are placed on the stern frame in such a position that the rudder cannot be turned more than 33 to 35 deg.   These stops are usually in the form of projecting lugs on the sides of the rudderpost in line with the uppermost rudder lug, which is enlarged and faced off so as to make the required angle with the rudder stop when the rudder is on the center line.   A rudder stop of this type is shown in Fig. 129.   On ships having the rudder controlled by a

Fɪɢ. 131. The Goldschmidt contraguide rudder and propeller post. This balanced type of hydrofoil unbalanced rudder in complement with an offset propeller post is used on the USMC C-3 vessels. See Fɪɢ. 132 for effect.

quadrant on the rudderhead, an auxiliary rudder stop is often fitted in the form of a channel stanchion filled with wood. This rudder stop is placed so that it may act as a quadrant bumper, limiting the swing of the rudder to the desired angle on each side of the center line. It is interesting to note here that the turning radius of a ship with the angle of the rudder kept constant is almost

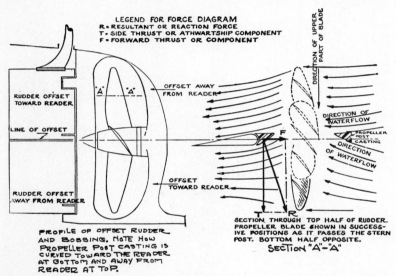

LEGEND FOR FORCE DIAGRAM
R = RESULTANT OR REACTION FORCE
T = SIDE THRUST OR ATHWARTSHIP COMPONENT
F = FORWARD THRUST OR COMPONENT

RUDDER OFFSET TOWARD READER

LINE OF OFFSET

RUDDER OFFSET AWAY FROM READER

OFFSET AWAY FROM READER

OFFSET TOWARD READER

PROFILE OF OFFSET RUDDER AND BOSSING. NOTE HOW PROPELLER POST CASTING IS CURVED TOWARD THE READER AT BOTTOM AND AWAY FROM READER AT TOP.

DIRECTION OF UPPER PART OF BLADE

DIRECTION OF WATERFLOW

PROPELLER POST CASTING

DIRECTION OF WATERFLOW

SECTION THROUGH TOP HALF OF RUDDER. PROPELLER BLADE SHOWN IN SUCCESSIVE POSITIONS AS IT PASSES THE STERN POST. BOTTOM HALF OPPOSITE.
SECTION "A"-"A"

FIG. 132. Diagrammatic view of the action of a Goldschmidt contraguide patent rudder.

the same regardless of *the* speed; *i.e., the vessel will follow about the same path when turning at* 10 *knots as it does when turning at* 20 *knots.*

   3. Stern Types. There are in general four types of sterns that are fitted to normal-type ships, the fantail, the merchant cruiser, the cruiser, and the transom. The *fantail stern* is now practically obsolete but may still be seen on many older vessels. Figure 133, sketch *A*, shows this type of stern. The *merchant-cruiser*, or *bath-tub*, stern is at present the most popular stern for merchant vessels. This is primarily because it reduces the resistance of the vessel and makes it easier to drive. In tests carried out at the Newport News

Towing Tank on a series of similar ships, it was found that the merchant-cruiser stern reduced the total resistance of the model by about 3 per cent. This reduction is mainly due to the increase in water-line length, which decreases the wave-making resistance (see Fig. 133, sketch *B*; see Chap. XIV).

The regular *cruiser stern*, from which the merchant-cruiser stern was developed, is now seen most often on large naval vessels, such

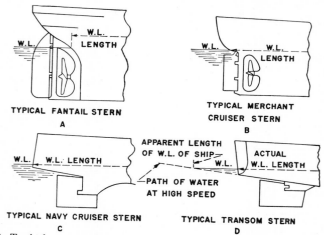

FIG. 133. Typical sterns. The naval architect continually attempts to reduce the speed-length ratio (page 176) of the vessel as much as possible without lengthening the vessel. Sketch *B*, *C*, and *D* show how some gain may be made.

as battleships and airplane carriers. Until recently, it was generally used on cruisers; hence its name (see Fig. 133, sketch *C*).

The *transom stern*, familiarly referred to as the *barn-door stern*, is shown in Fig. 133, sketch *D*. This type of stern is now fitted on high-speed vessels in the United States Navy, such as cruisers and destroyers, and on small high-speed pleasure cruisers and runabouts. This type of stern is broad and fairly flat underneath, which is helpful in preventing "squatting" of the hull at high speeds. Resistance is reduced at high speeds about 3 to 5 per cent. This reduction is accomplished by an "apparent" increase in the water-line length of the vessel which is due to the water flowing aft at such a rate that it does not come level with the undisturbed water surface for some distance behind the vessel. This leveling-off distance is the apparent increase in the length of the vessel (see Fig. 133).

Questions

1. What are the functions of the stem?
2. Discuss briefly the advantage of fitting a soft-nosed stem.
3. Sketch a typical riveted flat-bar stem.
4. What are the advantages of the clipper bow?
5. In what length waves is the spoon bow most effective?
6. What is the function of the stern frame?
7. Make a sketch of a single-screw stern frame and label the parts.
8. Why are semibalanced rudders almost invariably fitted on large vessels?
9. In the normal-form rudder what is the maximum efficient angle?
10. Is the weight of the rudder supported by the pintles?
11. What is the advantage of the double-plate rudder?
12. Why does the merchant-cruiser stern decrease the resistance (total) of a vessel?
13. How does a transom stern increase the apparent length of a vessel?

CHAPTER XIII

TYPES OF SHIPS

Most students are familiar with the automobile family and the work that each member performs. In the table below a comparison is given of the work of the members of the familiar automobile and the not so familiar ship family. In some cases the comparison is not exact but will serve for the purpose of this chapter.

On Land	On the Sea
Tractors	Tugs
Tractor trailer trucks	Tugs with barges
Heavy-duty 10-ton trucks	Full-scantling, maximum-draft freighters
Light-chassis trucks (large vans)	Shelter-deck vessels
Gasoline and oil trucks	Tankers
Coaldealers' trucks	Colliers
Station wagons	Small passenger-cargo vessels
Passenger cars	Yachts
Day buses	Bay steamers, cross-channel steamers, ferries
Transcontinental sleeper buses	Transoceanic liners

This does not begin to cover all types of ships, but it does give us an insight into the purpose of the most usual types. In the above we have entirely ignored the hundreds of specialized ships, such as whalers, cable layers, dredges, etc.

The design of a ship is based on a combination of some or perhaps all of the following considerations:

1. The cargo deadweight (the weight of the cargo to be carried).
2. The number of passengers.
3. The speed at sea.
4. Density of the cargo, *i.e.*, whether it will carry a heavy or a light cargo in relation to the space occupied.

5. Maximum draft is limited by the depth of some harbors.

6. Type of machinery—steam turbine, turboelectric, Diesel, Diesel-electric, etc.

7. Type of fuel—coal, fuel oil, Diesel oil.

8. Number of crew required.

9. Type of cargo—bales, crates, liquids, grains, etc.

10. Cruising radius required.

11. Safety requirements for the particular trade.

12. Other special requirements.

The determination of the above requirements is based on the owner's past experience, class of business, route of trade, and ability to look into the future, or on an analysis of cost data applied to a series of proposed ships of varying types, length, speed, draft, etc., the type that would return the greatest revenue to the owner being the one chosen.

A ship must operate at a profit. While the ideal vessel is one that is designed for and operates at its intended "trade," a number of vessels have been designed to operate in several trades and have been highly successful. Hard and fast rules are difficult to make in shipbuilding. Each case must be decided on its own merits.

We shall take up the ship types listed at the beginning of this chapter and briefly discuss their design and purpose. In Chap. XXIV we shall discuss the characteristics and present particulars and sketch drawings of some of the outstanding types of vessels built just prior to, during, and after the Second World War.

The Tug. This is a ship of many uses. The construction is heavy to withstand rough usage over a long period of time. The tug *Dorothy*, built at Newport News in 1891, is still in use more than 60 years later.

Tugs carry no cargo and are in reality floating power plants. They are useful in handling and docking large vessels, towing, fire fighting, and ocean salvage. The harbor tugs are usually small vessels about 70 to 100 ft in length. They very seldom venture far from their home port. The seagoing tugs, which range up to 200 ft in length, may be classified into two groups. The first is the ocean towing tug. This tug is ordinarily used for long ocean hauls, perhaps towing dredging or other equipment halfway around the world. The second type is the salvage tug. This type is very fast and powerful. Speed is necessary, for salvage[1] usually goes to the first tug, or vessel, that arrives on the scene of the disaster, takes the vessel in tow and brings her safely to port, or aids and assists in getting her safely to port. If the ship is lost, saving the cargo is also salvage. Salvage tugs are usually fitted with fire-fighting, life-

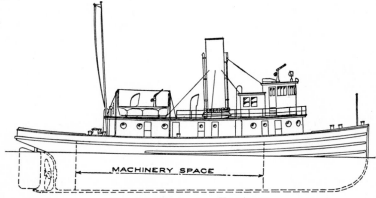

Fig. 134. Harbor tug *Huntington*.

saving, and salvage equipment, in addition to their powerful propulsion engines.

Full-scantling Maximum-draft Freighters. Full-scantling vessels are designed to carry heavy, dense cargoes such as heavy freight, ore, and sulphur. The term "full scantling" means that the

[1] "Salvage" is a term used in admiralty law to denote, not only the act of saving life and property from the perils of the sea, but also the amount of money given to the salvor for his risk and work in performing this act. Salvage to be paid must be complete; that is, the vessel and/or part of the cargo, if any, must actually be saved. The salvor receives salvage based on the risks taken and the value of the salvaged cargo and vessel. The author knows of no case where the salvage has been 100 per cent of the value of the ship and cargo, but does know of many cases where it has been less than one half the value. The owner of the salvaging vessel usually receives two thirds of the money paid and the crew receives one third.

framing, plating, etc., are heavy and strong and that the vessel is designed to load to the maximum allowable draft based on her length.   These vessels may be thought of as the heavy-duty trucks of the sea.   The *S.S. Angelina* of the Bull Line is a ship of this type. Figure 135 shows a poop, bridge, and forecastle (P. B. and F.), full-scantling vessel.   The Liberty-type vessels built between 1940 and 1946 are full-scantling ships.

Shelter-deck Vessels.   The other extreme from the full-scantling vessel is the "shelter-decker."   This is a type of ship that will give the most space per ton of cargo.   If the owner wishes to carry a

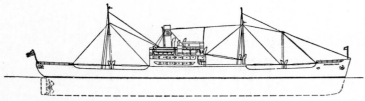

FIG. 135. *S.S. Angelina.*   Full-scantling poop, bridge, and forecastle type.

cargo that occupies much space but has very little weight, such as automobiles or cellulose, he would choose a vessel of this type.

It takes about 220 cu ft of automobiles and about 240 cu ft of cellulose to make up a ton of cargo.   However, 7 cu ft of copper slab or 17 cu ft of asphalt will weigh a ton.   If the automobiles were loaded on the full-scantling ship, the vessel would be full of automobiles long before she was brought down to her maximum allowable draft (Plimsoll mark), which would mean a loss of many tons of cargo.   On the other hand, if the shelter-decker were loaded with copper slab, she would be down to her "marks" before the holds were one-third full.   This would also mean a loss, for this vessel would travel to her destination two-thirds empty.   Loading the copper slab on the full-scantling vessel and the automobiles on the shelter-decker would practically double the amount of cargo transported.   Whether to build a shelter-decker or a full scantling or some type in between becomes, then, a question of the cubic feet required for each ton of cargo.   The design of both these types is also closely tied up with the American Bureau of Shipping rules (page 10) and the tonnage laws (pages 239 to 243). Figures 135 and 136 show sketches of a typical full scantling, P. B. and F., and a shelter-decker. The USMA design C-1A, C-2 and C-3 are all shelter-deck vessels.

Tankers. Oils, gasoline, molasses, and like liquid-bulk cargoes are usually transported by means of a type of ship known as a *tanker*. Most tankers have their machinery located aft and separated from the main tank spaces by means of twin bulkheads forming a narrow empty compartment called a *cofferdam*.

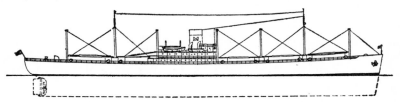

Fig. 136. *S.S. Hawaiian Planter*, a typical shelter-decker.

Tankers may be divided into three general classes, ocean-going, coastwise, and river craft. These classes differ very little except in respect to size and service.

Most of the world's modern tankers (about 83 per cent) are propelled by internal-combustion engines. Most American owners, however, still prefer steam propulsion. The steam power plant consumes more fuel than the Diesel, but fuel oil is plentiful and relatively cheap in the United States compared with its abundance and price in foreign countries. Most American designers feel that the steam plant's reliability and freedom from repairs more than make up for the increased cost of fuel. Furthermore, it should be kept in mind that fuel consumption is but one of many factors in the final cost of operation of the propulsion machinery.

Figure 137 shows the *Esso Richmond*, a modern steam-propelled high-speed Standard Oil tanker, and Fig. 138 shows a smaller river tanker belonging to the same company. It will be noted that no inner-bottom plating is fitted in way of the tank spaces. A tanker does not require a second skin; if the shell is punctured, water would simply flood the tank and, as the tanker is designed to carry liquid cargo, the inflowing water would simply become cargo.   A small cargo hold is fitted forward of No. 1 tank to provide space for the carrying of dry cargo, to give sufficient buoyancy to the bow when

FIG. 137. *S.S. Esso Richmond*, a 553-ft high-speed ocean tanker.

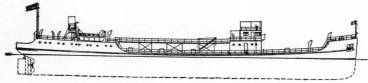

FIG. 138. *M.S. Esso Delivery No.* 11, a 260-ft river tanker.

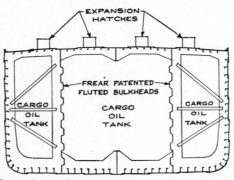

FIG. 139. Midship section of *S.S. Esso Richmond*, a modern twin-bulkhead type.

all tank spaces are filled, and to balance the relative emptiness of the engine room.

The sections through the ship in Fig. 139 show the longitudinal framing that is almost universal in tanker construction.   As mentioned before, this system gives great longitudinal strength, and the deep webs required do not interfere with the liquid stowage.

Figure 139 shows the modern twin-bulkhead design, and Fig. 140 the older centerline-bulkhead summer-tank design.

Collier. Colliers are ships specially designed for carrying coal in bulk. There are numerous other ships that are closely akin to the collier. The ore carrier operating on the Great Lakes is an example of one of these. These bulk-carrying ships may be roughly divided into two classes, the "self-unloaders" and those which must rely

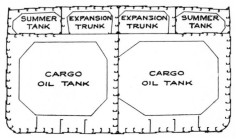

Fig. 140. Midship section of *S.S. John D. Archibold*, a centerline-bulkhead type.

Fig. 141. *S.S. Huron*, a Great Lakes self-unloading collier.

on shore-based unloading equipment. Modern scientific loading equipment has made it possible to load as much as 12,000 tons of coal aboard a collier in as little as 4 hr. An equal amount of iron ore has been loaded on a lake freighter in 16½ min and later unloaded in 2½ hr. The self-unloaders can deliver their own cargoes on the dock, 100 ft from the ship's side, at the rate of 1,000 tons per hr or more.

The machinery space on these bulk carriers is almost invariably aft to facilitate rapid loading and unloading, for the shaft tunnel necessary with machinery amidships interferes with unloading operations. A typical self-unloading collier is shown in Fig. 141.

The Medium Passenger-cargo Vessel.   A good example of this type of vessel is the *S.S. President Jackson*, a Maritime Commission C-3 design.   These vessels are 465 ft long by 69 ft 6 in. beam by 42 ft 6 in. deep, with a 26-ft 9-in. keel draft; the corresponding displacement at this draft is 16,175 tons, with a deadweight carrying capacity of 9,937 tons.   Her gross tonnage is 9,255.86, and her net tonnage is 5,151 (see Chap. XVIII for a discussion of gross and net tonnage).

The *S.S. President Jackson* carries 96 passengers in 38 staterooms. A crew of 122 persons is required for her operation.   Speaking in

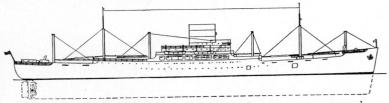

Fig. 142. *S.S. President Jackson,* a shelter-deck cargo-passenger vessel.

general and for ocean voyages only, every 3 passengers require 1 crew member.   This does not include deck and engine-room crew. This ship is a good example of a shelter-deck cargo-passenger vessel. A typical C-3 is shown in Fig. 142.

The C-3 type vessel is designed to operate as a "liner"; *i.e.,* she will have a fixed schedule and a fixed course, or "line," of travel. A liner can be thought of as an oceanic ferry shuttling back and forth with predetermined, or fixed, ports of call.   The tramp steamer, on the other hand, has been compared to a cruising taxi; *i.e.,* she picks up her cargo where she finds it and goes to any destination.   The tramp has no fixed schedule or line of travel.

Yachts.   The yacht is the pleasure car of the sea.   Standard-designed factory-type yachts are now built in large quantities. However, many persons prefer to have their yachts custom-designed by one of the numerous yacht architects, while others prefer to design their own.   Numerous yachts are built according to rule-of-thumb methods or to no design at all.   The results in the last three cases may be good but are more often ludicrous.

A large percentage of the errors in yacht design is due to the fact that the designer ignores the peculiarities of the waters in which the yacht is to operate. As an example of this, a deep-draft sailing yacht that behaves beautifully in the deep water off the coast of Maine will find its ports of call very limited in Chesapeake Bay and if it ventures out of the main channel may find itself hard aground. Likewise, shallow-draft boats designed for bay use are usually at a distinct disadvantage off the coast of Maine. However, excellent compromises suitable for general use are often possible.

Bay, Sound, and River Vessels. These are the vessels that are most familiar to inhabitants on the East or West coast or on the great river systems of the Middle West.

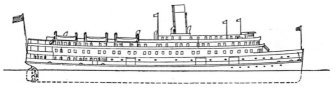

Fig. 143A. *S.S. Yorktown*, a Chesapeake Bay steamer.

The bay and sound vessels are usually shoal draft (not over 10 to 15 ft) and fairly fast. Most of them are now screw propelled. While the hull is of steel, the superstructure is usually of wood. Wood superstructures form a distinct fire hazard; no doubt steel, or some other fireproof material, will be substituted in the future. If they operate in protected waters, such as Chesapeake Bay, they almost invariably have a midship section shaped as in Fig. 143*B*. This type of section gives a low stability factor (or *GM*, as we shall see in Chap. XVI), when the vessel is upright. This small stability causes the vessel to have an easy roll. Should the vessel roll to a dangerous angle, the sponsons would become immersed, thus increasing the stability, as explained in Chap. XVI. This type of hull is not suitable for ocean use owing to the large waves encountered.

Most of these vessels carry the passenger's automobile as well as cargo. Some are designed as double-enders and can operate in either direction. If they are double-operating, they will have a propeller and rudder at each end of the vessel. The propellers are usually connected to opposite ends of the same shaft, and both rotate. If of the paddle-wheel type, they have a rudder at each end. Double pilothouses are a feature of this double-ended type of boat, the forward pilothouse controlling the after rudder, and vice versa. On the Hudson River and Great Lakes, some of the

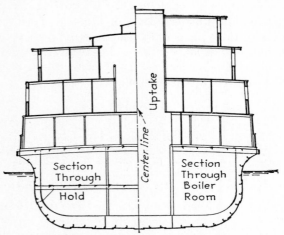

Fig. 143*B*. Midship section of a Chesapeake Bay steamer.

steamers are still of the paddle-wheel type and are fast and efficient boats.

The Mississippi River boats were usually "side-wheelers" or "stern-wheelers." Tunnel-type propellers are now in great use, especially on the towboats. These vessels must of necessity be of very shallow draft, which accounts for the stern-wheel and tunnel-type propulsion. They usually load and unload by coming right up to the river bank and putting over a gangway. At times the vessel is moored to a tree. The newer boats are usually loaded and unloaded at special docks. Their draft very seldom exceeds 6 to 8 ft, for the limiting draft from Pittsburgh to the Gulf of Mexico is about 9 ft. Figure 144 shows a typical old-style Mississippi River packet. Note the steel rods that support the ends.

In this same category we might place the swift channel steamers plying between England and the Continent. These are like the bay and sound steamers in that they are high speed (18 knots or more) for their size, and their runs are comparatively short. Most of the bay, sound, and cross-channel ships have runs that are timed to a train schedule; *i.e.*, they act as a link in a railroad system. They must function in all sorts of weather and run on schedule whether the water is rough or smooth. Some of these ships are propelled by paddle wheels, but the great majority have screw

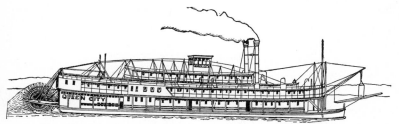

Fig. 144. The *Queen City*, an old-style Mississippi River steamer.

propulsion. Internal-combustion engines are used to a great extent for powering.

Large Transoceanic Vessels. These vessels operate on all the oceans of the world. Some are built primarily for passenger service and are called passenger liners. Others carry passengers and cargo. The number of passengers in relation to the amount of cargo usually determines whether they are called passenger vessels, passenger-cargo vessels, or cargo vessels.

The *S.S. Queen Mary* carries very little cargo and is primarily a passenger vessel. The *S.S. America* has fairly large cargo spaces but is still thought of as a passenger liner.

Between the leviathans, represented by the *S.S. Queen Mary*, *Queen Elizabeth*, and *United States*, and the small vessels plying the coastal waters, there are thousands of types. We have touched on only a few in this chapter. A. C. Hardy's "Ships at Work"[1] is

[1] Chemical Publishing Co., New York.

recommended as instructive and entertaining reading for the young shipbuilder.

Another interesting type of ship known as a *weight lifter* is exemplified by the "Bel" ships, so called because the first part of their names always start with "Bel," as the *Belnor, Beljeanne,* etc. There is very little difference between a "Bel" ship and a full scantling except that the "Bel" ship has extra-heavy masts, booms, and hoisting machinery. To quote from A. C. Hardy's book mentioned above:

One of the record cargoes achieved by the Bel fleet was that of the *Belpareil*, a twin-screw ship, which loaded three hopper barges, each weighing no less than 150 tons.

Prior to lifting the barges, two tugs stowed athwartships on the foredeck had already been shipped. In comparison with the barges these seem almost insignificant, but they measured 75 ft in length and weighed no less than 100 tons apiece.

Naming Ships. An owner may give his vessel any name he chooses; however, some companies, and during the Second World War the Maritime Commission, chose methods of naming vessels according to types. While some of the better-known systems may vary in certain cases, the general naming tendencies are outlined below:

Vessels	Source of Name
American President Lines	After presidents (*S.S. President Garfield*)
United Fruit Company	After banana-raising republics, cities, or provinces (*Antigua*)
Liberty ships	After history-making Americans (*John Morton*)
Victory ships	By the addition of the word Victory to names of one of the United Nations (*Greece Victory*), an American town (*Laconia Victory*), or an American college (*Kingspoint Victory, Hampden-Sydney Victory*)
Mariner class	By the addition of the word Mariner to the nickname of a state (*Tarheel Mariner*)
Atlantic Refining Company supertankers	By the addition of the word Atlantic (*Atlantic Seaman*)
Esso Shipping Company	By the addition of the word Esso to the name of a city (*Esso Raleigh*)

Vessels	Source of Name
Farrell Lines	The word African attached to some name, as *S.S. African Enterprise.* Operates to South Africa
Matson Line	The word Hawaiian added to a name, such as *S.S. Hawaiian Merchant.* Hawaiian trade
American Export Lines	Names beginning with Ex (*S.S. Exbrook*)
Navy tankers (T-2)	By the addition of the word Mission to a Christian outpost in the far west (*U.S.S. Mission San Luis Obispo*)
Battleships (Navy)	After states (*U.S.S. Missouri*)
Cruisers (Navy)	After cities (*U.S.S. Newport News*)
Destroyers (Navy)	After heroic personnel (*U.S.S. Mustin*)
Submarines (Navy)	After fish (*U.S.S. Tuna*)
Carriers (Navy)	After battles except *U.S.S. Roosevelt* and *U.S.S. Forrestal* (*U.S.S. Coral Sea*)

Questions

1. Name the three types of tug. For what is each used?

2. What is salvage?

3. Tell in a few simple words what the term "full scantling" means.

4. For what types of cargo is a shelter-decker used?

5. What type of propulsion is used in most tankers?

6. Why is double bottom not required in way of the liquid cargo spaces on a tanker?

7. Why is the machinery space on bulk carriers located aft?

8. About how many crew members would be required by an ocean-going passenger liner with a passenger list of 900?

9. Why is the sponson-type hull unsuitable for ocean-going vessels?

10. Where does the term "liner" come from?

NOTE: Chapter XXIV elaborates on this chapter and may well be read by the student at this time for information as to the type of ships now in operation. The inboard profiles will be found of especial value in fixing ship types in mind. Chapter XXIV is not combined with Chap. XIII because the material in Chap. XXIV will continually change and the author has made this the last chapter so that changes may be made without disturbing the preceding text.

CHAPTER XIV

LINES AND OFFSETS

The form of any solid body, such as a ship, can be determined by cutting it into sections and then noting its shape as revealed by the outlines of the cut surfaces. Each surface outline, since it lies in one plane, can be measured and then reproduced on a drawing, using the dimensions obtained by measurement.

In the early days of shipbuilding, and even during the clipper-ship era, the naval architect or the builder of a hull would make a small model of a proposed ship and lift lines from this model. The model was usually built of horizontal planks in sandwich fashion. The temporarily attached planks would then be shaped by taking a little off here and there until the experienced hand and eye of the model builder were satisfied that a good, fair form had been obtained. The planks of the model were separated; and measurements, or offsets, were taken from the model at different plank levels. These offsets were used to lay out the frames, planking, etc., of the full-sized ship.

A full-sized ship cannot be sawed apart and measured, but its form can be determined in the same way as that of the model by passing sets of parallel planes through its hull and measuring the outlines of these planes. The plan that defines the form of the ship by the use of such planes is called the *lines plan*.

The lines plan shows the outlines of all the cross-sectional planes and decks required to define the molded surface of the hull. This surface is bounded at the top by the sheer, or fore-and-aft curvature of the decks, and at the ends by the stem and stern profiles. All other lines shown on this plan represent the intersections of three sets of parallel planes with the molded form of the ship, or in

166

other words, the traces of these planes on the molded surface of the hull.[1]

The planes in one of these three sets are horizontal, or parallel to the base line, and their intersections with the molded form are known as *water lines*. These water-line planes correspond to the upper and lower surfaces of the planks composing the designer's wooden model. In making the model, alternate planks of light and dark wood were often used, or else the wood was put together with dark glue, to show the water-line shapes more distinctly.

The planes in the second set shown on the lines plan are vertical and longitudinal, or parallel to the fore-and-aft center line, and their intersections with the molded hull surface are called *buttock lines*. If the designer's model were built up out of longitudinal planks set on edge instead of being laid flat, the surface of these planks would correspond to the buttock planes.

The planes in the third set are also vertical, but they run transversely, or square to the fore-and-aft center line. Their surface intersections are the frame lines corresponding to the surfaces of the transverse vertical planks, which sometimes were used instead of horizontal planks, in the earliest designer's models mentioned previously.

THE LINES DRAWING

For the purpose of showing the relationship of the three sets of intersection curves to each other, the lines plan is made up of three principal views of the ship's form, known as the *half-breadth plan*, the *profile*, or *sheer plan*, and the *body plan*. These three views show the ship's form as it appears from above, from the side, and from the end, respectively. In each view, the molded surface intersections of one of the three sets of planes, being seen in outline, appear as curves, while the other two sets of planes, being seen edgewise, appear only as straight lines. All three views are laid out from two fore-and-aft reference planes, one horizontal through the base of the molded form and the other vertical and longitudinal through its

[1] The Castle Film Co., New York, has issued a film (No. 24), *Preparing and Setting a Keel Block and Bottom Cradle*. This film gives an excellent presentation of a ship's lines and is highly recommended as a teaching aid.

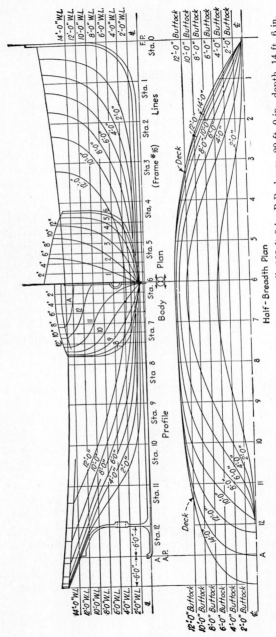

Fig. 145. Harbor tug *Huntington*, lines plan. Length, 109 ft, 0 in. over-all, 103 ft 0 in. B.P., beam, 29 ft, 0 in., depth, 14 ft, 6 in.

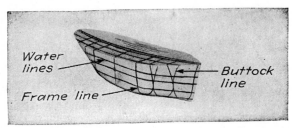

Fɪɢ. 146*A*. The intact model showing water lines, buttock lines, and frame lines painted on the outside where they intersect the shell.

Fɪɢ. 146*B*. Water planes. Model cut parallel to the base line and lifted vertically to show the shape of the water planes. Outline at shell corresponds to water lines on half-breadth plan.

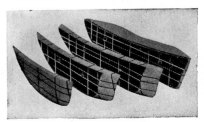

Fɪɢ. 146*C*. Buttocks. Model cut vertically parallel to the centerline plane and pulled apart laterally to show shape of the buttock planes. Outline at shell corresponds to buttock lines on profile.

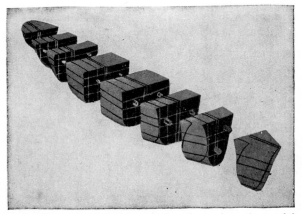

Fɪɢ. 146*D*. Frame lines cut at transverse intervals to show shape of frame lines. Outline at shell corresponds to frame lines as shown in body plan.

center.   The intersection of the horizontal reference plane with any view is called the *base line* and the similar intersection of the vertical reference plane is called the *center line*.   The fact that these lines represent planes viewed edgewise explains why the base line runs longitudinally on the profile and transversely on the body plan, while the center line is vertical on the body plan and horizontal on the half-breadth plan (see Fig. 145).

1. Half-breadth Plan.   The half-breadth plan is usually drawn for the port side only, since both sides of the ship are alike.   This plan is made looking down on the ship, showing its hull cut horizontally by the first set of planes, which are parallel to the base. The curved outlines of these planes are the water lines, which reveal the form of the hull at various heights above the base.   The half-breadth plan also gives the location and spacing of the frame stations and buttock planes, both appearing edgewise as straight lines.   The decks, bulwark rail, and stern knuckle, if any, also appear as curves in this view.

2. Profile.   The profile is a longitudinal side elevation, generally drawn with the bow to the right.   It shows the contour of stem and stern and the sheer of the decks, rail, and knuckle.   Its main purpose is to show the molded form of the ship at the center line and at the longitudinal vertical planes called *buttocks*, parallel to the fore-and-aft center line.   It also shows the location of frame stations and water-line planes, which are both seen edgewise as straight lines in this view, while the sheer lines of the decks, rail, and knuckle are curved.

3. Body Plan.   The body plan is an endwise view of the ship's molded form, showing its shape at each transverse frame-station plane, and it also locates the decks, rail, knuckle, longitudinal girders, sheet lines of shell plating, and frame endings.   All these lines appear as fair curves in this view, while the water lines and buttock planes are shown as straight lines.   The body plan is drawn for one side of the ship only.   The sections forward of amidships, making up the *forebody*, are shown to the right of the center line, while the sections aft of amidships, in the *afterbody*, are shown to the left.

Additional planes, known as *diagonals*, are also used to define the longitudinal molded form through the turn of the bilge and just above and below it.   These planes run diagonally downward from the center line toward the bilge, more or less normal (perpendicular) to the molded hull surface.   They are seen edgewise as straight lines in the body plan, but their true form does not appear in either of the other two views of the lines plan and must be shown in a separate view, often combined with the half-breadth plan.

Fig. 147. View of the mold loft.   The mold loft is of sufficient size so that the lines of a ship may be laid down full scale.   The rectangular patterns shown are templates of shell plates.   The lines on the mold-loft floor are frame lines.

OFFSETS

The measured dimensions to the outline of the ship's molded form, as revealed by the various planes on the lines plan, are known as *offsets*.   This name is derived from the fact that these outlines can be reproduced, either to full size or to any reduced scale, by "setting off" these dimensions from the base line, center line, or any other fixed reference line.   When set off vertically above base, an offset is

called a *height*.   When set off horizontally from the center line, it is
a *half breadth* or *half width*.

When three planes intersect each other at right angles, as the
various planes on the lines plan do, any point in the line of intersection between two of these planes can be definitely located by a

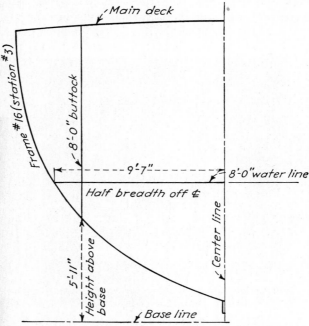

FIG. 148*A*. Frame offsets for section 3 (frame 16), see FIG. 148*B*.

single dimension, measured from the third plane along this intersection line.   This principal is followed in measuring the offsets for a
ship's molded form, which are generally taken at each frame station,
as half widths to each water line or as heights to each buttock line.
Since the offset is measured along the intersection of the frame-
station plane with the water line or buttock plane for which it is
given, *only this one dimension or offset is required to locate each point
in the sectional outlines of the molded form.*

Figure 148*A* shows offsets for points on a frame curve at a water line and buttock. Figure 148*B* illustrates the fact that, since each point lies in two planes, these offsets determine not only the half width and height of the frame at a water line and buttock but also the half width and height of the water line and buttock at this frame.

Preliminary Lines. The lines of a new ship as determined by its designer are drawn up to reduced scale (usually about one-fiftieth or

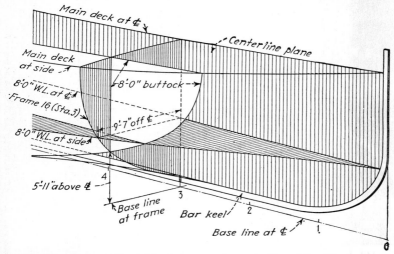

FIG. 148*B*. Skeleton half model of the tug shown in FIG. 145. The section at frame 16 (station 3) is shown also in FIG. 148*A*.

one-hundredth of the full size) by the hull technical office of the shipyard hull-design division, as the preliminary lines plan. On this plan, the transverse sections are drawn, not at frames, but at stations equally spaced between the forward and after perpendiculars of the ship. These stations divide the length of the vessel into an even number of intervals, for convenience in calculating the displacement by the rules explained in the next chapter. Another reason why the designer draws the preliminary lines at displacement stations, instead of at frames, is that the frame spacing is usually not determined until long after these lines have been drawn.

From the preliminary lines, offsets are measured with a scale and
made up into a table known as the *preliminary offsets*, usually
included in the lines plan.   Blueprint copies of the preliminary lines
and offsets are then sent to the mold loft, where they are used in
laying down the lines of the ship to full size, on the mold-loft floor,
and in fairing them up.   The mold-loft lines are first laid down at

Fig. 149. Lifting a steel plate. At times it is difficult to pick up accurately the
shape of a plate from the mold-loft floor. In such a case, a mold, or template, is
made directly from the ship. This is known as lifting a plate. The plate is laid
off, cut, and rolled to the shape indicated by the lifted template.

displacement stations; but as soon as the frame spacing has been
settled, a full-sized transverse section is drawn for every frame,
forming the working body plan.   From this body plan, molds are
made for the fabrication of the steel plates and shapes making up
the ship's hull.

Fairing the Lines.   Fairing the lines of a ship consists of two
processes, (1) smoothing out the curves representing sections
through the molded form until none of them shows any humps or

sudden changes in direction and (2) bringing the intersections of these curves into agreement with each other in all three views of the lines plan. The first object is attained by pinning springy wooden battens in a fair line through the spots determined by the offsets. The second is accomplished by adjusting these battens until the offset to any curve intersection is the same in both the two views in which it is definitely located. In the third view, both the intersecting curves lie in planes seen edgewise as straight lines; hence, the intersection is indefinite and cannot be checked (see intersections on Figs. 146A, B, and C).

As already stated, the lines are laid down in the mold loft to full size, on a scale fifty to one hundred times larger than that of the lines plan. It is therefore easier for the loftsman to notice any *unfairness* or any discrepancies between the same intersections in two different views than it was for the *draftsman* who drew the lines plan. The lines as completed on the mold-loft floor are much more nearly fair than on the preliminary drawing. A set of corrected offsets at frame stations is now scaled by the loftsman from the full-sized lines and returned to the hull drawing room. Here they are made up on tracing-cloth sheets, which are combined to form the book of offsets. Blueprint copies of this book are then sent to the hull and engine drawing rooms for use in developing the plans for the ship and to various yard departments needing them in their work.

Sectional-area Curve. The lines of a new vessel generally are drawn by its designer in accordance with a predetermined sectional-area curve, based on model-basin results obtained by towing models of previous ships of the same type and proportions as the proposed vessel. The data thus obtained have been studied and analyzed until the best distribution of sectional area for minimum resistance to propulsion has been well established (see page 180).

The sectional-area curve is drawn on a base line representing, to some convenient scale, the length adopted for the vessel (see Fig. 162). On this base line, ordinates are set up at the same displacement stations to be used in drawing the lines. The length of each ordinate is made to represent, on a suitable scale, the area of a transverse section through the ship's molded form at that station, up to the designed water line and on one side of the fore-and-aft center line.   These areas can be summed up by one of the calculating rules described in the next chapter, so as to give the ship's displacement.

Since the form of this sectional-area curve depends on the ship's displacement and length, both these factors in the design must be

Fig. 150. The *R.J. Bowman* on trial running at a speed of 15 knots.   As this vessel is 100 ft long the speed-length ratio is: $V/\sqrt{L} = 15/\sqrt{100} = {}^{15}\!/_{10} = 1.5$.   As a speed-length ratio of 1.5 is the maximum at which a displacement-type hull may be pushed, she is running at her top speed even though she has 1,000 hp.   It will be noted that at this speed-length ratio the ship sinks into the trough, or "hole," between the wave crests formed at the bow and stern.   It would take much more horsepower to push her over her bow wave, and if this power were available she would begin to plane.

determined before the curve can be drawn.   The displacement can be approximated by the use of a likely ratio of deadweight (carrying capacity) to displacement (total weight of the ship), which should, for example, vary from 0.65 to 0.75 for cargo vessels.   The length must be chosen to give suitable relationships between displacement, length, and speed.   For convenience, those relationships are expressed as dimensionless coefficients, known as the *speed-length ratio* and *displacement-length coefficient*.   The speed-length ratio is the ratio of the speed in knots to the square root of the effective length in feet and may be written

$$\text{Speed-length ratio} = \frac{V}{\sqrt{L}}$$

This ratio for normal merchant hulls is seldom greater than 1.0 and usually is about 0.70. At a speed-length ratio of about 1.5 the hull forms a wave crest at the bow and stern and sinks into the trough between. To get a vessel out of this "hole" in the water takes a tremendous expenditure of power. If this expenditure is made and the hull is forced over the bow wave, the phenomenon of "planing" takes place and the hull is no longer of the displacement type. This phenomenon of planing begins at a speed-length ratio of about 2.5 to 3.

Sailing yachts of the displacement type never have the power required to push themselves over their own bow wave; consequently, their maximum speed-length ratio is 1.5.

Below are two examples illustrating the use of the speed-length ratio.

Example 1: Calculate the maximum top speed of a displacement-type sailboat with a water-line length of 36 ft.

Solution: $\sqrt{36} = 6$, maximum $\dfrac{V}{\sqrt{L}} = 1.5$

$$V = 1.5 \times \sqrt{L} = 1.5 \times 6 = 9 \text{ knots}$$

Example 2: If the speed-length ratio of the *Queen Mary* is 1.0 and her length is about 1,000 ft, what is her speed?

Solution: $\dfrac{V}{\sqrt{L}} = 1$, $\sqrt{L} = \sqrt{1,000} = 31.8$

Then

$$\text{Speed} = 1.0 \times 31.8 = 31.8 \text{ knots}$$

The displacement-length coefficient is the ratio of the displacement in tons of salt water to the cube of the length in hundreds of feet and may be expressed as

$$\text{Displacement-length ratio} = \frac{\text{displacement}}{\left(\dfrac{L}{100}\right)^3}$$

The 100 is used as a divisor to make the coefficient number small. This coefficient is useful in comparing the relative *fatness* of vessels.

Form Coefficients. The other dimensions of breadth, draft, and depth, as well as the general character of the lines, are chosen so as

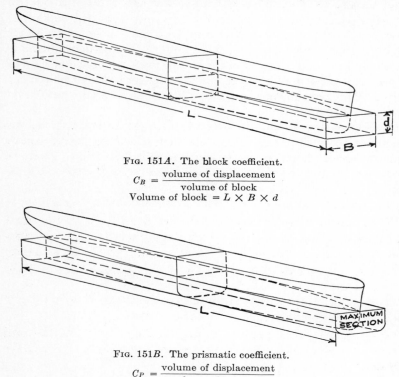

Fig. 151*A*. The block coefficient.

$$C_B = \frac{\text{volume of displacement}}{\text{volume of block}}$$

Volume of block $= L \times B \times d$

Fig. 151*B*. The prismatic coefficient.

$$C_P = \frac{\text{volume of displacement}}{\text{volume of prismoid}}$$

Volume of prismoid $= L \times \text{maximum section area}$

to agree with suitable coefficients of fineness, known as the *block coefficient, prismatic coefficient, maximum-section coefficient,* and *water-plane coefficient.* The final choice of the breadth is subject to considerations of stability; the draft is usually the maximum available in the harbors on the ship's route; and the depth depends on freeboard and carrying capacity. These coefficients express the fineness of the vessel by giving the ratio of its underwater volume or cross-sectional area to the maximum volume or area allowed by the dimensions. The lower the coefficient, the finer the form.

The block coefficient is the ratio of the volume of displacement to the volume of the enclosing rectangular block having the same dimensions as the ship's hull. It may be written

$$C_B = \frac{\text{displacement}}{L \times B \times d}$$

where L = length.
B = beam.
d = draft.

The maximum-section coefficient is the ratio of the maximum sectional area to the area of the enclosing rectangle, having as its dimensions the breadth and draft of the ship. This may be written

$$C_M = \frac{\text{maximum sectional area}}{B \times d}$$

The prismatic coefficient is the ratio of the displacement volume to that of a prismoid having the same length and maximum cross-sectional area as the ship. It is equal to the block coefficient divided by the maximum-section coefficient.

$$C_P = \frac{C_B}{C_M}$$

The water-plane coefficient is the ratio of the area of the load water plane to the area of the enclosing rectangle. It may be written

$$C_{WP} = \frac{\text{area of water plane}}{L \times B}$$

Figures 151*A* and *B* illustrate the relationship of the underwater form of the ship to the enclosing rectangular or prismatic block, as expressed by the block coefficient and prismatic coefficient. Figure 152 shows graphically the areas whose ratios constitute the maximum-section coefficient and water-plane coefficient. It also shows that the prismatic coefficient represents the ratio of the area under the sectional-area curve to that of the enclosing rectangle, since the height of this curve, by definition, is equal to the maximum-section area and its length is the same as the ship's length.

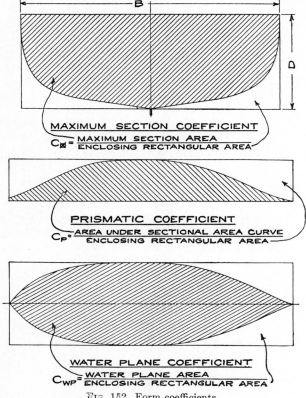

Fig. 152. Form coefficients.

In using the sectional-area curve as the basis for drawing a ship's lines, the designer must consider the forms found to be best for the frames forward and aft, whether U-shaped or V-shaped, and the most desirable form for the water-line endings, whether full, straight, or hollow. The lines are started by sketching in a freehand body plan, drawn to the correct breadth, draft, and depth and made up of transverse sections having the areas obtained from the sectional-area curve (refer to Figs. 145 and 148). This sketched body plan will be unfair, and the first line to be faired is the load water line, from which the half breadths for this water line can be corrected on the body-plan sketch and the sections redrawn to suit, without altering their areas. The next line faired will be the bilge diagonal, and the same process will be continued and extended through the other two views on the lines plan until all water lines, buttocks, and sections at stations are fair and in complete agreement. See Fig. 145 and check for any unfairness. The observant student may find several spots that are *not quite in agreement.*

Use of the Form Coefficients. The coefficients of fineness (form coefficients) are particularly valuable to the designer, for they are dimensionless; *i.e.*, they will apply to forms of all sizes because they are not in feet, tons, barrels, or other confining units but are merely numbers. The following table covers the field from a tug to an ocean liner.

TABLE OF TYPICAL SHIPS AND THEIR FINENESS COEFFICIENTS*

The ships in this table are arranged in declining order of their speed-length ratios. It will be noted that the tug *Huntington* is a faster ship for her length than the *S.S. America.*

Ship	Type	L'	Knots	$V/\sqrt{L}$	C_B	$C_{\bowtie}$	C_P	C_{WP}	$\dfrac{\Delta}{(L/100)^3}$
Nenemoosha...............	Yacht	121	12	1.09	.464	.760	.611	.677	132
Huntington...............	Tug	100	10	1.00	.532	.853	.663	.776	489
S.S. Acadia...............	Pass-Cargo	400	20	1.00	.536	.947	.566	.701	106
S.S. Hawiian Planter......	C-3 Cargo	465	18	.835	.670	.982	.682	.790	178
S.S. Esso Richmond	Tanker	547	18	.770	.660	.985	.670	.754	142
S.S. Pres. Jackson........	Pass-Cargo	465	16.5	.765	.660	.982	.673	.768	165
S.S. America...............	Pass-Cargo	686	23	.765	.588	.979	.600	.727	106
S.S. Nightengale..........	C-2 Cargo	435	15.5	.743	.683	.980	.697	.762	167
S.S. Angelina............	Cargo	385	13	.663	.714	.986	.724	.804	185
Liberty Ship (1941).......	Cargo	416	11	.540	.748	.983	.761	.848	178
S.S. Clairton (1917).......	Cargo	389	10.5	.533	.785	.985	.797	.873	196

* NOTE: The *S.S. Clairton* type was the Liberty ship of the First World War.

These ratio numbers enable the designer to compare a 400- and a 1,000-ft ship directly. For example, a 400-ft ship with a prismatic coefficient of 0.56 and a speed-length ratio of 1.0 would be similar to a 1,000-ft ship with the same prismatic and speed-length ratio.   As these two ships are similar, the shape of the sectional-area curve will also be similar, regardless of the vast difference in size.

In the same way, the water-plane coefficient gives us an idea of the water-line fineness.   A water-plane coefficient of 1.0 would indicate a rectangular barge, and a water-plane coefficient of zero would indicate a straight line with no breadth.   In between these two extremes are our ship-shaped forms.

The same is true of the midship-section coefficient, which tells us the general shape for the midship section.   For a further discussion of these coefficients and their relationships, see any standard work on naval architecture.   (See pages 387 and 388.)

Questions

1. What is meant by the lines of a ship?
2. Define sheer, water-line plane, buttock.
3. How were the lines of a ship developed about the year 1850?
4. Draw a rough sketch of the three views that delineate the lines drawing.
5. What is a diagonal?
6. Define base line; where is it located?
7. What is an offset?   What is its purpose?
8. Why is the preliminary lines plan drawn at equally spaced sections instead of at frame lines?
9. What is the purpose of the sectional-area curve?
10. Name the four coefficients of fineness.

CHAPTER XV

WEIGHT AND DISPLACEMENT CALCULATIONS

The area of any regular figure, such as a triangle, or the volume of any regular figure, such as a pyramid, can easily be calculated by simple and exact arithmetical means. Thus the area of a triangle is simply

$$\frac{\text{Base}}{2} \times \text{altitude} = \frac{b}{2} \times A = \text{area}$$

and the volume of a pyramid is

$$\frac{1}{3} \text{ area of base} \times \text{altitude} = \frac{B}{3} \times A = \text{volume}$$

We run into difficulty, however, when we attempt to ascertain areas and volumes bounded by curved lines or surfaces. This problem could be most serious for the shipbuilder; for very few of the areas and volumes with which we have to deal in shipbuilding are regular in shape, and as a consequence the simple and exact mathematical formulas are of little value to us. Fortunately, there are several mathematical rules, or "tricks," if you will, that enable us to ascertain by simple arithmetical means the approximate area or volume of almost any figure.

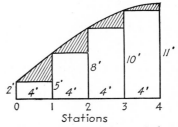

Fig. 153. The shaded area is lost by using this method.

One method (not particularly accurate and used here merely for illustration) for finding the approximate area of a curved steel plate is to divide the area into small rectangles, find the area of each rectangle, and add these values together to obtain the area of the whole plate. Consider the steel plate shown in Fig. 153. We could measure the length of this plate and then lay off spots 4 ft apart and measure the width of the plate at each spot, these being designated as stations 0, 1, 2, 3, and 4. Using the ordinate measurements shown in the figure, we should obtain

Station	(1) Length, ft	(2) Height, ft	(1) × (2) Area, sq ft
0 to 1	2	4	8
1 to 2	5	4	20
2 to 3	8	4	32
3 to 4	10	4	40
Total of four rectangles (= area of plate)...			100

This answer would not even be close to the correct answer, for we did not obtain in our total the area shown shaded in the figure; and this method, therefore, is of little value. We could obtain a more nearly correct answer by taking measurements halfway between our ordinates and considering the parts so measured as trapezoids rather than rectangles. This is the idea behind the trapezoidal rule.

THE TRAPEZOIDAL RULE

A trapezoid is a figure formed of four straight lines, two of which are parallel. Consider Fig. 154*A*. If the lengths of the parallel

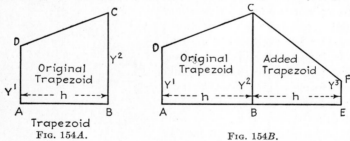

Trapezoid
Fig. 154*A*.

Fig. 154*B*.

sides *AD* and *BC* are Y_1 and Y_2, respectively, and *h* is the distance between them, the area of this trapezoid is given by

$$\tfrac{1}{2}(y_1 + y_2)h$$

or one-half the sum of the parallel sides multiplied by the distance between them.

If we now add another trapezoid beside the first one, we should have a figure such as that shown in Fig. 154*B*.

The area of the original trapezoid was given by

$$\text{Area} = \tfrac{1}{2}(y_1 + y_2)h$$

The area of the added trapezoid would be

$$\text{Area} = \tfrac{1}{2}(y_2 + y_3)h$$

The area of the whole figure would be simply an addition of the two areas.

$$\text{Area of both} = \tfrac{1}{2}(y_1 + y_2)h + \tfrac{1}{2}(y_2 + y_3)h$$

Or simplifying and rearranging we should have

$$\text{Area of both} = h(\tfrac{1}{2}y_1 + y_2 + \tfrac{1}{2}y_3)$$

If we then added another trapezoid of the same width, the total area of the three would become

$$\text{Total area} = h(\tfrac{1}{2}y_1 + y_2 + y_3 + \tfrac{1}{2}y_4)$$

This could be continued indefinitely.

We can put this rule into words as follows: To find the area under a curve by the trapezoidal rule, divide the base into *any* number of *equal* parts, and erect perpendiculars from the base to the curve at these points. Then determine the lengths of these perpendiculars, or ordinates, and to half the sum of the first ordinate and the last ordinate add the sum of the intermediate ordinates; multiply this result by the common distance between them (which is h in this case), and the result will be the required area.

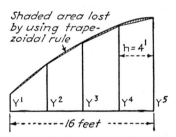

Fig. 155. The trapezoidal rule applied to a curved plate.

As the curved plate illustrated in Fig. 153 and again in Fig. 155 is very nearly a series of trapezoids, let us solve for the area of this plate using the trapezoidal rule.

Substituting the above measured (page 183) ordinate values in the trapezoidal-rule equation

$$\left(\frac{y_1 + y_5}{2} + y_2 + y_3 + y_4\right)h = \text{area}$$

we should obtain

$$\left(\frac{2 \text{ ft} + 11 \text{ ft}}{2} + 5 \text{ ft} + 8 \text{ ft} + 10 \text{ ft}\right) \times 4 \text{ ft} = 118 \text{ sq ft}$$

Comparing this area with the one obtained by adding rectangles (page 184) we can see that our accuracy has increased considerably, for we have added in the triangular-shaped tops of the rectangles, thus obtaining 18 sq ft more. However, this is not yet the correct answer, for these top portions are not true triangles inasmuch as one side of the triangle is a curved line.

We can reduce this error by increasing the number of ordinates. It is conceivable that if we used an infinite number of ordinates the answer would be correct.

There is however, another "rule" for finding areas and volumes that is more accurate and that is therefore used to a greater extent than the trapezoidal rule.

SIMPSON'S FIRST RULE

Simpson's rule is of British origin and is extensively used by naval architects of all nations. It is based on the assumption that all curves for which it is to be used are parabolas of the second order, *i.e.*, parabolas whose equation when referred to the coordinate axes is of the form $y = a_0 + a_1 x + a_2 x^2$, the constants being a_0, a_1, and a_2. This assumption gives excellent results in our work, for most ship curves do approach parabolas of the second order. The answers given by this rule are of course not exact unless the figure we are calculating is bounded by a curve that is a parabola of the second order; however, *the answer is sufficiently accurate for all practical purposes.*

We shall not attempt to prove this rule mathematically, for the mathematics involved lies beyond the scope of this work. (For a mathematical proof see Attwood and Pengelly's "Theoretical Naval Architecture," Appendix A, page 452.[1]) We can, however, solve some simple regular figures by use of the rule and then solve the same figure by the simple exact formula and compare the answers. This process will illustrate the method and give us more

[1] Longmans, Green and Company, New York.

faith in the answers obtained when we apply Simpson's rule to more complicated areas and volumes.

To make use of Simpson's rule we must divide the length of the figure into any *even* number of intervals that will give us an *odd* number of ordinates. (This differs from the trapezoidal rule, which permits us to use either an even or an odd number of ordinates.) The next step is to multiply the length of each ordinate by a series of numbers known as *Simpson's multipliers*. The sum of the products of this multiplication, called *functions* and designated by f, is then multiplied by one-third the common interval (distance between ordinates). The result is the area.

NUMBER OF ORDINATES USED AND THE CORRECT MULTIPLIER TO USE WITH ITS CORRESPONDING ORDINATE

Number of ordinates used	Ordinate number												
	1	2	3	4	5	6	7	8	9	10	11	12	13
	Corresponding multiplier												
3	1	4	1										
5	1	4	2	4	1								
7	1	4	2	4	2	4	1						
9	1	4	2	4	2	4	2	4	1				
11	1	4	2	4	2	4	2	4	2	4	1		
13	1	4	2	4	2	4	2	4	2	4	2	4	1

Simpson's multipliers are very simple to remember if we keep their sequence in mind. Set up in tabular form are the multipliers to be used with 3, 5, 7, 9, 11, and 13 ordinates. Of course any *odd* number of ordinates may be used, the correctness of the answer usually increasing with an increase in the number of ordinates. It will be noted that the multipliers always start with 1; the next number is always 4; and they will always end with 4-1. Furthermore, it will be noted that we can continue the multipliers indefinitely by simply inserting 2's between consecutive 4's.

To illustrate the rule and the multipliers, consider the triangle in Fig. 156. As we are using three ordinates, the multipliers will be

1-4-1.   As the triangle is 6 ft high, the common interval between the spaces will be 3 ft.

Multiplying the length of the ordinates by Simpson's multipliers and adding the results gives us a total of 12.   Multiplying this sum first by $\frac{1}{3}$ and then by the distance between stations, of the common

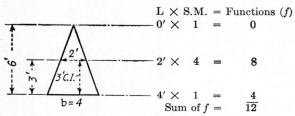

L $\times$ S.M. = Functions (f)

0′ $\times$ 1 = 0

2′ $\times$ 4 = 8

4′ $\times$ 1 = $\underline{4}$

Sum of f = 12

Fig. 156.

By Simpson's rule:

$$\frac{1}{3} \times \text{C.I.} \times \text{sum } (f) = \text{area}$$
$$\frac{1}{3} \times 3 \text{ ft} \times 12 = 12 \text{ sq ft}$$

By arithmetical methods:

$$\text{Area of triangle} = \frac{b}{2} \times d = \frac{4 \text{ ft}}{2} \times 6 \text{ ft} = 12 \text{ sq ft}$$

interval (C.I.), gives us 12 sq ft for the area of the triangle.   It will be noted in Fig. 156 that the arithmetical formula for the area of a triangle gives the same result.

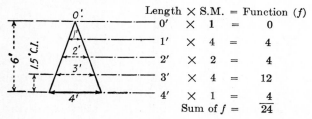

Length $\times$ S.M. = Function (f)

0′ $\times$ 1 = 0

1′ $\times$ 4 = 4

2′ $\times$ 2 = 4

3′ $\times$ 4 = 12

4′ $\times$ 1 = $\underline{4}$

Sum of f = 24

Fig. 157.

$$\frac{1}{3} \times \text{C.I.} \times \text{sum } (f) = \text{area}$$
$$\frac{1}{3} \times 1.5 \text{ ft} \times 24 = 12 \text{ sq ft (as in Fig. 156)}$$

To illustrate how the multipliers can change without changing the answer, we shall recalculate the area of the same triangle, using five instead of three ordinates.   (Notice that there must be—and still are in our case—an odd number of ordinates.)

It will be noted in Fig. 157 that although the number of multi-pliers has increased, the answer remains the same because the common interval decreases with the increase in the number of ordinates used.

Let us now apply this rule to finding the weight of a steel plate ½ in. thick and of the shape indicated in Fig. 158. It should be noted that this is the same plate shown in Figs. 153 and 155, and therefore the answers should be somewhat alike. The answer given by Simpson's rule will be closer to the correct answer, for reasons heretofore mentioned, than the answers given by the two previous methods.

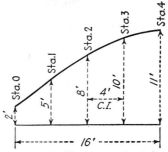

Fig. 158. Measurements taken on a steel plate at equal intervals. Plate thickness = ½ in.

In working with Simpson's rule it is best to arrange the work in a tabulated form as below.

Station number	Width in feet	Simpson's multiplier	Function
0	2	1	2
1	5	4	20
2	8	2	16
3	10	4	40
4	11	1	11
Sum of functions.			89

⅓ × C.I. × sum of function = area in sq ft
⅓ × 4 × 89 = 118.67 sq ft area of plate

Using the trapezoidal rule on this same plate gave us 118 sq ft. The gain in area of 0.67 sq ft is due to the fact that Simpson's rule considered the curve to be a parabola of the second order while the trapezoidal rule considered it to be a straight line between ordinates. Had the curve been bending upward instead of downward, the area given by Simpson's rule would necessarily have been less than that given by the trapezoidal rule, but the answer still would have been more accurate.

We now have the area of the plate, and we wish to know its weight. A square foot of steel 1 in. thick weighs 40.8 lb as noted on page 33. As our plate is $\frac{1}{2}$ in. thick, the weight will be 20.4 lb per sq ft, and the entire plate will weigh

118.67 sq ft $\times$ 20.4 lb per sq ft = 2,421 lb (approx.)

THE DISPLACEMENT CALCULATION

We have heretofore applied Simpson's rule only to areas. We shall now apply it to determining the volume of a simple geometric figure and then to finding displacement volume, or weight, of a ship.

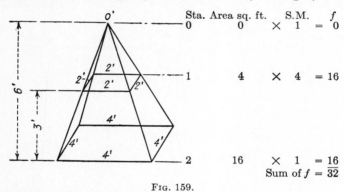

Sta.	Area sq. ft.		S.M.		f
0	0	$\times$	1	=	0
1	4	$\times$	4	=	16
2	16	$\times$	1	=	16
			Sum of f =		$\overline{32}$

Fig. 159.

Volume is by Simpson's rule:

$$\frac{1}{3} \times C.I. \times \text{sum of } (f) = \text{volume}$$
$$\frac{1}{3} \times 3 \text{ ft} \times 32 = 32 \text{ cu ft}$$

By arithmetical means:

$$\text{Volume of pyramid} = \frac{\text{area of base}}{3} \times \text{altitude} = \frac{16 \text{ sq ft}}{3} \times 6 \text{ ft} = 32 \text{ cu ft}$$

In this case Simpson's rule gives the exact answer.

Consider the pyramid shown in Fig. 159. In this case, instead of multiplying distances directly by Simpson's multipliers, we multiply areas. Distances in feet, when multiplied by feet, give areas in square feet; and areas in square feet, when multiplied by feet, give volumes in cubic feet. To clarify this, we shall solve for the areas through the pyramid at stations 0, 1, and 2 and plot the points on a sheet of graph paper, obtaining the curve shown in Fig. 160. After we plot the curve, it will be apparent that we are then simply performing the same operation as when we obtained the area of the steel plate; *i.e.*, we are finding the area under a curve. It should be noted that, in this case, we are finding the area under an area curve,

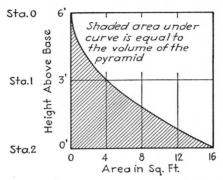

FIG. 160. Curve of sectional areas for the pyramid shown in FIG. 159.

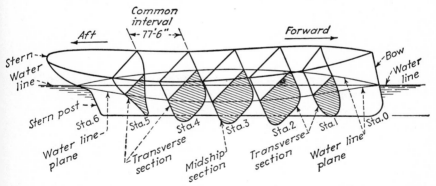

FIG. 161. Transverse sections below the water line are shown as shaded areas. The area of the curved portions when plotted as shown in FIG. 162 gives the sectional-area curve for the ship.

which is already in square feet, and therefore the answer will be a volume, which will be in *cubic feet* (see Figs. 159 and 160).

The answers given by Simpson's rule and the arithmetical exact formula are, in this case, identical. It should be borne in mind, however, that Simpson's rule *is exact only when the boundary curve is a parabola of the second order.*

In Fig. 161 we have an isometric drawing of the profile of a ship. If we obtain the area of each section through the ship up to the water-line plane (this can be done by Simpson's rule, for the areas are bounded by curved lines) and plot these areas at their respective stations on a piece of graph paper, we should obtain the sectional-

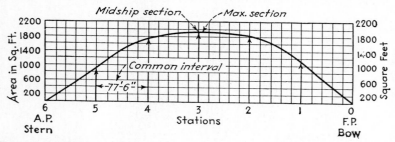

Fig. 162. Section-area curve. The area of any section through the vessel from the keel to the water line may be read from this curve. The area under this area curve is equal to the volume of water displaced by the ship when floating at the draft for which this curve was plotted. The area under the curve is easily found by the use of Simpson's rule.

area curve shown in Fig. 162. We are again simply finding the area under an area curve, and in this case, as previously, we shall obtain a volume.

This curve will give the area up to the water line of any section along the length of the ship. The area under this curve will be the volume of the ship below the water-line plane. Arranging the work as on page 189 we have the following:

Station number	Area sq ft	Simpson's multiplier	Function of the area
0	0	1	0
1	1,041	4	4,164
2	1,801	2	3,602
3	1,859	4	7,436
4	1,751	2	3,502
5	924	4	3,696
6	0	1	0
Sum of f..............................			22,400

$\frac{1}{3} \times$ C.I. $\times$ sum of $f(A)$ = volume of underwater portion of ship

$$\frac{1}{3} \times 77.5 \text{ ft} \times 22,400 = 578,659 \text{ cu ft}$$

We remember from our high-school physics that any object floating in water is displacing an amount of water equal to its own weight. One cubic foot of salt water weighs 64 lb (very nearly); therefore, in one ton (2,240 lb) of salt water we should have $\dfrac{2,240}{64} = 35$ cu ft.

Our ship is displacing 578,659 cu ft of salt water; so the weight of salt water that she is displacing would be $\dfrac{578,659}{35} = 16,533$ tons. As the weight of water she displaces is equal to the weight of the ship, the ship must weigh 16,533 tons when fully loaded.

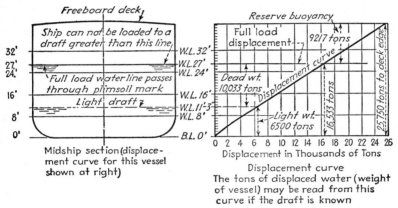

Midship section (displacement curve for this vessel shown at right)

Displacement curve
The tons of displaced water (weight of vessel) may be read from this curve if the draft is known

Fig. 163. A typical displacement curve.

In actual practice, we calculate the displacement of the ship at several water lines and plot the result on a sheet of graph paper (see Fig. 163). We can then read off the displacement at any intermediate water line from the graph. In other words, to determine the weight of a vessel at a particular draft, we read her draft marks and obtain an average of the bow and stern drafts. Then we use this average draft to enter the displacement curve and read the corresponding weight of water she is displacing, which will, of course, equal the weight of the ship. Conversely, if we know the weight of a ship before launching, it is a very simple matter to look on the displacement curve and read the corresponding draft. The draft corresponding to the displacement will be the water line at which she will float. (Actually, the displacement curve is calculated with the vessel on an even keel and at zero trim.) If the vessel is not on an even keel or is out of trim, the displacement will not be exactly the amount read from the curve and will have to be corrected. To make this correction, which is usually small, see any standard work on naval architecture.

It will be noted from Fig. 163 that the light draft of the ship is 11 ft 3 in. and that the corresponding weight is 6,500 tons. This is known as the *light weight* of the vessel, *i.e.*, the weight of the vessel with no fuel, water, passengers, crew, baggage, mail, stores, or cargo aboard. These last items make up the difference in weight between the light weight of the vessel and the total displacement and are called *deadweight items*. The weight of the deadweight items that can be carried is known as the *deadweight carrying capacity* of the ship. The deadweight carrying ability of a ship is vitally important to the owner, for it is from this that he receives his revenue and profits.

Questions and Problems

1. Why are the trapezoidal and Simpson's rules of such importance to the shipbuilder?

2. Which of the above rules is most accurate for ship calculations?

3. Using the trapezoidal rule, calculate the area of the following plate. The five ordinates are spaced 4 ft apart. Ordinate lengths are as follows:

$$0 = 3 \text{ ft}, \quad 1 = 4.75 \text{ ft}, \quad 2 = 6 \text{ ft}, \quad 3 = 8 \text{ ft}, \quad 4 = 5 \text{ ft}$$

4. Calculate the area of the plate in Prob. 3, using Simpson's first rule.

5. What would be the weight of the plate in Prob. 3 if it were $\frac{3}{4}$ in. thick?

6. What is the relation between the displacement of a vessel and its weight?

7. What is meant by the term "deadweight"?

8. How could you determine the water line at which a vessel will float before the vessel is launched?

9. What does the area under an area curve represent?

CHAPTER XVI

STABILITY, TRIM, THE INCLINING EXPERIMENT, AND DAMAGE CONTROL

STABILITY

Stability is the tendency of a ship to return to its original position when inclined from that position by external or other forces.

There are three types of stability. These may be illustrated by discussing the stability of a cone resting on a table. Such a cone is

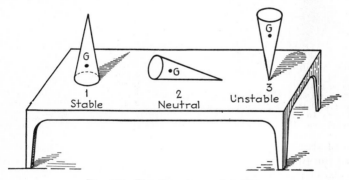

FIG. 164. The three types of stability.

said to be

1. *Stable* when resting on its base. If a force is applied to the cone, tilting it slightly, the center of gravity of the cone is raised relative to the surface of the table. (The center of gravity of any object is a point at which we may consider its entire weight to be concentrated, or the point at which the object would balance.) If the force is removed, the cone will come to rest in its original position.

2. *Neutral* when resting on its side. If a force is applied to the cone when resting on its side, the center of gravity is neither raised

nor lowered.   If the force is removed, the cone will roll until friction overcomes the force applied and it will have no tendency to return to its original position.

3. *Unstable* if balanced on its apex.   Even a slight touch will cause a cone in this condition to capsize, owing to a lowering of its

Fig. 165. A ship may have considerable heel and still be perfectly stable.   The *S.S. Leicester* at anchor in Bermuda Harbor.   This is a British Liberty.   This vessel had a cargo of grain in the 'tween decks.   The grain boards gave away in an August hurricane and the vessel was abandoned.   She was found after the hurricane by a passing vessel and towed to Bermuda.   The grain was removed and she righted herself, only to be driven on the rocks.   Another salvage was made, and she is now back in service.

center of gravity.   The movement of the cone will be out of proportion to the force applied.

A vessel can have neutral stability and remain upright.   A vessel with negative stability, or in the unstable condition upright, will not necessarily capsize, for she may become stable when she heels even slightly, as will be discussed later.   It should be further noted that a vessel floating bottom side up may be perfectly stable in that condition.   In all the following discussion on stability, however, we are referring to the stability of the vessel in the upright or nearly upright condition. The stability that tends to return the vessel to the upright condition when heeled away from that position will be referred to as *positive stability*. It should be noted that off-center weights can cause a vessel to list; therefore, a list to one side or the other does not always indicate negative stability (Fig. 165).

Some Elementary Trigonometry. Two expressions, or terms, used in trigonometry, the sine and tangent, are used in investigating

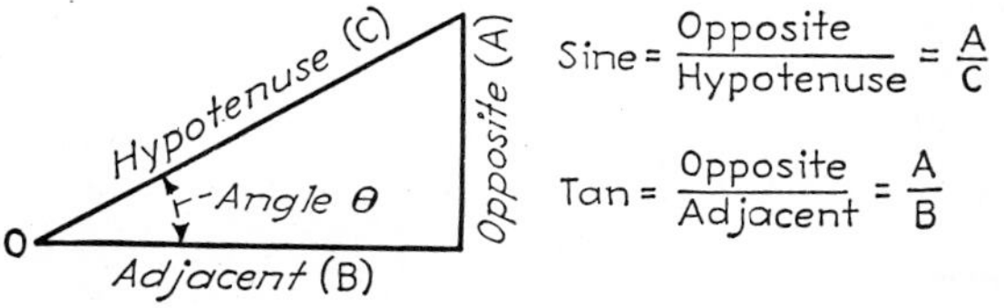

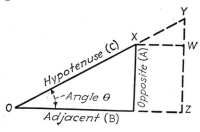

$$\text{Sine} = \frac{\text{Opposite}}{\text{Hypotenuse}} = \frac{A}{C}$$

$$\text{Tan} = \frac{\text{Opposite}}{\text{Adjacent}} = \frac{A}{B}$$

FIG. 166.

the stability of a ship. As some students may not have studied trigonometry, we shall discuss these two terms briefly.

Figure 166 shows a right-angle triangle, *i.e.*, a triangle one angle of which is 90 deg.

FIG. 167.

The sine and the tangent are simply ratios between the sides of the triangle. To illustrate this, consider Fig. 167. If the angle is kept constant and the hypotenuse is made longer by the length xy, then

$$\frac{\text{Hypotenuse}}{\text{Opposite side}} \propto \frac{\text{hypotenuse} + xy}{\text{opposite side} + yw} \qquad (\propto = \text{proportional to})$$

The proportion between the sides of the triangle has not changed with an increase in the size of the triangle. We can change these proportions, or ratios, only by increasing or decreasing the angle; *i.e.*, the sine and the tangent are a function of the number of degrees in the angle. If we know the sine or the tangent we can find the angle, or if we know the angle we can obtain the sine or the tangent.

Figure 168 shows these relationships worked out for a 30-deg and a 60-deg triangle. These values will change with a change in angle.

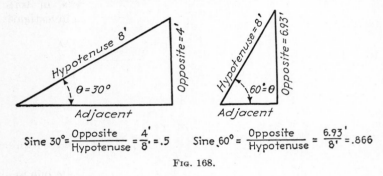

$$\text{Sine } 30° = \frac{\text{Opposite}}{\text{Hypotenuse}} = \frac{4'}{8'} = .5 \qquad \text{Sine } 60° = \frac{\text{Opposite}}{\text{Hypotenuse}} = \frac{6.93'}{8'} = .866$$

Fig. 168.

The values for any angle may be obtained from a table of trigonometric functions found in any trigonometry book. If we know the sine or tangent and the length of one side, we can find the length of the other two sides. These relationships are invaluable in stability work, surveying, gunnery, etc. The relationships, or equations, that we shall use are listed below (see Fig. 168).

$$\sin \theta = \frac{\text{opposite side}}{\text{hypotenuse}} = \frac{A}{C}, \qquad A = C \sin \theta$$

$$C = \frac{A}{\sin \theta}$$

$$\tan \theta = \frac{\text{opposite side}}{\text{adjacent side}} = A, \qquad A = B \tan \theta$$

$$B = \frac{A}{\tan \theta}$$

Note in the table below that *for small angles, the values of the sine and tangent are very nearly the same.* This is fortunate, for we can use them interchangeably without serious error, up to an angle of about 6 deg.

Angle, deg	sin θ	tan θ
2	0.0349	0.0349
6	0.0697	0.0699

Equilibrium. A vessel to remain at rest and afloat in still water must fulfill two conditions.

1. The weight of the vessel and everything on board must equal the weight of the water displaced by the hull.

2. The center of gravity of the ship and everything on board must be directly in a vertical line with the center of gravity of the displaced water.

Displacement. To understand what is meant by displaced water and the center of gravity of the displaced water (center of buoyancy), assume that we have a ship floating in still water and that we are able to freeze the water around the ship and remove the ship from the ice. A hole is left in the ice that is the exact shape of the ship. If we weigh the ship and then pour into the hole a weight of water equal to the weight of the ship, the hole will be filled exactly level with the top of the ice. The weight of this water is equal to the weight of water displaced by the ship, and the center of gravity of the displaced water is known as the *center of buoyancy.*

The Couple. The weight of the vessel acts downward at its center of gravity, and the pressure resulting from the displacement of the water acts upward at the center of buoyancy (center of gravity of the displaced water) to form two equal and opposite forces.

As long as these two forces are equal and in a vertical line, the vessel is in equilibrium. When they move out of a vertical line, a *couple* is formed. This couple may be either a righting or an upsetting couple.

Two parallel forces that are opposite in direction and equal in amount and with different lines of action constitute a couple, as

WB (Fig. 169). The perpendicular distance between them, *d*, is known as the *arm of the couple.* The product of either force (the two forces being equal) times the arm is known as the *moment of the couple* (see page 12 as a memory refresher).

$$Wd = Bd = \text{moment of couple}$$

From this formula it is obvious that the moment of the couple may be increased by increasing either *B* and *W*, or *d*.

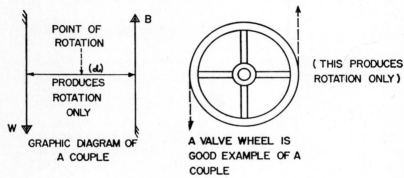

B
POINT OF
ROTATION
(d)
PRODUCES
ROTATION
ONLY
W
GRAPHIC DIAGRAM OF
A COUPLE
(THIS PRODUCES
ROTATION ONLY)
A VALVE WHEEL IS
GOOD EXAMPLE OF A
COUPLE

FIG. 169. The couple.

Statical Stability. Figure 170 shows a ship on even keel floating in still water. Point *G* is the center of gravity of the ship, and point *B* is the center of buoyancy.

As the center of gravity is over the center of buoyancy and as the weight of the vessel equals the weight of the water displaced by the vessel, the vessel is in equilibrium and at rest.

In Figure 171, the vessel has been heeled to an exaggerated degree by some momentary external force, and the vessel is tending to return to the upright position after this force has been removed. A study of this figure shows why it returns to the upright. The following is an analysis of the righting process:

1. *G* has not moved. This is to be expected unless some weights in the ship have shifted or fallen overboard.

2. *B* has moved outboard along the arc of a circle whose center is at the intersection of a vertical line through *B* and the center line

of the vessel. This point of intersection is designated as *M*. *B* becomes *B'* in its new position.

3. *M* is known as the *metacenter*. The Greek word *meta* means "above"; "metacenter" means "above the center" of buoyancy.[1]

4. The distance from *G* to *M* is known as *GM*, or the *metacentric height*, and is a measure of the vessel's stability in the upright or nearly upright condition.

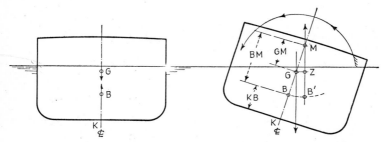

Fig. 170. Ship at rest. Fig. 171. The couple (weight × *GZ*) is tending to right the vessel.

5. The distance from *B* to *M* is known as *BM*. This height is found by the equation $BM = I/V$, which will be discussed more fully on page 211.

6. *K* denotes the keel, and *KB* the distance from the keel to the center of buoyancy.

7. A new letter, *Z*, has been added. This is a point opposite *G*, and the line *GZ* is parallel to the water line.

8. A little study will make it evident that *G* acting downward and *B* acting upward will form a couple whose arm is *GZ*. The moment of this couple will depend on the weight of the vessel and the distance *GZ*.

9. The couple formed is tending to return the vessel to the upright. When the vessel is back in the upright condition, the arm

[1] NOTE: Point *M* does not coincide with the center line of the vessel except at small angles of heel. However, as its transverse movement is small, and in any case does not affect our reasoning here, it is, for simplicity, shown on the center line.

of the couple, *GZ*, becomes zero, as in Fig. 170, the righting moment becomes zero, and the vessel will remain at rest in that position.

Figure 172 shows sections through four vessels. The first two have the same beam (and the same *KM*) but different vertical *CG*'s and the last two have the same vertical *CG*'s but different beams.

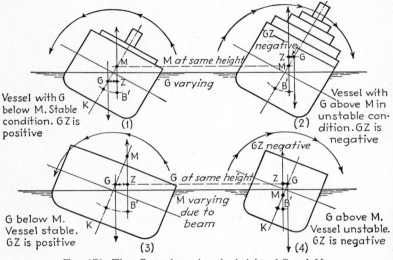

FIG. 172. The effect of varying the height of *G* and *M*.

These sketches illustrate the relation of stability to *GM*.

1. If *M* is above G, the ship has positive stability.
2. If *M* is at *G*, the ship has neutral stability.
3. If *M* is below *G*, the ship has negative stability.

Figure 173 shows a cross section of a ship to a large scale and illustrates the use of the tangent of the angle of inclination (heel) to obtain *GZ*, the arm of the couple.

GZ is the opposite side of the triangle of which *GM* forms the hypotenuse and *ZM* the adjacent side. If we know the angle of heel, θ, and *GM*, we can find *GZ*, which is the righting lever, by the equation

$$GZ = GM \sin \theta$$

Tangent θ is easier to measure on a ship than sin θ; and as the tangent and the sin are very nearly the same at small angles we may substitute tan θ for sin θ and our *GZ* equation becomes

$$GZ = GM \tan \theta$$

Example: Assume that the *GM* of the vessel shown in Fig. 173 was 4 ft and that she was heeled to an angle of 2 deg. What is the value of *GZ*?

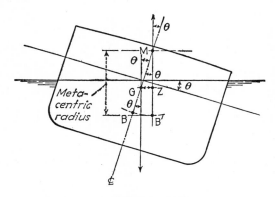

In triangle GMZ
GM= Hypotenuse; GZ= Opposite; ZM= Adjacent;
θ= Angle of inclination. ∴ Sin θ = $\dfrac{GZ}{GM}$
and rearranging GZ = GM x sin θ, and for small
angles; GZ= GM x tan θ (approx.)

Fig. 173. The relation of *GZ* to *GM* at small angles.

Solution: The value of the tangent of 2 deg (from page 199) is 0.0349. Substituting in the equation

$$GZ = GM \tan \theta$$

we have

$$GZ = 4 \text{ ft} \times 0.0349 = 0.1396 \text{ ft}$$

To find the moment tending to right the ship we multiply the arm of the couple, *GZ*, by the weight of the vessel. Assume this weight to be 10,000 tons, then

Moment of statical stability = $W \times GM \sin \theta = W \times GZ$
= 10,000 tons $\times$ 0.1396 ft = 1396 ft-tons

Rocking-chair Analogy. The rocking-chair analogy is the basis of an interesting experiment relating to the stability of a ship that any student may perform at home.

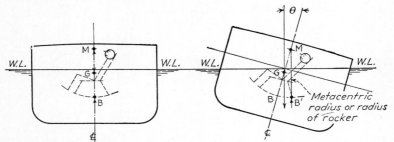

M is at the center of curvature of rocker. B moves along a curve whose center is at M

Ship and chair at a slight angle

FIG. 174. A rocking chair and occupant superposed on a midship section of a ship to illustrate the similarity between the stability of a ship and a rocking chair.

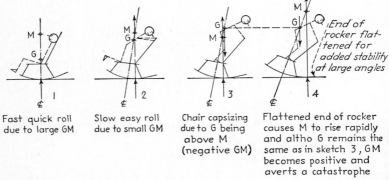

Fast quick roll due to large GM

Slow easy roll due to small GM

Chair capsizing due to G being above M (negative GM)

Flattened end of rocker causes M to rise rapidly and altho G remains the same as in sketch 3, GM becomes positive and averts a catastrophe

FIG. 175. The rocking-chair analogy. The stability characteristics of a rocker are similar to the stability characteristics of a ship.

Figure 174 shows the three points B, G, and M sketched in the section of a ship and also these same three points sketched in corresponding positions on a rocking chair.

The center of support for the rocker is on the arc of the circle along which the center of buoyancy moves. The center of this circle is at M, which is the center of curvature of the rocker. The center of gravity, G, of the chair includes the person in the chair.

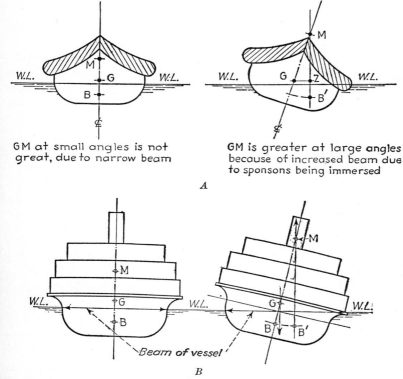

GM at small angles is not great, due to narrow beam

GM is greater at large angles because of increased beam due to sponsons being immersed

A

Beam of vessel

B

FIG. 176. *A*, sponsons on a canoe. *B*, sections through a bay steamer. If the ship gets dangerously close to capsizing, the sponsons go into the water, increasing the beam of the vessel. This increase in beam raises M and thereby increases GM.

If the curvature of the rocker is constant, the height of M will remain constant. The height of G, which can be easily varied, will change GM. We can then note with each change in GM the corresponding change in the behavior of the chair (Fig. 175).

1. Sit in the chair in the normal way.   The chair will rock back and forth at its normal rate (Fig. 175, sketch 1).

2. Put the knees in the chair and the hands on the back of the chair.   This will cause G to rise, making GM smaller.   The chair will have a long, easy, slow roll (Fig. 175, sketch 2).

3. Now stand up in the chair, grasp the back of the chair with the hands, and start the chair rocking. G is now above M, and the chair will probably capsize (Fig. 175, sketch 3).

Figure 175, sketch 4, shows why rocking chairs have the rear ends of the rockers flattened.   As M is at the center of curvature of the rocker, flattening the curvature causes M to rise, thus increasing the GM should the chair get dangerously close to capsizing. This same effect is produced by the sponsons on pleasure canoes and the wide flare on Chesapeake Bay steamers (Fig. 176).

THE INCLINING EXPERIMENT

To work out stability problems we must find G, the center of gravity of the vessel, and M, the metacenter.

When a ship is in the design stage, the naval architect's staff works out the weights of the individual parts, or groups of parts, of the vessel and the center of gravity of each part.   During the design of the *S.S. United States* this was done very painstakingly, even the weights and centers of the pillows on the beds and the chairs in the staterooms being carefully estimated and included in the total weight and center of gravity of the whole ship.

When the ship is complete, or nearly so, it is usual to have an inclining experiment (sometimes called erroneously "rolling the ship"), which is a very simple method of locating exactly the vertical center of gravity of the vessel.   Quite often the question is asked by men in the yard: *"How can you obtain the center of gravity of a ship by rolling a weight across the deck?"*   The answer is obtained by simple arithmetic.

Shift of the C. G. of a Vessel Due to Shift of a Weight Already on Board.   Consider the small rectangle in Fig. 177.   In Fig. 177, sketch A, we have a rectangle 10 by 12 ft or 120 sq ft in area.   The center of gravity is, of course, 6 ft above the base.   In Fig. 177, sketch B, we have cut 2 ft from the height of the rectangle, leaving an area of 100 sq ft with a center-of-gravity height of 5 ft above the base. In Fig. 177, sketch *C*, we have added the 2- by 10-ft rectangle to the base of the original rectangle, giving us the original area of 120 sq ft with a center of gravity 4 ft above the original base or 6 ft above the new base. We shall work this mathematically and endeavor to derive an equation for what we have done.

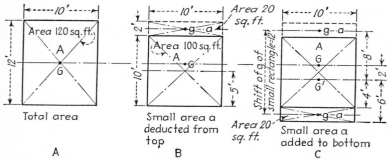

Fig. 177. Effect on center of gravity of shifting a portion of the figure.

First consider the following areas:
Area of small part = a = 10 ft $\times$ 2 ft = 20 sq ft
Area of original rectangle = A = 10 ft $\times$ 12 ft = 120 sq ft
It can be seen from Fig. 177, sketch *C*, that the center of gravity of the original rectangular area has dropped 2 ft owing to shifting the small area from the top to the bottom. The center of gravity of the small rectangular area was shifted a total of 12 ft. Using the areas obtained above, we can now equate these results.

Original Rectangle $\qquad$ Small Rectangle
Area A $\times$ shift of CG (GG') = area a $\times$ shift of cg (gg')
120 sq ft $\times$ 2 ft = 20 sq ft $\times$ 12 ft
240 = 240

or algebraically,

$$A \times GG' = a \times gg'$$

We can substitute weight W for area A and not disturb our equation. We should then have

$$W \times GG' = w \times gg'$$

Rearranging,

$$GG' = \frac{w \times gg'}{W}$$

To perform an inclining experiment we shift a weight, placed on a large jumbo truck, transversely across the deck of the vessel. Unless prevented by external forces, the vessel will heel to such an

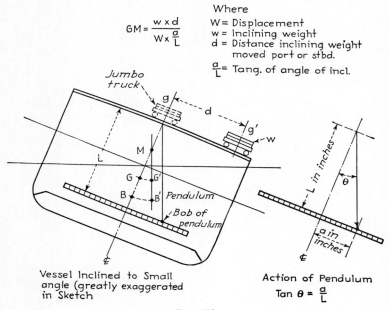

$$GM = \frac{w \times d}{W \times \frac{a}{L}}$$

Where
W = Displacement
w = Inclining weight
d = Distance inclining weight moved port or stbd.
$\frac{a}{L}$ = Tang. of angle of incl.

Jumbo truck

Vessel Inclined to Small angle (greatly exaggerated in Sketch)

Action of Pendulum
Tan $\theta = \frac{a}{L}$

Fig. 178.

angle that the center of gravity of the weight shifted in combination with that of the vessel will be directly over the center of buoyancy of the ship. Figure 178 shows a ship in this condition. The angle of inclination is small, being about 1 deg. (The angle is greatly exaggerated in the sketch.)

If we call the angle of inclination to the upright θ and GM the metacentric height, then, for small angles where the values of the sine and the tangent are very nearly equal,

$$\tan \theta = \frac{GG'}{GM}$$

or

$$GG' = GM \tan \theta$$

Substituting this value for GG' in the formula from the top of this page we should have

$$GG' = \frac{w \times gg'}{W}$$

$$GM \tan \theta = \frac{w \times gg'}{W}$$

or

$$GM = \frac{w \times gg'}{W \times \tan \theta}$$

W is equal to the weight of the vessel.   This can be obtained by reading the draft marks and reading the corresponding displacement from the displacement curve.   (Refer to page 193, for a memory refresher.)   Therefore, W is known.   Likewise, w is the inclining weight and truck, which is weighed before being placed on the ship. Therefore, w is known.

gg' is the distance the inclining weight is moved.   This can be measured with a tape and so is known.

The only thing we do not know is the angle the ship inclines when the weight is moved.   This is usually determined by hanging three pendulums down convenient hatchways and measuring the distance that the plumb bob moves when the weight is shifted.   The pendulums should be 20 ft or longer so that the reading will be reasonably accurate.

If we know the length of the pendulum and the distance it swings, it is easy to obtain the tangent of the angle, for

$$\tan \theta = \frac{\text{distance pendulum swings}}{\text{length of pendulum}} = \frac{a}{L}$$

The tangent can be measured directly from the ship by measuring the pendulum length and the distance it moves.   This is the reason why $\tan \theta$ was substituted for $\sin \theta$ in the equation $GZ = GM \sin \theta$.

We can now write our formula in its final form.

$$GM = \frac{w \times d}{W \times \dfrac{a}{L}}$$

Note that for convenience we have substituted d for gg' and a/L for tan θ.

To illustrate the above we shall work through the data obtained from the inclining experiment on the *S.S. Coamo*, which was built at Newport News.

Inclining Experiment.   Name of vessel = *S.S. Coamo*
Vessel heading = due east
Wind = E $\times$ NE 4 miles
Draft of vessel (mean) = 18 ft 3 in.
Corresponding salt-water displacement (from curves) = 6,197 tons
Density of James River water (from hydrometer) = 1.01735
Correction to salt-water tons = $\dfrac{1.01735}{1.026} \times 6{,}197$

$$= 6{,}143 \text{ tons actual}$$

Length of pendulum (middle) = 21 ft 4¾ in. = 256.75 in.
Distance weight moved = 18.25 ft from center line to port
Inclining weight including truck = 21.96 tons
Distance (a) middle pendulum moved to port = 7.71 in.

Tangent of inclined angle = $\dfrac{a}{L} = \dfrac{7.71 \text{ in.}}{256.75 \text{ in.}} = 0.0300$

$$GM = \frac{w \times d}{W \times \tan \theta} = \frac{21.96 \text{ tons} \times 18.25 \text{ ft}}{6{,}143 \times 0.030} = 2.17 \text{ ft}$$

The tabulation above has been considerably shortened and should not be taken as a model. Actually, three pendulums are used, the inclining weight is moved across the deck about nine times, and pendulum readings are taken after each movement. (For a complete description of an inclining experiment see any standard work on naval architecture.)

We have seen how we can find *GM*.   This is not exactly what we were looking for; we wished to find *G*, the vertical center of gravity of the vessel.   Knowing *GM*, we can find *G* if we know the height of *M*.

Determining the Height of the Metacenter.   In order to find *M*, we must make use of a term not heretofore discussed, namely, the *moment of inertia*.   The moment of inertia of a plane area about any axis is the sum of the product of each elementary area times the

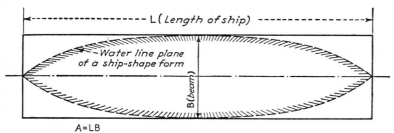

Fɪɢ. 179. Moment of inertia of a rectangular form.   The moment of inertia of a rectangle about its own center line is $AB^2/12 = LB^3/12 = I$.

square of the distance from the inertia axis.   To discuss moment of inertia completely would require higher mathematics.   Here we shall confine ourselves to a discussion of the moment of inertia of a rectangle which should be sufficient for an understanding.   For a rectangle with the axis taken at the center line the equation would be

$$I = \frac{AB^2}{12}$$

where I = moment of inertia.

A = area of rectangle.

B = breadth of rectangle.   See Fig. 179.

The moment of inertia I depends on the shape of a figure; therefore, different equations are used for calculating the moment of inertia of each figure.   The moment of inertia of the water plane may be found by the proper use of Simpson's rule.   We shall discuss only the moment of inertia I of a rectangle about its own center line, for this will amply illustrate the effect of beam on the stability of a ship (Fig. 179).

The equation $BM = I/V$ was given on page 201. BM is the distance from the center of buoyancy to the metacenter; I is the moment of inertia of the water plane; V is the volume of displacement of the vessel in cubic feet (Fig. 180).

We found the distance GM from the inclining experiment. We must now find the distance BM and KB, for $BM + KB = KM$ and $KM - GM = VCG$, which is the vertical center of gravity of the ship—exactly what we were looking for.

To illustrate the use of our BM formula we shall find the height of the metacenter of a rectangular barge with a rectangular midship section as in Fig. 181.

Example: Calculate the height of M in the rectangular figure as sketched. GM is 3 ft as determined by an inclining experiment. Find the vertical center of gravity.

Solution:

$$I \text{ of rectangle} = \frac{AB^2}{12} = \frac{100 \text{ ft} \times 24 \text{ ft} \times (24 \text{ ft})^2}{12}$$

$$= \frac{2{,}400 \times 576}{12} = 115{,}200 \text{ ft}^4$$

Displacement of rectangular barge

$$= L \times b \times d = 100 \text{ ft} \times 24 \text{ ft} \times 12 \text{ ft} = 28{,}800 \text{ cu ft}$$

$$BM = \frac{I}{V} = \frac{115{,}200 \text{ ft}^4}{28{,}800 \text{ cu ft}} = 4 \text{ ft}$$

Height of center of buoyancy = ½ draft = 6 ft

Then

Height of $M = BM + KB = 10 \text{ ft} = KM$

If the GM of this barge, as determined by an inclining experiment, was 3 ft, then

$$VCG = KM - GM = 10 \text{ ft} - 3 \text{ ft} = 7 \text{ ft above base line}$$

Importance of GM. It is important that we know the center of gravity of a ship, for the behavior of a ship at sea depends upon the value of GM. The point M changes somewhat as the vessel

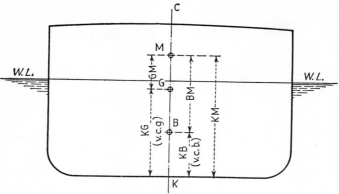

G = Center of gravity of Vessel
B = Center of buoyancy of Vessel
M = Metacenter
K = Keel (usually the base Line)

FIG. 180. The relation between *BM*, *GM*, *KB*, and *KG*.

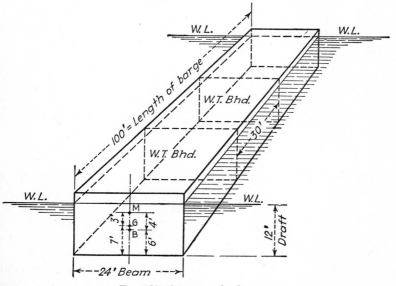

FIG. 181. A rectangular barge.

increases or decreases draft, but the point G can be made to vary widely by changing the cargo-weight distribution. A change in either G or M varies GM. The value of GM for ordinary merchant ships should be about 5 per cent of the beam when loaded. If this value of $0.05B$ is greatly exceeded, the ship will become so stiff that if it is thrown over by a wave it will come back to the upright with a jerk. This jerky motion is very uncomfortable for the passengers and crew and may even endanger the vessel. Ships with small GM values usually ride with a long, easy roll; however, low GM values may endanger a ship if her shell is punctured, for she may lose stability and capsize owing to the free surface of the flooding water. A happy medium is required in this as well as in other design work.

Free-surface Effect. The surface of a liquid in contact with air, *i.e.*, with a free surface, remains parallel to the surface of the earth when the container is inclined from the vertical. Free-surface effects become particularly important when they occur inside a ship, for they reduce the stability of the vessel.

It can be seen from our now familiar equation

$$BM = \frac{I}{V}$$

that it is the moment of inertia of the water plane that keeps a ship right side up, for BM increases with an increase in I. Furthermore, I depends entirely on the beam of the vessel, because, for a rectangle

$$I = \frac{AB^2}{12}$$

It will be noted that I increases as the *square* of the beam. Thus a rowboat 6 ft wide has four times the BM of a similar one only 3 ft wide. (*Note that length is not a factor.*)

The effect of the inertia of the water plane of a vessel is neutralized if an equal free surface exists within the hull. This fact is generally overlooked by the layman and was the cause of the capsizing of the *S.S. Segovia* at Newport News, Va., and more lately the *S.S. Normandie* in New York. It will pay shipbuilders, ship

operators, operating personnel and firemen to know something of the
effects of free surface within a floating object.

Assume that we have a ship with one hold flooded as indicated in
Fig. 182. The free surface in the hold will neutralize an amount
of water plane equal to the area of the free surface of the flooded
water. Also, the tank (which is shown about one-third full) will

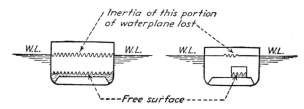

FIG. 182*A*. Section through a flooded hold and a flooded tank.

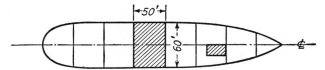

FIG. 182*B*. Plan view of the flooded hold and the flooded tank.

FIG. 182*C*. The remaining water plane.

neutralize the water plane in way of the tank. This causes a
reduction in the metacentric height *GM*.

As

$$BM = \frac{I}{V}$$

Then

$$\text{Loss in } GM = \frac{i}{V}$$

where

$$i = \text{moment of inertia of the flooded space}$$

Our rectangular barge whose *VCG* was calculated on page 212 had a *GM* of 3 ft 0 in.   Let us assume that a small amount of water, say ⅛ in. deep, is pumped into a space amidships 30 ft long, which is shut off by watertight bulkheads.   This small amount of water would affect the draft very little, and so the rise in *KB* could be neglected (see Fig. 180).

The free surface of the flooded area would be as follows:

$$\text{Flooded area} = 30 \text{ ft} \times 24 \text{ ft} = 720 \text{ sq ft}$$

$$i \text{ (in this case)} = \frac{AB^2}{12} = \frac{720 \times 24^2}{12} = 34{,}560 \text{ ft}^4$$

$$\text{Loss in } GM = \frac{34{,}560 \text{ ft}^4}{28{,}800 \text{ cu ft}} = 1.2 \text{ ft}$$

It should be noted that in the above equations no account was taken of the depth of the water in the hold.   This is correct, for the volume of water *plays no part* in the stability loss—it is the moment of inertia of the free surface that counts.

As our original *GM* was 3 ft, the *GM* remaining would be 3 ft − 1.2 ft = 1.8 ft which would still be sufficient as a safe margin of stability.

However, had the barge been flooded only ⅛ in. deep throughout its total length, we should have

$$\text{Flooded area} = 100 \text{ ft} \times 24 \text{ ft} = 2{,}400 \text{ sq ft}$$

$$I = i = \frac{AB^2}{12} = \frac{2{,}400 \times 24^2}{12} = 115{,}200 \text{ ft}^4$$

$$\text{Loss in } GM = \frac{115{,}200 \text{ ft}^4}{28{,}800 \text{ cu ft}} = 4.0 \text{ ft}$$

Our remaining *GM* after flooding 100 ft of the 100 ft total would be

Original *GM* − *GM* loss = 3 ft 0 in. − 4 ft 0 in = −1 ft 0 in.

The barge would have negative stability and would heel over slightly.   This small inclination would cause the free water to run to the low side.   The barge would then come to rest at a slight angle, for the area of the free surface would be considerably reduced.

Had the flooding water been deeper, capsizing would have been almost certain.

Had the firemen ceased to increase the number of holds they were flooding the moment they noticed the vessel listing, we should not have had to right the *S.S. Segovia* before rebuilding and the *S.S. Normandie* before scrapping. The effect of free surface on stability will be illustrated conclusively to the student if he steps into a rowboat about half full of water.

LONGITUDINAL TRIM

Using what we learned about transverse stability, we can shift to longitudinal stability without changing our reasoning, for the same principles hold.

The trim of a ship is the algebraic sum of the draft forward and aft; or, better, it is the difference in the draft mark readings.

Example: A ship is on an even keel with a draft of 10 ft 0 in. A weight already on board is shifted aft so that the draft marks on the extreme bow and stern now read 7 ft 0 in. forward and 13 ft 0 in. aft.

Solution: She has risen 10 ft − 7 ft = 3 ft at the bow and sunk 13 ft − 10 ft = 3 ft at the stern, which would give a total of 6 ft 0 in. trim by the stern. The same result could be obtained by subtracting the readings of the new draft marks; *i.e.,*

$$13 \text{ ft } 0 \text{ in. } - 7 \text{ ft } 0 \text{ in. } = 6 \text{ ft } 0 \text{ in. trim by stern}$$

A ship when changing trim very seldom trims about amidships or about the center of buoyancy. A ship *will always trim* about the center of flotation, which is the center of gravity of the water plane of the vessel.

Longitudinal stability is similar to transverse stability. The only difference is that we use the longitudinal *GM* in place of the transverse *GM*. The longitudinal *GM* will be very large compared with the transverse *GM*. Longitudinal *GM* is about $1\frac{1}{4}$ times the length of the ship.

The change of trim in inches resulting from moving a weight already on board would be

Change of trim in inches

$$= \frac{12 \times \text{weight} \times \text{distance moved} \times \text{ship length}}{\text{displacement of ship} \times \text{longitudinal } GM}$$

$$= \frac{12 \times w \times d \times L}{W \times LGM}$$

It is more convenient for us to work out a *moment to change trim* 1 in. for our vessels than to use the above equation. As a moment is equal to a weight times a distance, it is possible, if we know the moment to trim 1 in., to work out the trim resulting from a weight shift aboard a vessel or from adding a weight to a vessel at a certain point.

The moment to change trim 1 in. at load draft is approximately one-tenth the displacement in tons, and the *tons per inch* immersion for a normal-form 400-ft freighter is approximately 50 (50 tons would cause the freighter to sink 1 in.). It should be borne in mind that these figures are only approximations and that the hull technical division works out the exact values for moment to trim 1 in., tons per inch immersion, etc. The values used here are merely for illustration. For exact values a copy of the displacement and other curves calculated for the particular vessel in question should be consulted.

To illustrate the method of calculating trim and sinkage we shall use the approximations above and work two sample problems.

Example 1: *Trim Resulting from Shifting a Weight Already on Board.* Assume that we have a 400-ft 8,000-ton-displacement cargo vessel floating at a draft of 19 ft 0 in. forward and aft and that we are going to move a 35-ton tank from No. 5 hold to No. 1 hold. Calculate the approximate change in trim resulting from this change (see Fig. 183).

Solution: The moment to change trim is approximately one-tenth the displacement; so

$$\tfrac{1}{10} \times 8,000 \text{ tons} = 800 \text{ ft-tons}$$

The tons per inch immersion is approximately 50. This is not used in Example 1, for no weight has been added to the vessel;

we are simply shifting a weight already on board. Assuming that the center of flotation of the vessel is amidships (which is not usually true as it is usually somewhat aft of amidships), our trimming moment would be

Trimming moment = (162.5 ft + 162.5 ft) × 35 tons = 11,375 ft-tons

$$\text{Trim in inches} = \frac{\text{trimming moment}}{\text{moment to trim 1 in.}} = \frac{11,375 \text{ ft-tons}}{800 \text{ ft-tons}} = 14.22 \text{ in.}$$

The stern would rise 14.22/2 = 7.11 in. and the bow would immerse the same 7.11 in.

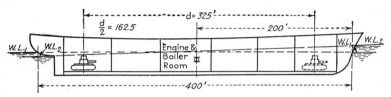

Fig. 183. Change of trim resulting from moving a weight already on board.

The new drafts would be

Bow = 19 ft 0 in. + 7⅛ in. = 19 ft 7⅛ in. (approx.)
Stern = 19 ft 0 in. − 7⅛ in. = 18 ft 4⅞ in. (approx.)

Example 2: Trim Resulting from Adding a Weight to a Vessel. Let us say that we now add two 50-ton landing barges in No. 5 hold. Calculate the new draft.

Solution: We are now adding a weight to the vessel; she will therefore (1) sink a certain amount and (2) change trim.

1. To calculate the sinking: The tons per inch is approximately 50; therefore,

$$\text{Sinkage} = \frac{\text{weight added}}{\text{tons per in.}} = \frac{100 \text{ tons}}{50 \text{ tons per in.}} = 2 \text{ in.}$$

The drafts, not including trim, will be

Bow = 19 ft 7⅛ in. + 2 in. = 19 ft 9⅛ in.
Stern = 18 ft 4⅞ in. + 2 in. = 18 ft 6⅞ in.

2. To calculate the trim: The trimming moment is obtained by multiplying the weight added times the distance from the added weight to the center of flotation.

The center of flotation in our case was assumed to be amidships and the weight added is 100 tons; therefore,

Trimming moment $= 162.5$ ft $\times$ 100 tons $= 16,250$ ft-tons

The moment to trim 1 in. is still 800 ft-tons. Therefore,

$$\text{Trim} = \frac{16,250}{800} = 20.31 \text{ in.} = 20\tfrac{3}{8} \text{ in. approx.}$$

The new and final drafts would be

$$\text{Bow} = 19 \text{ ft } 9\tfrac{1}{8} \text{ in.} - \frac{20\tfrac{3}{8}}{2} \text{ in.} = 18 \text{ ft } 11 \text{ in. approx.}$$

$$\text{Stern} = 18 \text{ ft } 6\tfrac{7}{8} \text{ in.} + \frac{20\tfrac{3}{8}}{2} \text{ in.} = 19 \text{ ft } 5 \text{ in. approx.}$$

It should be noted that the above is only an approximation and is used merely as an illustration of the method. With a copy at hand of the displacement and other curves calculated for the particular vessel, the calculation can be made exact.

DAMAGE CONTROL

The above method of calculating trim may be used in making the calculations for *flooding-effect diagrams*. These diagrams are made up for every warship and, at present, for most merchant ships. They furnish trim and heel information in a simple form to the damage-control officer, so that in case a part of the vessel becomes flooded he may quickly bring her back to even keel.

The principle of damage control is a simple one. A vessel afloat is a balanced object. If a vessel's shell is punctured, an amount of water flows in that is proportional to the size of the space that is flooded.[1] We consider this to be an added weight.

---

[1] Any cargo stowed in the space will exclude an amount of water equal to the volume of the cargo. If the flooded space is filled with lumber, very little water can enter. If the space is empty at the time of flooding, a large amount of water will enter.

The vessel will heel and trim a certain amount depending on the weight added and the distance of the center of gravity from the center of flotation and from the center line.

FIG. 184. Normal torpedo damage extends approximately 40 ft fore and aft. The *S.S. Malay* in dry dock, after being torpedoed off the Virginia Capes. This is a one-compartment ship and as the vessel was torpedoed between bulkheads, no bulkheads were damaged, and only one compartment was flooded. Although the side, double bottom, and bottom were partially missing, the vessel was back in service in 16 days.

To return the vessel to an even keel the damage-control officer must adopt one of the following methods:

1. Add a weight that has an equal and opposite heeling and trimming moment.

2. Shift weights already on board that will give equal and opposite heeling and trimming moments.

3. Remove a weight that has the same trimming and heeling moment.

Method 1 is accomplished by flooding tanks that are located

on the opposite side of the center line and the center of flotation from the damaged part.

Method 2 is accomplished by pumping liquids from tanks on the damaged side to tanks on the intact side.

Method 3 is accomplished by emptying tanks on the same side of the center line and center of flotation as the damaged part. This is the most satisfactory procedure.

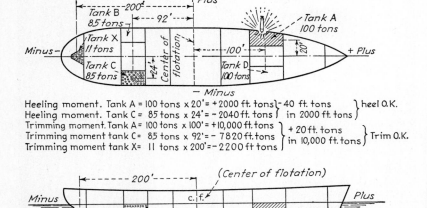

Heeling moment. Tank A = 100 tons x 20' = +2000 ft. tons ⎫ -40 ft. tons ⎫ heel O.K.
Heeling moment. Tank C = 85 tons x 24' = -2040 ft. tons ⎭ in 2000 ft. tons ⎭
Trimming moment. Tank A = 100 tons x 100' = +10,000 ft. tons ⎫ +20 ft. tons ⎫ Trim O.K.
Trimming moment tank C = 85 tons x 92' = -7820 ft. tons ⎬ in 10,000 ft. tons ⎭
Trimming moment tank X = 11 tons x 200' = -2200 ft tons ⎭

FIG. 185. Correcting list and trim by counterflooding.

As an illustration, consider Fig. 185. The vessel shown has just been torpedoed. The vessel's shell has been punctured in way of tank *A*. This tank will flood and the vessel will (1) trim by the bow and (2) heel to port.

The damage-control officer attempts to correct this heel and trim. The heel could be corrected by flooding tank *D*; however, this would increase the trim (for tank *D* is forward of the center of flotation), which may be undesirable.

Tank *A* has a heeling moment of +2,000 ft-tons and a trimming moment of +10,000 ft-tons. Figure 185 shows that tank *C* has a negative heeling moment of −2,040 ft-tons. Filling this tank would correct the heel. Tank *C*, however, has only a negative trimming moment of −7,800 ft-tons, which would not be sufficient to bring the vessel back to an even keel fore and aft. Tank *X*, the afterpeak tank, holds 11 tons and is 200 ft aft of the center of flotation. Flooding this tank would give a trimming moment of −2,200 ft-tons. Tank *X* has no heeling moment, for its center of gravity is on the center line. This trimming moment added to the negative trimming moment produced by flooding tank *C* would bring the vessel back to an even keel fore and aft. The vessel would have increased her draft, however, owing to the addition of 296 tons of water. Even-keel conditions might be obtained by flooding tank *C* and pumping tank *Y*, the forepeak tank, provided that the proper moment is obtained by so doing. Emptying full tanks is usually more desirable than flooding empty ones, for it decreases rather than increases the draft.

Heeling and trimming moments are calculated for every compartment and tank. These moments are placed on a drawing of the vessel in their proper places so that the damage-control officer can ascertain at a glance the trimming and heeling moments resulting from filling or emptying any tank or compartment.

Questions and Problems

1. What are the three types of stability?
2. Will a vessel that has negative stability necessarily capsize?
3. What two conditions are necessary for a vessel to float at rest in still water?
4. From your own experience give a simple illustration of a couple.
5. Describe in your own words the relation of *GM* and stability.
6. Make a rough sketch of a midship section slightly heeled, and spot in the points *G*, *M*, *B*, *B'*, *Z*, and *θ*.
7. Try the rocking-chair analogy at home.
8. Why is excessive *GM* as great a danger in some cases as deficient *GM*?
9. What is the purpose of the inclining experiment?
10. Tell in your own words the procedure to follow in performing the inclining experiment.

11. About what *GM* should you expect to find in a normal modern passenger vessel of 90 ft beam?

12. What caused the capsizing of the *S.S. Normandie?*

13. On a vessel, is it always best to put out a fire by pouring water into the holds?

14. Define moment to trim 1 in. and tons per inch immersion.

15. State in your own words the principle of damage control.

CHAPTER XVII

LAUNCHING

The actual launching operation itself is simply a transfer of the vessel from the building stocks into the water. However, the preparations preceding the launching must begin before the keel is laid. We shall discuss these preparations in this chapter.

PREPARING THE SHIPWAY

The preparation of the shipway, or berth, is one of the most important operations in shipbuilding. As the ground under shipways is usually too soft to support the concentrated weight of a large vessel, the ways must be extensively piled. This piling is driven down to a depth of 30 to 50 ft. A pile driven into the soil under the shipways at Newport News will support about 1 ton per foot of driven length. Sometimes under one shipway there are as many as 6,000 piles, averaging about 40 ft in length. These piles are closely spaced (about 2 ft 6 in. apart) under the standing and sliding ways because they must take the weight of the vessel and its cradle. As the vessel slides down the ways, these piles are called upon to resist the pivoting load that is thrown upon them at a certain period of the launch.

The keelblocks take the greater part of the weight of a vessel during the construction stages, and the bilge blocks and shores take the remainder.

There are in general, three types of building ways, upright stocks, semisubmerged concrete building ways, and submerged shipways.

Stock Ways. Most stocks are constructed of timber or concrete uprights set on cross balks in the ground, these latter being supported by piling. The tops of the stocks are set to a

Fig. 186. Bow view of vessel ready for launching. Note the relation between the size of the fore poppet and the vessel.

grade of about $\%_{16}$ in. per ft.   The ends of the stocks extend into the water about 100 ft, in the case of the smaller ones, to 250 ft, in the case of the larger.

Semisubmerged Ways. Semisubmerged building ways are usually constructed entirely of concrete, extensively piled as mentioned before.   At their outboard ends they have floating gates, which may be pumped out and removed after the ways have

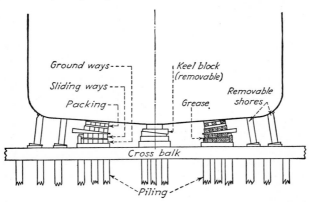

Fig. 187. Section through ship and ways showing the system of piling and hull support prior to launching.

been partially flooded through special valves.   The depth of the water over the sills of semisubmerged ways averages about 20 ft.

Submerged Ways. Completely submerged ways are sometimes used for the construction of large vessels.   They are also valuable as dry docks when not being used for construction.   The *U.S.S. Midway* and the *S.S. United States* were constructed in submerged ways due to their great weight and length which would complicate a sliding launching.

LAUNCHING TERMS

The following applies only to fore-and-aft launching operations from inclined ways.   Figure 188*A* shows in barest outline a vessel resting in its cradle ready for launching and illustrates some of the terms that will be used in the following section.

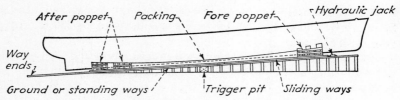

FIG. 188A. Ship poised on ways ready for launching.

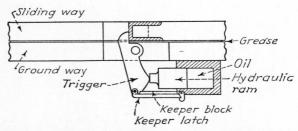

FIG. 188B. Typical hydraulic-trigger arrangement (one trigger is placed in each way). Mechanical triggers with a system of levers replacing the hydraulic ram are also used extensively.

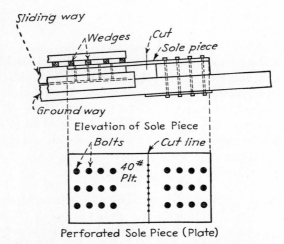

FIG. 188C. Ship-releasing arrangement making use of a solepiece.

The *ground ways,* or *standing ways,* are supported by the pile foundations. The top of these ways is coated with launching grease. Launching grease is put on in layers, the total thickness usually being about 1 in. To launch the aircraft carrier *Yorktown,* 43,400 lb of launching grease was used to coat the two ways.

The *sliding ways* rest on top of the grease that coats the ground ways. When the vessel is released, the sliding ways slide on this grease and carry the vessel into the water.

The *wedges* shown in Fig. 187 extend from the forward end to the after end of the cradle and are driven up hard before the shores

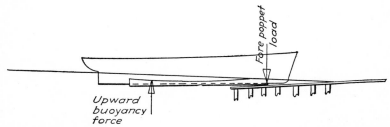

Fɪɢ. 189. Ship pivoting. Load on fore poppet is the difference between the upward buoyancy force and the weight of the vessel.

and the keelblocks are removed. *They do not lift the vessel* but merely bring the cradle up close to the bottom of the ship so as to prevent excessive settling when the shores and keelblocks are removed. (Sometimes in side launching small boats, wedges are used to lift the vessel.)

The *hydraulic,* or *mechanical, triggers,* of which there is one in each standing way, keep the sliding ways from moving until the shores and keelblocks are removed. Sometimes, in launching small vessels, solepieces are used to hold the vessel just before the launch. The type of solepiece shown in Fig. 188*C* is cut with a burner's torch to release the vessel.

The *fore poppet* (Fig. 189) takes the poppet load that is thrown upon it when the vessel pivots during the launch (see below).

At a certain stage of the launch the *way ends* exert a strong pressure on the ship's bottom (Fig. 191).

THE LAUNCHING PROCESS

Let us assume that we have a hypothetical ship poised on the ways, with all shores and keelblocks removed and held only by the hydraulic or mechanical triggers. The triggers are released, and the vessel starts down the ways. As long as the cradle is still largely supported by the ways, very little can happen, for the vessel still slides along on most of its original support. However, as shown in Fig. 190, the time arrives when the afterpart of the sliding ways begins to slide out beyond the ground ways. When this happens, the vessel may "tip," which would cause

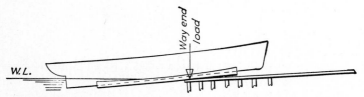

Fig. 190. Ship tipping over way ends (insufficient buoyancy at stern).

the stern to lower and the bow to rise, thus putting severe pressure on the way ends and the bottom of the vessel. The buoyancy of the stern of the vessel counteracts this tipping tendency.

Finally, the buoyancy of the vessel becomes great enough to lift the stern. Then the afterpart of the cradle lifts from the ways, and the remaining weight of the vessel is thrown on the fore poppet (Fig. 189). This is known as *pivoting*, and the weight thrown on the fore poppet is known as the *poppet pressure*.

After the ship pivots, it continues to enter the water, supported by the buoyancy of the water and by the fore poppet until the latter drops off the standing ways; or, if the supporting buoyancy equals the weight of the vessel, it simply floats off with no drop. The vessel is now free of the ways and must have sufficient stability when afloat to remain upright (Fig. 194).

Factors Influencing the Launching. A launching to be successful depends upon the following four factors:

1. *The ship must start.* Starting depends upon the declivity (slope) of the ways, the weight per square foot on the grease, the temperature at the time of the launch, and the type of grease used. The declivity is usually set at ⅝ in. to the foot; but it may be necessary to increase this for small vessels, for the tendency to slide decreases as the weight per square foot on the grease decreases.

The weight per square foot on the grease can be controlled within limits by decreasing or increasing the width of the sliding ways. For example, suppose we have a vessel 400 ft long and weighing about 3,230 tons when launched. The length of the sliding ways would be about 350 ft. If the width of each sliding way was, say, 2 ft, then we should have an area of

$$350 \text{ ft} \times 2 \text{ ft} = 700 \text{ sq ft for one way}$$

and both ways would have an area of 1,400 sq ft. The weight per square foot would be

$$\frac{3,260 \text{ tons}}{1,400 \text{ sq ft}} = 2.33 \text{ tons per sq ft}$$

If possible, a width of sliding way is used that will give a pressure per square foot of between 2 and 2½ tons. Above a pressure of 2½ tons per sq ft the grease has a tendency to squeeze out and burn. Below a pressure of 2 tons the vessel may not slide down a ⅝ in. per foot slope.

2. *Pressure on the way ends, due to tipping, must not be great enough to buckle the bottom of the ship or to cause damage to the way ends* (Fig. 190). This pressure can at times be reduced to a safe value or to zero by increasing the declivity of the keel, cambering the ways, or by extending the ways farther into the water. Adding ballast forward is of doubtful value. Before the *S.S. America* was launched, the open floors were shored internally so that they might resist an expected high way-end pressure. The amount of way-end pressure would be proportional to the difference between the weight moment tending to cause the vessel to tip and the buoyancy moment tending to lift the stern.

3. *The fore poppet must be of sufficient strength to receive the load thrown upon it when the stern lifts and the vessel pivots.* When the *S.S. Normandie* was launched, her pivoting load was 7,000 tons, or 25.3 per cent of her total launching weight (27,666 tons). As 7,000 tons is greater than the light weight of the C-3 type 492-ft cargo and passenger vessel *S.S. President Jackson*, it is easy to visualize the reason for the massive fore poppets used under some of the larger vessels.   As the vessel pivots, the keel

Fɪɢ. 191. A near view of the fore-poppet structure just before the launch of the *S.S. America*.

lifts, which throws the entire poppet load on the first saddle (Fig. 192).   It is structurally undesirable to concentrate this load on such a small area, for to do so would endanger the ship, the fore poppet, and the ways.   There are several methods of distributing this pivoting load over a fairly large area.

The method used at Newport News and at many other yards was developed by William Gatewood, former naval architect at that yard.   Figure 192 shows diagrammatically and in profile the arrangement of this type of fore poppet.

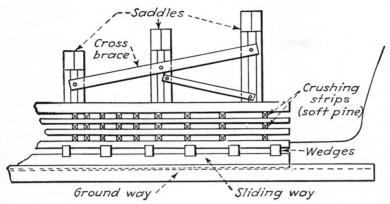

Fig. 192. Elevation of fore poppet showing crushing strips and wedges. (Note increased spacing of crushing strips forward.)

The saddle straps are flat steel U- or V-shaped plates that pass under the hull and are welded at their upper edge to steel brackets. Wood packing is placed between the steel saddle strap and the hull to prevent damage to the hull. On large vessels, concrete is usually poured in at the top to make a strong close fit in way of the poppet-timber bracket (see Fig. 193). The poppet timbers rest on longitudinal beams separated by *crushing strips* about 3 by 3 in. in cross section and made of some soft wood. The crushing strips are spaced farther apart under the forward end of the saddles than under the after end so that, when the ship begins to pivot and the load is thrown on the

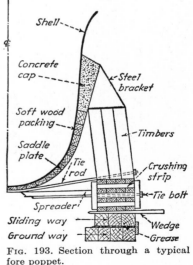

Fig. 193. Section through a typical fore poppet.

forward saddle, the widely spaced crushing strips (being unable to carry as much load as the closely spaced ones) crush downward, throwing a portion of the load on the second saddle, which in turn

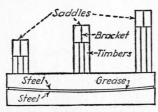

crushes downward, throwing a portion of the load from the first two saddles on the third. This progressive crushing continues until the pressure is approximately equalized among the saddles. Five rows of crushing strips were used in the fore poppet on the aircraft carrier *U.S.S. Yorktown;* the actual maximum amount of crushing was $6^{15}\!/_{16}$ in.

Fig. 194. Rocker-type fore poppet shod with steel and greased.

Figure 194 shows another method of spreading the poppet load. This fore poppet is known as the *rocker type* and has been

Fig. 195*A.* Instability at launching would be catastrophic. The *S.S. Principessa Jolanda* poised for the launching at La Spezia, Italy in 1907. This vessel was practically complete and ready for trials. Thousands of people were in attendance both on the ground and in yachts clustered about the ends of the ways. (*Courtesy of the Mariners Museum, Newport News, Va.*)

used by the New York Shipbuilding Co. It is essentially a circular joint, shod with steel and greased.

4. *The ship must not capsize when afloat.* This was discussed

in Chap. XVI. The 105-ft tug *Sommers N. Smith* capsized in the James River during launching in 1896. Her instability was due to the fact that her machinery had not been installed. She was later righted and after her machinery was installed was suffi-

Fig. 195*B*. A few moments after the vessel was waterborne, she took a sharp list to port and tugs and yachts rushed to the rescue.

Fig. 195*C*. A few moments later the huge 500-ft vessel lay on her side and began to settle in the waters of the harbor. The vessel was almost a complete loss; only the boilers were salvaged.

ciently stable. The *S.S. Principessa Jolanda* capsized during the launching at La Spezia, Italy. All that was salvaged was some of the boilers (Figs. 195*A*, *B*, *C*). In 1952 the Italian motor-ship *Pio Riego Gambi* capsized at Naples, Italy, during launching.

Failure of the ship to start or too great a way-end pressure is serious. A fore-poppet failure or lack of stability after launching is catastrophic.

Launching Routine. The actual transfer of the weight of the vessel from the keelblocks, cribbing, and shores on which the vessel

FIG. 196. The *S.S. America* has just pivoted and thrown the weight not supported by buoyancy on the fore poppet, which is easily taking the load. There was no drop-off as the buoyancy of the bow and the length of the ways allowed a smooth run.

was built to the launching ways takes place the day of the launch. The following description outlines a typical routine but applies to no particular ship. (1) The grease irons, which are spaced about 20 ft apart and which keep the load of the sliding ways and packing from bearing on the grease until just before the launch, are removed. (2) The wedges are driven up, which brings the poppets and packing up tight against the shell. (3) The shores are removed from between the ways. (4) The wedges are again driven up. (5) The removal of the keelblocks and the remaining shores can now take place simultaneously. When these are removed, the vessel is resting on the launching cradle and is ready for release.

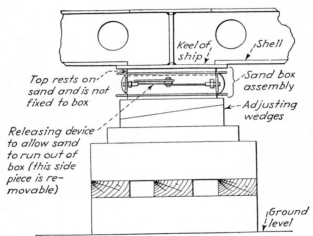

Keel of ship

Shell

Top rests on sand and is not fixed to box

Sand box assembly

Adjusting wedges

Releasing device to allow sand to run out of box (this side piece is removable)

Ground level

Fig. 197. Keelblock assembly with a quick-releasing sandbox.

Keelblocks. A number of ingenious methods have been devised to facilitate the removal of the keelblocks. Under some ships, wedge-shaped filler blocks are placed under the flat top blocks and are removed by knocking out the wedge-shaped filler pieces. As the size of the vessel increases, the difficulty of knocking out the blocks increases. Also, as each keelblock is removed, its load is partly thrown on to the adjacent blocks. In the yard at Newport News collapsible sandboxes (Fig. 197) are usually placed on alternate keelblocks. The top of the sandbox is supported only by the sand contained in the box. Just before the vessel is ready for launching, a releasing lever is pulled and the forward side of the box is removed. The sand then runs out, and the support is thus removed from the top of the box, which in turn drops to the bottom of the sandbox. The blocks are then easily removed, for they have no pressure on them.

A system similar to the above was used at the launch of the *S.S. Normandie* except that salt was used in the boxes instead of sand. Steam forced through the box condensed into water, and the water dissolved the salt. The salt solution ran out of a small hole in the bottom; the support of the keelblocks was thus removed and this load transferred to the cradle. These collapsible blocks are installed about two weeks prior to the launching.

Questions and Problems

1. Name and describe three types of building ways.
2. Why is extensive piling required under most shipways?
3. What is the difference between a trigger and a solepiece?
4. What are the four critical periods during a launch?
5. Why are ways sometimes cambered?
6. What is meant by tipping? What counteracts tipping?
7. Why are crushing strips used only under the fore poppet?
8. Make a freehand sketch of a section through a fore poppet.
9. Describe in your own words the routine followed in launching a vessel.
10. Describe two ingenious devices developed to facilitate the removal of the keelblocks.

CHAPTER XVIII

TONNAGE

History. Even in early Egyptian and Phoenician times, it became apparent that length, breadth, and depth did not adequately express the earning capacity of a vessel. Therefore, certain crude devices were used to determine a vessel's carrying capacity, in order to distribute equitably the various harbor dues, etc., among the vessel owners.

Tonnage measurements, as we know them now, began in the thirteenth century. At this time vessels were carrying large amounts of wine. Wine was usually stored and transported in a large cask or barrel known as a *tun*, which meant a measure of capacity. This tun when filled with wine held 250 gal, occupied about 57 cu ft of space in the ship, and weighed 2,240 lb. This capacity and weight for the tun were established by law in England in the fifteenth century. At that time the taxes or port dues were paid in actual barrels, or tuns, of wine, so that the payment came to be called *tunnage*, meaning the number of tuns a certain vessel had to pay as fees based upon the number of tuns she could carry. The spelling of the word was later changed and became *tonnage*.

Tonnage Measurements. As the word "tun" meant space occupied (57 cu ft) and also weight (2,240 lb), great confusion existed (and still exists) as to what should be used to express the earning ab__ty of a ship—the space in the vessel suitable for stowage of cargo or the actual weight that could be carried. The idea now is to base tonnage on the earning space in the vessel rather than on the weight the vessel can carry. Therefore, Simpson's rule is used to get the volume of earning space in cubic feet, and this volume is then arbitrarily divided by 100, giving the tonnage of the vessel. This tonnage is *space* tonnage, not weight tonnage.

The actual rules for working out the tonnage are complicated and archaic. They are contained in a booklet entitled "Measurement of Vessels."[1] Tonnage measurements are made by the government while the vessel is under construction in the builder's yard and must be completed before a carpenter's certificate will be issued. Without this certificate the vessel cannot be documented and therefore cannot leave the builder's yard. To calculate the actual tonnage of the vessel, the government uses the booklet "Measurement of Vessels."

The following discussion is a condensed general presentation of this very large subject and is based on the United States rules only.

Gross tonnage. Except for certain exempted spaces, the gross tonnage is the entire internal volume in cubic feet divided by 100 (100 cubic feet = 1 ton by law). This tonnage, in addition to including the volume in the hull, includes most of the volume in the deck houses.

Net tonnage is the tonnage that remains after the so-called "nonearning" spaces are deducted from the gross tonnage. It is intended to be a measure of the ship's earning ability. Tolls for canal transit, wharfage, etc., are based on net tonnage. The naval architect, therefore, tries to make this as small as possible.

Exemptions. Certain spaces are exempt from measurement and are *not included* in gross tonnage (see Fig. 198). They are

1. The entire double-bottom space.

2. The fore- and afterpeak space and deep tanks, if fitted to carry water ballast only.

3. Poop, bridge, and forecastle, if fitted with tonnage openings (see Fig. 200 for a sketch of a tonnage opening).

4. An entire shelter deck, if fitted with a small well and suitable tonnage openings (see Fig. 198*A*).

5. Passenger spaces on the deck above the uppermost continuous deck (see Figs. 199*A* and *B*).

6. Other miscellaneous spaces, such as companions, skylights, wheelhouses, vents, and some water closets.

The tonnage, exclusive of the above-mentioned spaces, is the gross tonnage of the vessel.

[1] Government Printing Office, Washington, D.C.

Deductions. From the gross tonnage, certain spaces may be deducted. These spaces are, in general, crew and working spaces. The machinery space is the principal deduction, which, in general, is as follows (see Figs. 198*A* and *B*):

1. If the machinery space is 13 per cent, or less, of the gross tonnage, the deduction shall be $1\frac{3}{4}$ times the actual space.

2. If the machinery space is over 13 per cent and less than 20 per cent of the gross tonnage, the deduction shall be 32 per cent of gross tonnage.

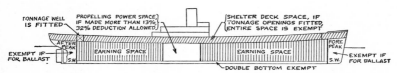

Fig. 198*A*. Shelter-deck vessel, type *A*, for light bulky cargo. Gives maximum capacity. Similar to *S.S. Hawaiian Planter* (Fig. 136).

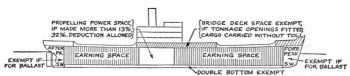

Fig. 198*B*. Full-scantling vessel, type *B*. For carrying heavy dense cargo. Allows minimum freeboard. Similar to *S.S. Angelina* (Fig. 135).

3. If the machinery space is over 20 per cent of the gross tonnage, the deduction goes back to $1\frac{3}{4}$ times the actual volume.

It follows from the above that the wise ship designer will make the volume of the machinery space over 13 per cent of the gross tonnage, even though this volume is not required by the machinery, thus obtaining the flat 32 per cent deduction, which would be much greater than $1\frac{3}{4}$ times the size of the actual space. To illustrate this, let us assume the machinery space to be 12 per cent of the gross; the deduction would be $1\frac{3}{4} \times 12$ per cent = 21 per cent. But by increasing the size of the space to 13 per cent we would be allowed to deduct 32 per cent of the gross tonnage, a deduction gain of 11 per cent.

In order to get crew and working spaces deducted, the builder must certify that they will be used for crew and working spaces only. Thus we see, above the doors to the crew and working spaces, "Certified for 8 seamen," "Certified for galley," etc. Certified for 8 seamen does not mean that eight seamen will be crowded into the one stateroom. Accommodation for one seaman by law is equal to 120 cu ft of space and at least 16 sq ft of deck space. A stateroom with a floor space 9 by 13 ft with 8 ft 3 in.

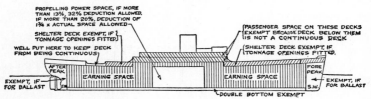

Fig. 199*A*. Freight and passenger shelter-deck vessel. Similar to *S.S. President Jackson* (Fig. 142).

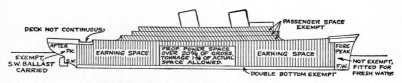

Fig. 199*B*. High-speed passenger-cargo vessel.

deck height would be certified for eight seamen although only three would probably occupy the room.

Tonnage openings. In order to help the shipowner further, the rules permit the exception of poops, bridges, forecastles, and even entire shelter-deck spaces, if certain nominally nonwatertight openings are fitted in the enclosing structure (see Fig. 7). These openings may be secured by bolted plates (no gasket allowed) or wooden battens and are known as *tonnage openings.* Vessels designed to transport light bulky cargoes make use of this device so as to deduct the entire shelter deck (see Fig. 198*A*).

The two major canals, Suez and Panama, have their own rules, which differ in some respects from the above, giving, in general, a greater tonnage than the United States rules discussed here.

Reasons for Tonnage Measurements. Most fees, tolls, and dues are based upon either gross or net tonnage. Dry docking is based upon gross tonnage and is usually about 16 cents per gross ton per day. Thus the fee for dry docking a 10,000 gross ton ship is about $1,600 a day.

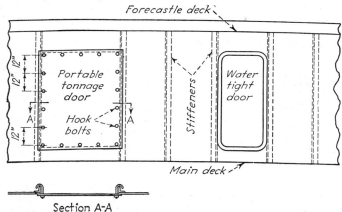

Fig. 200. Tonnage opening in bulkhead *nominally* nonwatertight (no gasket). Watertight door at right is used for access (see Fig. 7).

Harbor dues in foreign ports, foreign and American dockage dues, canal tolls, and sometimes pilotage are based on net tonnage. Note: See Chap. XV for a discussion of weight and displacement tonnage.

Questions and Problems

1. What is a tun?

2. A vessel has an internal volume of 200,000 cu ft, not including exempted spaces. What is her *gross* tonnage?

3. There are 50,000 cu ft of space in the above vessel of Prob. 2 that may be deducted under the present laws regulating tonnage. What would be her net tonnage?

4. Who makes the tonnage measurements?

5. What is the purpose of the tonnage opening?

6. Can cargo be carried in spaces fitted with tonnage openings?

7. Make a list of the more important exemptions.

8. What is the principal deduction allowed by law?

9. How are crew and galley spaces exempted from tonnage?

10. Why do we have tonnage measurements?

CHAPTER XIX

POWER AND ITS MEASUREMENT

The discussion of power, which is the motive force of a ship, is a somewhat different type of subject from our previous discussions as it approaches the field of marine engineering. However, we will touch briefly upon the main engineering phases of shipbuilding to give the student a foundation for further study, if he so desires. In this chapter we shall discuss power in a general way, and in the next chapter discuss what this power has to overcome in order to drive the ship. After we have fixed these two ideas in mind, we shall discuss methods of transmitting this power to the water to propel the vessel.

Work. Technically the term "work," as used in physics and engineering, is made up of two parts, force and distance. If we multiply the force applied by the distance moved, we obtain the measure of work done.

This is a little different meaning of the word work from that which we use in everyday life. It would have been difficult to convince Atlas that he was not working when, according to mythology, he held the world on his shoulders. However, since he was not moving the earth, only holding it, *he was not, in a technical sense, accomplishing work.* Work is measured in foot-pounds. One foot-pound is the work expended in lifting a weight of one pound through a distance of one foot.

Power. Power is defined as the *rate* of doing work. Here it should be noted that we have brought in the additional factor of how *quickly* the work is done. It is obtained as follows:

$$\text{Power} = \frac{\text{work}}{\text{time}} = \frac{\text{force} \times \text{distance}}{\text{time}}$$

Since

$$\frac{\text{Distance}}{\text{Time}} = \text{speed}$$

We may substitute in the above equation and obtain

$$\text{Power} = \text{force} \times \text{speed}$$

Power is usually expressed in foot-pounds of work per minute, foot-pounds of work per second, or more frequently, as *horsepower*.

Horsepower. Actually, for comparative purposes, we must introduce an expression that is more all-embracing than power. This expression, used by engineers throughout the world, is *horsepower*. This term, or expression, can be very confusing to the average person and a discussion of how it originated may give us better insight into its meaning.

In the middle of the seventeenth century English coal miners had to go to deeper and deeper levels to obtain coal. As they dug deeper into the ground, more and more water leaked into the mines, and because of the greater depths, the difficulty of keeping the mines water-free became very great.

In order to clear the water from the mines, a horse was harnessed to the end of a long sweep (Fig. 201) and the sweep was attached at its inner end to a pump. As the horse went round and round, dragging the sweep behind him, he thus operated the pump.

For many centuries man had tried to contrive a mechanical device that would take the place of the horse, and in 1706 the first steam engine was invented in England. This engine was very inefficient and was not used to any extent. In 1780, James Watt, a Scotsman, made some improvements on the original, but because of the earlier failures of steam engines, the coal-mine owners were prejudiced against this form of power. Watt asked himself this question, "How can I establish the value of my engine against the value of a horse and thereby sell the engine?" This question promptly led to, "How many horses will my engine replace?"

To settle this last question, Watt decided to find out just how much work a horse did in one day at the mines and, in general, used this procedure:

Watt attached a spring balance between the singletree and the end of the sweep (Fig. 201) to measure the pull of the horse in pounds, and then he measured the radius of the sweep in feet. Knowing the radius of the sweep and the number of revolutions per hour made by the sweep, he could determine how far the horse walked in one hour.   The calculated speed of the horse proved to

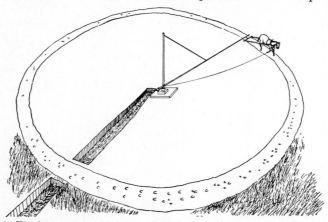

Fig. 201. The horse, attached to a long sweep, operated a pump which, through a reciprocating action, pumped water from the mines.   While watching the action of a horse operating a pump in this manner, James Watt conceived the idea of the now-common expression "horsepower."

be an average of 2½ mph for an entire day, and the spring balance showed an average steady pull (force) of 150 lb.

He then set down the following data:

$$1 \text{ mile} = 5,280 \text{ ft}$$
$$\text{Force} = 150 \text{ lb}$$
$$\text{Speed} = 2\tfrac{1}{2} \text{ mph}$$

Then

$$5,280 \text{ ft} \times 2\tfrac{1}{2} \text{ mph} = 13,200 \text{ ft per hr}$$
$$\frac{13,200 \text{ ft per hr}}{60} = 220 \text{ ft per min}$$
$$220 \text{ ft per min} \times 150 \text{ lb} = 33,000 \text{ ft-lb of work per min}$$
$$\frac{33,000}{60} = 550 \text{ ft-lb of work per sec}$$

wnich was the rate of work done by an average horse operating a pump.

Now if Watt could produce an engine that would do 1,100 ft-lb of work per sec, then his engine could, by the formula, 1,100/550 = 2, do the work of two horses, and for sales purposes he said he had a two-horsepower engine.

The rest was easy. All the businessman needed to do to decide whether a horse or a steam engine was the more economical was to calculate the expenses of both and then compare. Needless to say, the engine won out, and steam rapidly replaced the horse for pumping purposes at the mines.

Summarizing, we can say

1 horsepower = 550 ft-lb per sec (foot-pounds of work per second of time)

= 33,000 ft-lb per min

A kilowatt, the electrical equivalent of horsepower, is equal to 1.341 hp, or 737.6 ft-lb per sec.

The Measurement of Power. To measure power, we must measure a *force,* a *distance,* and a *time.* To do this we can (*a*) use a *force* and a *speed,* (*b*) use a *torque* and a *rate of revolution* (see page 249).

The following three examples illustrate the three types of power usually referred to in dealing with ships:

Example 1. *Towrope Horsepower.* If a rope is attached to a bow of a ship being towed through the water and we measure the pull on the rope and the speed of the ship, we can determine the power necessary to sustain this speed from the formula which we shall now derive. When

$$R = \text{resistance (pull on rope), lb}$$
$$v = \text{speed, ft per min}$$
$$V = \text{speed, knots}$$
$$1 \text{ knot} = 1 \text{ nautical mile per hour}$$
$$= 6{,}080 \text{ ft per hr}$$
$$= \frac{6{,}080}{60} = 101.33 \text{ ft per min}$$

Then

$$\text{Towrope hp} = \frac{R \times v}{33,000}$$

$$= \frac{R \times 101.33}{33,000}$$

$$= \frac{R \times 1}{325.7}$$

Substituting V for unity (1)

$$\text{Towrope hp} = \frac{R \times V}{325.7}$$

This is the reduced form in which we use this equation.   Towrope horsepower is also known as *effective horsepower*, ehp.

Example: Suppose we are towing a small boat and note that a balance attached to the rope shows a 1,000-lb pull when we are traveling at 10 knots.   Determine the towrope horsepower.

Solution: Substituting

$$\frac{1,000 \text{ lb} \times 10 \text{ knots}}{325.7} = 31 \text{ towrope hp}$$

If the small boat were driving itself, it would require about 50 shaft horsepower to maintain this speed, as will be explained later.

Example 2.   Power Transmitted by a Rotating Shaft.   This power may be measured at the engine coupling where it is known as *brake horsepower*, bhp, or aft of the thrust block and forward of any steady bearings where it is known as *shaft horsepower*, shp, or at the propeller hub where it is known as *delivered horsepower*, dhp.   The shaft horsepower is the common measured value for all types of shipboard power plants.

The shaft itself is calibrated as a torsion spring by measuring the torsional deflection (angular twist) on a given shaft length under a known applied torque with static conditions.   A torsion meter is the instrument used to measure this torsional deflection.   When the shaft is delivering power and the torsional deflection and revolutions per minute are measured at the same time, the shaft horsepower is computed as follows:

Q measured torque = say, 400,000 lb-ft (from the torsion meter)
N revolutions per minute = say, 110

Solution: The torque may be imagined as the force applied
at the end of a lever one foot long from the shaft center line; hence
the distance through which the force moves in one revolution is
2π ft and the work per revolution is $2\pi \times Q$ ft-lb. Therefore

$$\text{shp} = \frac{2\pi \times Q \times N}{33,000} = \frac{Q \times N}{5,252} = \frac{400,000 \times 110}{5,252} = 8,377$$

Since shp is proportional to the product of Q and N, the same
power at higher rpm will produce less torque, and hence a somewhat
smaller shaft diameter may be used.

Shaft horsepower of a ship is always considerably larger than the
towrope horsepower. The value of the ratio shp/towrope hp for
well-designed single-screw ships is around 1.3 and even higher for
multiple-screw vessels. For towboat service, values run up to 3 or
higher when towing, and when a tug is pushing at zero ahead speed,
the ratio is infinite. Factors affecting this ratio are shaft-bearing
losses, propeller design, the rudder, appendages such as struts and
bossings, and form and loading of the ship itself.

Example 3. IHP: Power Developed in a Reciprocating Engine.
IHP (indicated horsepower) is an expression for power developed
by the reciprocating engine. The reciprocating engine is simply
an improvement of the original engine developed by James Watt.
However, about 3,000 triple-expansion steam engines were built
during the Second World War primarily because of comparative
ease of fabrication and simplicity of operation, and are the prime
movers used in the Liberty-type vessels.

Types of Engines Used. The type of engine used in Liberty
ships is fairly expensive to operate, burning about 1.2 lb of oil per
shaft horsepower-hour at a pressure of 220 lb and a superheat
temperature of 450°F. The following table gives a comparison of
this reciprocating engine with a turbine at the same pressure and
superheat, a turbine at high superheat and pressure, and finally with
a Diesel engine. Pounds of fuel per shaft horsepower hour is the

amount of fuel in pounds required to be burned in the boilers of steam-generating plants or in the cylinders of a Diesel engine to produce one shaft horsepower for a period of one hour.

Engine type	Boiler pressure, lb per sq in.	Superheat temperature, °F	Oil, lb per shp hr
Reciprocating..................	220	450	1.2
Low-pressure turbine..........	220	450	0.9
High-pressure turbine..........	600	1000	0.5
Super-high-pressure turbine.....	1,000	1200	0.48
Diesel........................	.....	....	0.4

It will be observed that, as the pressure and temperature increase, the amount of fuel burned per shaft horsepower-hour decreases; so high-pressure high-temperature steam plants are being installed in most of the newer vessels.

It should be noted here, in fairness to steam-generating turbine plants, that they have neither the lubrication expense nor the problems of maintenance with which the Diesel installations are plagued. American owners prefer high-pressure superheated steam for large power installations that are in almost continuous operation, and Diesel for small installations intermittently operated.

To measure the power of reciprocating steam engines, a *steam engine indicator* is used. This device, which is attached to the engine cylinders, measures the pressure inside at all points of the cycle. The area of the diagram which the indicator makes is proportional to the work done per revolution of the engine. By dividing the area of the diagram (or card) by its length and using the proper scale, the *mean effective pressure*, mep, is obtained. This mep will do the same amount of work in one working stroke of the engine as actually is done in the cylinder per revolution, the back or exhaust stroke being considered as doing no work.

By knowing the mep for each cylinder end of the engine and the engine rpm, the indicated horsepower, ihp, can be computed.

$$\text{ihp} = \frac{(\text{mep})LAN}{33,000}$$

where mep = lb per sq in. for the cylinder end

L = length of piston stroke, ft

A = net area of the piston, sq ft

N = rpm of the engine.

The ihp of Liberty-type engines is 2,500 at 76 rpm. This is known as indicated horsepower and is usually abbreviated ihp.

Thrust Horsepower. Thrust horsepower is rarely used in powering discussions. It refers to the push (thrust) of the shaft on the ship and is measured by means of a *thrust meter* attached to the shaft aft of the thrust bearing. The thrust meter is usually operated on the hydraulic-oil diaphragm principle and registers a pressure on a gauge. As only ehp, shp, and ihp are important at this point, no discussion of thrust hp is attempted. However, thrust horsepower is useful in the proper design of thrust bearings and in some cases in propeller design.

Relations between EHP, SHP, and IHP. Ehp (or towrope horsepower) is only about 60 to 70 per cent of the shp. Most of this loss is in the propeller.

For a reciprocating engine, shp developed is only about 85 per cent of the ihp shown by the formula

$$\text{ihp} = P\frac{LAN}{33,000}$$

Most of this loss is from the mechanical friction of the sliding parts in the engine (the student will find the word "plan" a convenient memory aid).

From the above it may be said that the effective horsepower (ehp) developed by the reciprocating engine is only about 50 per cent of the indicated horsepower.

Questions and Problems

1. What is power? How is it defined?

2. Why did Watt derive the expression horsepower?

3. Is 100-engine horsepower really the power that could be exerted by 100 horses properly harnessed for a period of 5 min.?

4. As horsepower is a relative term, it is used only for comparison. Name some other comparable expressions such as Watts, lumens, etc.

5. What are the five types of horsepower most usually used in shipbuilding? List their abbreviations.

6. List the formulas used for determining three types of horsepower.

7. Why are some reciprocating engines expensive to operate?

8. A Liberty ship has a reciprocating engine with an ihp of 2,500. What is her shp?   *Ans.* 2,125 shp.

9. What is the effective (towrope) horsepower of the Liberty ship?
                                                                                                                              Ans. About 1,250 ehp.

10. Calculate the approximate amount of fuel oil a 10,800-ton deadweight 11-knot, 2,125-shp Liberty ship will burn per day at sea speed.

Form:

SHP × lb per shp per hr = pounds of fuel oil per hour
Lb per hr × 24 hr = pounds of fuel oil per day

As one barrel of fuel oil weighs 339.9 lb, then

$$\frac{\text{Pounds of fuel oil per day}}{\text{Weight of one barrel of fuel oil}} = \text{barrels of fuel per day}$$

                                                                                                                                     Ans. 180 barrels.

11. Calculate the approximate amount of fuel oil burned per day by a 16-knot 13,750-shp 26,000-ton deadweight supertanker, with a boiler pressure of 600 lb and a superheat of 1000°, when the vessel is cruising at sea speed.
                                                                                                                                     Ans. 485 barrels.

CHAPTER XX

METHODS OF DETERMINING POWER REQUIRED

RESISTANCE

When an attempt is made to force an object through a liquid, such as a ship through water, it is found that a positive force must be used to overcome the retarding force of the water. This retarding force, or *resistance* as it will hereafter be called, is made up of three main parts, namely, *frictional resistance, wave-making resistance* and *eddy-making resistance*. We shall take these up in order and in some detail.

Frictional Resistance. As frictional resistance is a rubbing resistance and as the hull plating of a ship is sometimes called the skin, the frictional resistance of a ship is called *skin friction*. If we take a long plank that is very thin and tow this plank through water with its narrow edge vertical the plank would make practically no waves and produce no eddies. These planks in model basins are called *friction planes* (see Fig. 204). We can measure the resistance, or force required to push or pull the plank, and we will find that it is caused almost solely by the friction of the water on the plank, or friction plane. Frictional resistance is surprisingly large, being about two-thirds of the total resistance of a normal merchant vessel and about 90 per cent of the total resistance of a 20-ft model of the same ship. The symbol for frictional resistance will be R_f.

Wave-making Resistance. Wave-making resistance is next in amount to frictional resistance. Just as frictional resistance is thought of as a rubbing resistance, we can think of wave-making resistance as a *pressure resistance;* that is, it is the resistance that results from pushing away water or of making and maintaining a set of waves that travel with the ship. The smaller the waves, the less the wave-making resistance of the ship (see Fig. 1).

Eddy-making Resistance. This is a whirling resistance and can plainly be seen behind a square-stern boat, a strut, or a rudder-post set across the lines of flow. On well-designed hulls, this eddy-making resistance is small. On old-type flat-plate rudders and

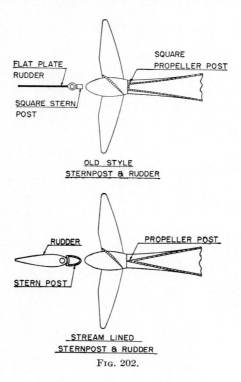

FIG. 202.

square rudderposts, it is surprisingly large. Streamlining the rudder of the 30-year-old *S.S. James Ellwood Jones* increased its speed from 10½ to 11¼ knots, primarily because of the reduction in eddy-making resistance.

As it is experimentally impossible to separate wave-making and eddy-making resistance, we lump them together and refer to them collectively as *residual resistance*, or R_r.

The resistance of a ship traveling fast enough to produce waves cannot be calculated mathematically by using theoretical considerations. Eminent mathematicians are working on the problem but, as yet, without complete success.

Therefore in order to solve this problem, we have two approaches for obtaining the resistance of a projected new vessel.

a. Obtain resistance data from a previous and similar ship and change the results to suit our new design.

b. Tow a model of the projected ship in a model basin and expand the results to ship size.

In case *a*, a small difference and in case *b*, a great difference in size must be considered, which brings us to the serious difficulty which plagued ship designers for centuries. This difficulty was that frictional resistance and residual resistance do not change with size similarly but follow entirely different laws.

In the eighteenth century, Benjamin Franklin towed models of canal boats and attempted to expand his results to full-scale sizes but with extremely poor results. Robert Fulton, in 1800, made use of Beaufoy's tests which were conducted in 1795, but because they had not yet realized that *frictional and residual resistance followed different laws when expanded,* he too failed to forecast full-scale results accurately.

William Froude was the first to realize (1874) that there is a different set of laws for the two types of resistance, and this realization made model testing an accurate method of forecasting the resistance of a full-sized hull.

MODELS

A model is a small-sized replica of a full-sized ship (see Fig. 203). Models commonly used in model basins vary in length from 4 to 20 ft or more. In general, the larger the model, the smaller the experimental error when the results are expanded. However, very good results have been obtained with 4-ft models of ships 750 ft in length. The experimental error in forecasting full-scale results from small models has been within 3 per cent of results obtained from actual trial runs of the ship on the measured mile at Rockland, Me., and as these *full-scale results are themselves not perfect*, 3 per cent is well within the scope of experimental error (see Fig. 234).

In order to make a model of a ship and tow it for resistance, we must first have the lines, dimensions, displacement, speed, and wetted surfaces of the proposed ship (see page 258). With this information in hand, we then make use of other contributions of Froude's to naval architecture known as *corresponding speeds* and

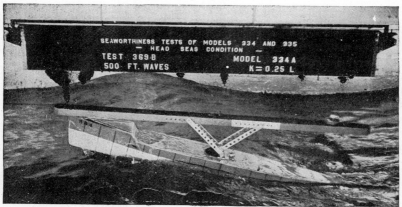

Fig. 203. Model of a 400-ft vessel in 500-ft waves. This model was towed to determine the pounding characteristics of a vessel with similar lines. Although the lines used on this model showed low resistance in smooth water, the model was discarded because of its tendency to pound. This pounding tendency is clearly shown in the photo. Also note that the stern is submerged. A slight change in the lines altered these unfavorable conditions.

the law of similitude. No full mathematical presentation of these laws will be made in this text; however, we can follow through the design of a model using these laws, thus giving the student an idea of how a model is prepared.

Corresponding Speeds. To obtain an idea of this procedure, we shall first discuss corresponding speeds. William Froude, who first propounded this law, stated it as follows:

"In comparing similar ships with one another, or ships with models, the speeds must be proportional to the square roots of their linear dimensions." A 400-ft vessel traveling at 15 knots is not unusual, a 100-ft vessel traveling at the same speed would be considered "fast." The speed of the 100-footer corresponding to the speed of the 400-footer at 15 knots would be:

Let X = corresponding speed of the 100-ft vessel, then

$$\frac{\sqrt{400 \text{ ft}}}{\sqrt{100 \text{ ft}}} = \frac{20}{10} = \frac{15}{X}$$

$$20X = 150$$

$$X = 7.5 \text{ knots.}$$

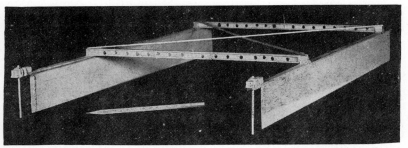

Fig. 204. Friction planes. These two very thin planks with aluminum stiffeners on the top to hold them straight are towed in the model basin to determine the frictional resistance per square foot of wetted surface at model speeds. This resistance is then multiplied by the square foot of wetted surface of the model and the result deducted from the total resistance, leaving residual resistance. Sand strips and match sticks are added to excite turbulent flow, or, in other words, give a rotary movement to the water, which simulates actual conditions in larger vessels.

We may then say that her speed corresponds to the speed of the 400-footer, size for size. So to compare the speeds of vessels, we must consider *size* as a factor and *reduce the speeds of vessels of dissimilar sizes by the law of comparison.* The law of similitude then goes on to say that at corresponding speeds the residual resistances of two similar vessels, or of a vessel and its model, are proportional to their displacements. That is, if the displacement of one is 1,000 times that of the other, then at corresponding speeds the residual resistance of one will be 1,000 times that of the other.

Applying this law, let us assume that we are required to design a 4-ft model of a 385-ft ship preparatory to having it towed in a model basin to predict the power necessary to drive a ship with this particular set of lines at its designed speed.

First make up a table as follows:

Characteristic	Ship	Model
Length....................	385 ft	4 ft
Wetted surface............	31,650 sq ft	Required
Displacement.............	10,583 tons of s.w	Required
Speed....................	13 knots	Required

We know that the model will be 4 ft long as we have chosen this length to suit our model-towing apparatus. What we must determine is the displacement (weight) of the model, its wetted surface, and the corresponding speed at which it must be towed to simulate the speed of the 385-ft ship at 13 knots.

Linear Ratio. First we obtain the *linear ratio*. The linear ratio (l) is the displacement length of the ship divided by the displacement length of the model or

$$(l) = \frac{\text{displacement length of ship}}{\text{displacement length of model}} = \frac{385 \text{ ft}}{4 \text{ ft}} = 96.25$$

The linear ratio is simply a *length ratio*. If we are to obtain surface, or area, we must multiply length by breadth or, to save time, simply square the linear ratio and obtain a *surface ratio*.

Surface Ratio. The surface-area ratio would be

$$\text{Surface ratio} = \text{linear ratio } (l) \text{ squared} = (l)^2$$
$$= (96.25)^2$$
$$= 9,264$$

Displacement Ratio. In order to obtain displacement which is measured as length by width by depth, or area multiplied by depth, (which gives an answer in cubic feet) we cube the linear ratio and obtain a weight or displacement ratio

$$\text{Displacement ratio} = \text{linear ratio cubed}$$
$$= (l)^3$$
$$= (96.25)^3$$
$$= 891,666$$

This is true if both ship and model are in water of the same density. Since ships usually float in salt water and model tanks use fresh water, the displacement ratio must include the ratio of the density (weight per cubic foot) of salt water to fresh water. This ratio averages about 1.024, the salt water being the heaviest. In our case the displacement ratio is

$$891,666 \times 1.024 = 893,806$$

Speed Ratio. As noted from Froude's law, the speed of two similar ships of different size (corresponding speeds) would be in the ratio of the square roots of their length; then

$$\text{Speed ratio} = \sqrt{\frac{385 \text{ ft}}{4 \text{ ft}}} = \frac{19.62}{2} = 9.81$$

or we can take the square root of their linear ratio (96.25), which also equals 9.81.

We now have the 4 ratios required to design our 4-ft model. We apply these ratios as follows, first to find wetted surface.

Wetted Surface. The linear ratio is not used directly here except to find the other ratios, so in our first calculation, we would use the surface ratio to give us the wetted surface of the proposed 4-ft model

$$\text{Wetted surface of model} = \frac{\text{wetted surface of ship}}{\text{surface ratio}}$$
$$= \frac{31,650 \text{ sq ft}}{9,264}$$
$$= 3.416 \text{ sq ft}$$

Finding the Displacement. Here we use the displacement ratio

$$\text{Displacement of model} = \frac{\text{displacement of ship, lb (salt water)}}{\text{displacement ratio} \times \text{f-w constant}}$$
$$= \frac{10,583 \text{ tons} \times 2,240}{891,666 \times 1.024}$$
$$= 25.85 \text{ lb}$$

Finding the Speed at Which to Tow the Model. We find the speed to tow the model which corresponds to the speed of the full-sized ship by using the speed ratio derived previously:

$$\text{Speed of model} = \frac{\text{ship's speed}}{\text{speed ratio}} = \frac{13 \text{ knots}}{9.81} = 1.327 \text{ knots}$$

We now have the required data to design and tow our model. The model is laid out to the exact lines of the ship but on a smaller scale, using the linear ratio to scale down all lengths, breadths, and depths. The wetted surface of the model will be 3.416 sq ft, the weight will be 25.85 lb and the speed that we are to tow it down the tank works out to be 1.327 knots. Actually, the model is towed at several speeds so that a curve of resistance may be plotted (see Fig. 207). We may now fill out our table:

	Ship	Model
Length...................	385 ft	4 ft
Wetted surface...........	31,650 sq ft	3.416 sq ft
Displacement.............	10,583 tons s.w.	25.85 lb (f.w.)
Speed...................	13 knots	1.327 knots

Having the model and necessary data, let us investigate a model basin.

THE MODEL BASIN

There are two basic types of model basins in existence. The more expensive type, usually operated by governments, is the carriage-track type, which consists essentially of a level track and a carriage which travels on the track and tows the model down the tank. The resistance of the model is measured by a sensitive dynamometer attached to the carriage. The speed is measured on a recording tape. The other type of model basin, which is smaller, uses the falling weight principle for acceleration and speed. In this type, a line is attached to the model and then to a weight which is allowed to fall down a well. After the inertia of the model is overcome, and the desired model speed is reached, the excess weight used for acceleration is automatically removed. The weight necessary to overcome the resistance of the model and maintain the desired speed continues to drop into the well until the model has completed its run. The weight required for acceleration and maintenance of the desired speed is determined by experiment. The time of travel is recorded on a self-recording tape on a chronograph. Of course, if we know the distance traveled and the time required to travel this distance, we can determine the speed. Some of the outstanding model basins, or tanks, in operation today are:

The D. W. Taylor Model Basin at Cardarock, Md., about ten miles outside of Washington. The most elaborate model basin for ships. Operated by the Navy. This basin has both types of tank.

The National Advisory Committee for Aeronautics, about three miles outside of Hampton, Va. This basin is primarily for seaplanes and high-speed boats. The length approximates a mile and the speed of the carriage approaches 80 knots.

The Wageningen Basin in Holland. Much experimental work has been done here. Recently an extensive series of model propellers of airfoil sections of various blade widths and numbers of blades from two to five have been completed at this tank by Prof. Laurens Troost. Results indicate that the curves and data obtained afford about the best basis for propeller design now available (see Fig. 232). A modified set of these curves and their use appear in the chapter on propulsion.

The William Froude Laboratory in England. This was the first successful model basin and is now one of the outstanding tanks in operation. Refer to Froude's law.

The Imperial Japanese Model Basin at Tokyo. Few results of their tests are available in the United States.

The Hamburg Tank. This basin carried on many experiments, especially tests on submarines. The German submarine with a speed of 25 knots submerged was not introduced into the war until April, 1945. Its effectiveness is unknown but feared by all navies, as this speed would permit it to slip through all known screens. Latest reports are that the Russians are now copying this undersea boat. Due to war action (1945) this tank was destroyed but is now being rebuilt.

University of Michigan Tank. This is an outstanding educational basin for the students as well as an experimental basin and does much work for outside interests.   It is one of the foremost private tanks in the United States and is of the carriage type.

The Stevens Tank.   This tank is operated by the Stevens Institute of Hoboken, N.J., and was the tank that developed and tested the lines of the now famous sailing yacht Ranger built for Harold S. Vanderbilt which successfully defended America's cup against the British yacht Endeavor in the yacht races in the summer of 1939 (see Fig. 218).   It is a carriage tank and also does a considerable amount of free-running small-scale self-propelled work in connection with steering and maneuvering characteristics.

The Newport News Tank.   Operated by the Newport News Shipbuilding and Dry Dock Company, Newport News, Va. Results from this tank were used in developing the lines for the *S.S. America,* and other noted vessels.   It is a gravity tank and has wave-making devices which can simulate the waves produced by a storm of any desired intensity (see Fig. 203).

The M.I.T. Towing Tank.   This is a new tank of the gravity type, similar to, but larger than, the Newport News tank.   It is to be used for educational and commercial purposes.

EVALUATING THE RESULTS

We have now discussed the types of resistance, the methods of preparing a model to determine the resistance, and the method of determining the resistance in a model basin.   We shall now evaluate our results.

Total Resistance.   The model basin test report will give us the total resistance of the model.   We know that the total resistance will be composed of frictional resistance (R_f), wave-making resistance, and eddy-making resistance.   As wave-making and eddy-making resistance cannot as yet be separated, we will lump these two and call them residual resistance (R_r).   Therefore, we now have only two resistances to deal with, namely, frictional (R_f) and residual (R_r) resistance.

As previously noted, William Froude pointed out that frictional and residual resistance did not expand from model size to ship size (or full size) by using the same multiples (or coefficients) of expansion. Froude overcame this difficulty by using *two methods of expansion*.   First he determined how frictional resistance expanded.

Frictional Resistance Expansion. Froude towed very thin planks of varying length and determined the resistance of these planks. Knowing the wetted surface (area made wet by the water) of the planks and the total resistance resulting from towing them at varying and progressing speeds, he divided the measured pull, or resistance, by the square feet of wetted surface and obtained the resistance due to rubbing or friction (as practically no waves were produced by the thin planks) per square foot of wetted surface. However, as Froude increased the length of the planks, he found that the resistance per square foot became less.   This was logical and was explained by Froude in the following way: "The leading portion of the plane (plank) must communicate on onward motion to the water which rubs against it and consequently the portion of the surface which succeeds the first will be rubbing, not against stationary water, but against water partially moving in its own direction and cannot therefore experience as much resistance from it."

Because of the limited size of Froude's tank, he was unable to tow planks, or planes, longer than 50 ft in length. He expressed a desire to do so but never completed the experiments. Froude did, however, present a table which assumed that the frictional resistance decreased as the length, due to the forward motion of the after particles, but because of experimental difficulties, he assumed that it decreased no further after 50 ft of length.   Curiously enough, this table corresponds closely enough to the data obtained experimentally on trial courses for its validity to be admitted. The Japanese did attempt to tow planks up to 500 ft long, but as they could not keep the thin 500-ft planks straight their experimental errors were very large, and the results are not generally accepted by naval architects.

Since Froude's time many other experimenters have measured frictional resistance. In 1932 Dr. Schoenherr plotted the results obtained by the many experimenters and drew a curve at a mean distance through these plotted points.   This has come to be known

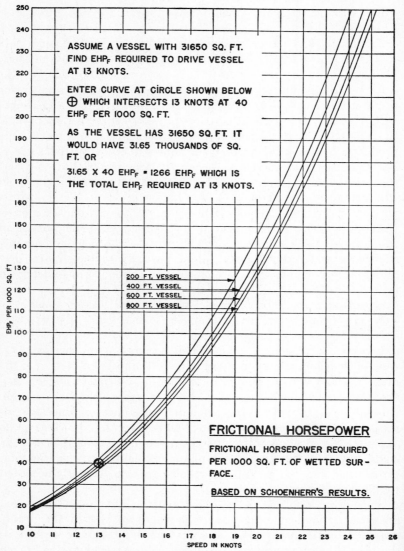

FIG. 205. Frictional horsepower based on Schoenherr's experiments.

as *Schoenherr's mean line.* From the curve represented by this mean line he developed a formula which fitted them all very well. His formula has since been generally adopted by American towing tanks. Figure 205 gives the frictional horsepower for each 1,000 sq ft of wetted surface calculated from Schoenherr's formula. Frictional resistance per thousand square feet is shown for four different lengths of ship, representing the average range of lengths. Lengths in between may be interpolated, those beyond may be extrapolated. Thus a 385-ft ship with 31,650 sq ft of wetted surface would have a frictional ehp of about 40 per thousand sq ft of wetted surface at 13 knots, or 40 ehp × 31.65 (thousands) = 1,266 ehp$_f$ (see Fig. 205).

Fig. 206. A 4-ft model of a projected high-speed tanker being towed at a model speed corresponding to a ship speed of 19 knots. In this photograph the bow wave crest and the following trough and the stern wave crest are all apparent. The hull should be so designed that a crest is formed at the stern in order that the propeller may gain from the wave-orbit wake which is rotating forward when the wave is cresting.

Residual Resistance. It has been pointed out in the above discussion how we may obtain frictional horsepower. We must now obtain the residual resistance (R_f), and horsepower, (ehp$_r$) before we can expand our results to ship size.

To discuss residual resistance, we first considered Froude's law in detail. We stated that at corresponding speeds, for two sizes of ships, the speeds are proportional to the square roots of the linear ratio, that is, if the linear ratio is 96.25 as derived on page 258, the square root would be

$$\sqrt{96.25} = 9.81$$

This would be the conversion factor for the speed ratio, and at corresponding speeds, residual resistance R_r is proportional to the displacement. It follows then that R_r is proportional to $(96.25)^3 \times 1.204 = 893,806$, which is the same as saying that R_r is proportional to the displacement ratio.

If, for illustration, the residual resistance of a model of the 385-ft ship we are using as an example should be 0.01 lb at a model speed of 1.327 knots, the residual resistance of the ship R_{rs} at the corresponding speed of 13 knots would be

$$R_{rs} = R_{rm} \times l^3$$
$$R_{rs} = 0.01 \times 893,806 = 8,938 \text{ lb}$$

In the above s and m have been added to denote *ship* and *model*.

MODEL TOWING PROCEDURE

We are now ready to tow our model in the basin, or tank. The model is placed in the basin and ballasted until it floats at the proper model draft corresponding to the draft of the ship. The model is towed at speeds corresponding to a ship speed of, say, 8, 10, 12, and 14 knots, approximately, which covers our speed range. During the runs we measure the total resistance of the model at the above speeds.

If we plot the resulting total resistance on graph paper, we obtain curve A in Fig. 207. This will be the total resistance of the model which, as previously noted, cannot be expanded directly.

The model basin has the number of pounds of pull necessary to overcome a square foot of frictional resistance when a model is towed at a certain speed. The frictional resistance per square foot of wetted surface is obtained by towing friction planes (very thin planks). We can now plot a curve of frictional resistance for our model, as we know the square feet of wetted surface. This is plotted on our original graph as curve B in Fig. 207.

If the frictional resistance R_{fm} at any point is subtracted from the total resistance R_{tm}, this would leave the residual resistance of the model R_{rm}, or

$$R_{rm} = R_{tm} - R_{fm}$$

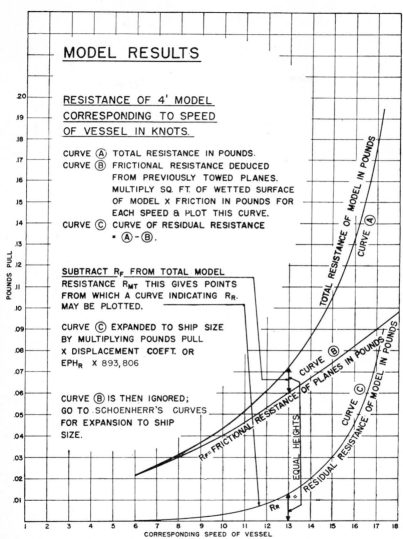

MODEL RESULTS

RESISTANCE OF 4' MODEL
CORRESPONDING TO SPEED
OF VESSEL IN KNOTS.

CURVE (A) TOTAL RESISTANCE IN POUNDS.
CURVE (B) FRICTIONAL RESISTANCE DEDUCED
FROM PREVIOUSLY TOWED PLANES.
MULTIPLY SQ. FT. OF WETTED SURFACE
OF MODEL X FRICTION IN POUNDS FOR
EACH SPEED & PLOT THIS CURVE.
CURVE (C) CURVE OF RESIDUAL RESISTANCE
= (A) - (B).

SUBTRACT R_F FROM TOTAL MODEL
RESISTANCE R_{MT} THIS GIVES POINTS
FROM WHICH A CURVE INDICATING R_R.
MAY BE PLOTTED.

CURVE (C) EXPANDED TO SHIP SIZE
BY MULTIPLYING POUNDS PULL
X DISPLACEMENT COEFT. OR
EPH_R X 893,806

CURVE (B) IS THEN IGNORED;
GO TO SCHOENHERR'S CURVES
FOR EXPANSION TO SHIP
SIZE.

POUNDS PULL

.20 .19 .18 .17 .16 .15 .14 .13 .12 .11 .10 .09 .08 .07 .06 .05 .04 .03 .02 .01

TOTAL RESISTANCE OF MODEL IN POUNDS
CURVE (A)

CURVE (B)
R_F = FRICTIONAL RESISTANCE OF PLANES IN POUNDS

CURVE (C)
RESIDUAL RESISTANCE OF MODEL IN POUNDS

EQUAL HEIGHTS

R_R =

CORRESPONDING SPEED OF VESSEL

1 2 3 4 5 6 7 8 9 10 11 12 13 14 15 16 17 18

Fig. 207. In the above figure we have received the total resistance of the model in
pounds. We then plot a curve of frictional resistance in pounds at various speeds
deduced by towing friction planes which gave no residual, or wavemaking, resistance.
The difference between the two curves is obviously the residual resistance. The
residual resistance is expanded by Froude's method, the frictional resistance by the
use of Schoenherr's curves.

267

In the above, *m* has been added after the symbols to denote that they are *model* results.

Expanding to Ship Size. We now have our model results broken down into residual and frictional resistance. The next step is to expand it to ship size by using the method of Froude.

Expanding Frictional Resistance. We ignore the model frictional resistance, which was obtained by multiplying the square feet of wetted surface of the model by the frictional resistance per square foot of wetted surface, obtained by towing the friction planes, and use Schoenherr's data directly, as they apply to full-sized ships. It should be noted again that the model frictional resistance was calculated solely to enable us to plot the curve B which, when subtracted from the total resistance of the model, left us curve C which is the residual resistance.

We first ascertain the wetted surface of our ship from the table on page 260. This will be found to be 31,650 sq ft. Referring to Schoenherr's curves (Fig. 205), find a corresponding frictional effective horsepower of 40 per thousand sq ft at 13 knots. Multiplying this by the thousands of sq ft (31.65) gives us a frictional ehp of 1,266. We calculate this at several speeds, say 8, 12, and 15 knots and make up a table as follows:

Speed, knots	ehp$_f$ per 1,000 sq ft	Thousands of sq ft	ehp$_f$*
8	10	31.65	316.5
12	32	31.65	1,013.0
15	59.5	31.65	1,833.0

Fig. 208. Table of fractional ehp$_f$; wetted surface of vessel = 31,650 sq ft.

From the data of the foregoing table, we may plot curve B, Fig. 209, for an ehp$_f$ ship.

Expanding Residual Resistance. We deduct model frictional resistance from model total resistance and have left model residual resistance.

* The above ehp is plotted on Fig. 209.

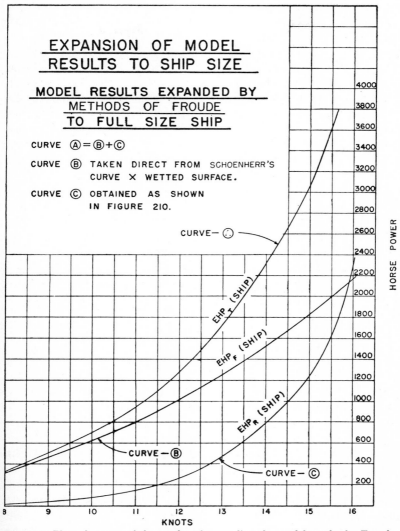

Fig. 209. Plotted curves of the results of expanding the model results by Froude.

The model residual resistance is expanded in proportion with the linear ratio cubed; that is, the model residual resistance in pounds, is multiplied in all cases and at the various speeds by $(l)^3 \times 1.024$, which is equal, in our case, to 893,806. *Note that this is the displacement ratio.*

From curve C of Fig. 207, our model resistance in pounds of pull is 0.002 lb at 8 knots, 0.0078 lb at 12 knots, and 0.0297 lb at 15 knots, all of these speeds being the corresponding speeds of the ship. NOTE: Work out corresponding model speeds. As a starter, the model speed corresponding to an 8-knot ship speed is 0.815 knot. Indicate these speeds on the bottom of Fig. 209.

Knowing the various residual pulls of the model at the speeds as noted, we may prepare the following table:

Speed, knots	Model pull, lb	Displacement coef $(l^3 \times 1.024)$	$R \begin{cases} \text{ship } R_r \\ \text{pull, lb} \end{cases}$	S	$R \times S$	$\text{eph}_r = \dfrac{R \times S}{325.7}$
8	0.002	893,806	179	8	1,432	4
12	0.0078	893,806	6,972	12	83,664	257
15	0.0297	893,806	26,546	15	398,190	1,223

FIG. 210. Table of expansion using Froude's method of expansion of residual resistance. In this equation

$$\text{Towrope hp} = \frac{R,\text{ lb} \times \text{speed, knots}}{327.5} = \frac{R \times S}{327.5} \text{ (see page 248)}$$

Note that while the model pull is small, the displacement coefficient, 891,666, is so great that the resultant ship's ehp_r is normal.

With this information in hand we may plot curve C for ehp_r ship, as shown in Fig. 209.

To find the total effective horsepower that has to be installed is now simple. We add the ehp_r to the ehp_f as read from the two curves at the various speeds and obtain the ehp_t which has to be installed. Curve A, Fig. 209, is drawn to illustrate this.

Figure 211 is an extension of Fig. 209 and shows the results of a self-propelled test on a similar but larger model than the one used to obtain the results shown in Fig. 207. As this was a self propelled test, the curves showing the propulsive coefficient, wake

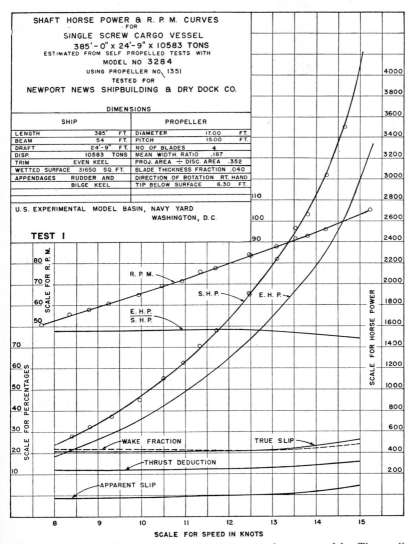

FIG. 211. Result of a Washington model-basin test on the same model. The small, slightly irregular spots are the results of each individual test or run. Their irregularity is due to experimental error. A fair curve is drawn through a mean of the spots.

271

fraction, thrust deduction, and true and apparent slip have been plotted.

A study of Fig. 211 will show that, up to our designed speed, the power is reasonable. However, to increase the speed of our ship from 13 to 15 knots, a gain of 2 knots, *requires almost double the horsepower*, (2,150 to 4,100). A speed of 16 knots is about all that can be obtained *regardless of the horsepower with the type of lines being used*. If a faster ship is required, a finer set of lines must be used, if the length is held constant.

The following important information may be read from the curves of Fig. 211:

At the designed speed of 13 knots

rpm.............................	87
shp.............................	2,180
ehp.............................	1,680
Propulsive coef. $\left(\dfrac{\text{ehp}}{\text{shp}}\right)$..........	78%
True slip.......................	21.8%
Wake fraction...................	21.3%
Thrust deduction................	13%
Apparent slip...................	0.5%

It may also be noted that when the rpm drops below 73, at a speed of 12 knots, *the apparent slip becomes negative*.

RESISTANCE FACTORS

Propulsive Coefficient. As will be discussed in the next chapter, the *shaft horsepower* necessary to drive the ship must be sufficiently greater than the *effective horsepower* if it is to overcome the losses in the propeller and other losses brought about by the effects of fouling, and rough water. The propulsive coefficient is

$$\frac{\text{Effective horsepower}}{\text{Shaft horsepower}}$$

With modern streamlining of stern arrangements and rudder, and modern propellers of good airfoil design, the propulsive coefficient may run as high as 80 per cent for single-screw and 72 per cent for multiple-screw vessels. On old-style vessels where no attention was paid to the streamlining of sternpost, rudder, and propeller blades, and where reciprocating engines were used, it was customary to use a value of

$$\frac{\text{Effective horsepower}}{\text{Indicated horsepower}} = 50 \text{ per cent}$$

This value included some margin for service conditions.

Resistance Due to Fouling.   Fouling of a ship's bottom causes astonishing resistance in ships and an even more astonishing resistance in small boats of low speed, such as sailboats, where wave-making resistance is negligible.

In his "Practical Naval Architecture," Lovett tells of a vessel that loaded out of England with a clean bottom, making 12 knots on the run to South Africa.   It took several weeks to unload due to berthing difficulties, and on the way back *her maximum speed was only* 8 *knots*.   When this vessel was dry-docked over 40 tons of barnacles were scraped from her bottom.

The new high-toxic plastic and regular paints do much to eliminate this fouling condition.   The secret of most antifouling paints is in the poison they liberate by dissolving, or *leaching,* when in contact with water.   This toxin is usually a compound of copper or mercury, or both, which is soluble in sea water and forms a belt of poisonous solution around the hull of the ship.   The dissolving, or leaching, rate must be so controlled in the manufacture of the paint that enough toxin dissolves to discourage the marine growth but not so much that the paint loses its toxins before the next dry-docking.

The Navy *"hot plastic"* has been known to protect the bottom of a vessel for a period of 24 months in the South Pacific.   The cold plastics hold up for a period of 18 months.   As a merchant ship is usually dry-docked every 12 months for inspection of sea valves, etc., a period of 12 months seems sufficient for paint antifouling protection.   Most operators dry-dock every six months for better over-all protection to the bottom plating.   (NOTE: The American Bureau of Shipping requires dry-docking every 4 years for the special survey.)

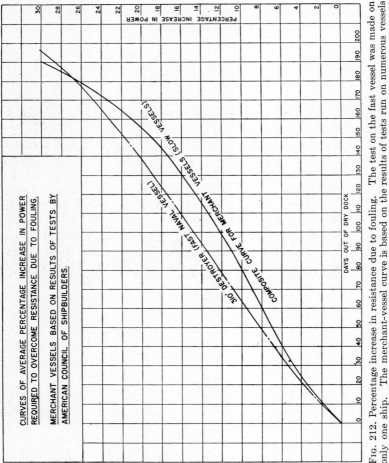

FIG. 212. Percentage increase in resistance due to fouling. The test on the fast vessel was made on only one ship. The merchant-vessel curve is based on the results of tests run on numerous vessels operating in the temperate zone. Any particular vessel may vary in fouling conditions as much as 50 per cent from the above, depending upon the time at anchor or at the berth and many other conditions.

Figure 212 shows a curve of increase in percentage of power required to overcome resistance due to fouling. This curve, drawn as a mean of the increases encountered by numerous ships, is an average based on the number of days out of drydock. Laying at piers or at anchor in warm water increases the percentage of power loss. Continuous operation in cold water would show considerably less power loss due to fouling. Vessels operating in

Fig. 213. Model of a proposed aircraft carrier (never built) being towed in 600-ft waves. The length of the vessel approached 900 ft. The water cascading from the forward end of the flight deck, if dimensions were expanded to ship size, would be well over 500 tons and would crush the structure of the flight deck. This photo was taken as the model pitched out of the wave.

fresh water, such as the Great Lakes, have little or no trouble with fouling or corrosion.

Wind Resistance. Wind resistance on a ship is small. If the vessel is traveling in still air, wind resistance is only 2 to 4 per cent of the water resistance. If the ship is running into a strong head wind, and the ship can maintain her speed, it may reach 25 per cent of the total resistance in still air. The ship is forced to slow down, not because of wind resistance, but because it is buffeted by the large waves caused by the strong head wind. Also, as the wind blows from any quarter, fore-and-aft streamlining is only 25 per cent effective, at best. Streamlining of some ferryboats has driven passengers from the open decks because the smoke, from the stack, hugs the deck.

In view of the above observations we can say that, as in the case of streamlined typewriters, streamlining ships is of aesthetic and advertising value only.

Shallow-water Resistance. The behavior of a ship in shoaling, or shallow water, is amazing. There are two kinds of increases in resistance due to running in shoal water.

1. There is a slight, but measurable, increase beginning when the ship advances into water whose depth is from one-half to one-quarter the length of the ship. At high speeds, it begins when the ship advances into water whose depth is equal to the length of the vessel.

2. There is a phenomenal and sudden increase in resistance beginning when the speed of the ship equals 2 times the square root of the depth of the water in feet, or, $V = 2\sqrt{H}$ in which V = speed in knots and H = depth of water in feet. When $V = 2\frac{1}{2}\sqrt{H}$, we have almost reached the limit at which the ship can be driven in such shallow water. When $V = 3.36\sqrt{H}$, we are at the utmost limit of speed for the ship unless the vessel begins to plane, in which case the vessel begins to outrun the waves that normally would be produced in deep water. As she travels faster than her wave train, few waves can be produced; residual resistance decreases, and we have the phenomenon of full planing such as there is in the case of fast outboards and racing hydroplanes.

Example: Assume a 400-ft vessel is traveling at 12 knots in deep water and enters water about 36 ft deep; then

$$V = X\sqrt{H}$$
$$12 = X\sqrt{36}$$

whence

$$X = 2$$

which means that the vessel would slow down appreciably as the speed of the ship equals 2 times the square root of the depth of the water. The stern waves, which are trailing the ship at an angle of about 45 deg to the center line, will now take a position

90 deg to the center line, the engines will begin to throb under the additional load and excessive vibration will become apparent throughout the vessel.

Many small-boat owners watch the angle of the stern wave to keep from running aground when traveling in shoal water. When the stern wave begins to set at right angles, they slow down or head for deeper water.

Fig. 214. A complex machinery casing in model form. As it is difficult to evaluate mathematically the stresses on a complex form, models are built and the results determined experimentally. Since we know how the simple beam at the left should behave under known loading, a known load is placed on this beam and the resulting behavior noted. By comparison, stresses on the complex structure may be obtained. The material of the beam and the casing is the same and was constructed during the same period.

Figure 215 shows the results of tests made to determine the maximum speed of a proposed high-speed ferryboat as she entered varying depths of shoaling water. The results show that the power curve rises vertically at $11\frac{1}{2}$ knots in 20 ft and at $16\frac{1}{4}$ knots in 40 ft of water. As a large portion of the ferry's run was to be in water approximately 27 ft deep, a speed of about $13\frac{1}{2}$ knots was all that could be expected, regardless of the power, if the vessel remained a displacement boat. Of course, if sufficient power were installed to make the vessel plane (which in a vessel of this size

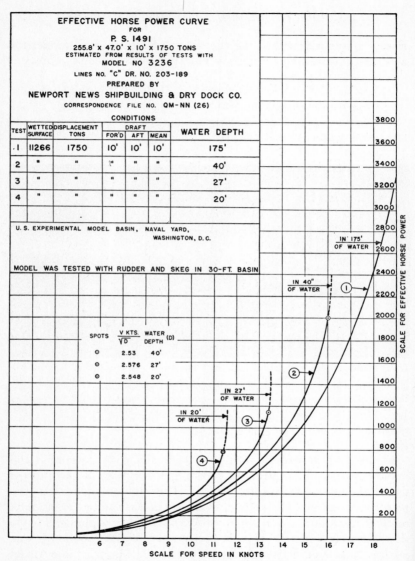

EFFECTIVE HORSE POWER CURVE
FOR
P. S. 1491
255.8' x 47.0' x 10' x 1750 TONS
ESTIMATED FROM RESULTS OF TESTS WITH
MODEL NO 3236
LINES NO. "C" DR. NO. 203-189
PREPARED BY
NEWPORT NEWS SHIPBUILDING & DRY DOCK CO.
CORRESPONDENCE FILE NO. QM-NN (26)

CONDITIONS

| TEST | WETTED SURFACE | DISPLACEMENT TONS | DRAFT | | | WATER DEPTH |
			FOR'D	AFT	MEAN	
1	11266	1750	10'	10'	10'	175'
2	"	"	"	"	"	40'
3	"	"	"	"	"	27'
4	"	"	"	"	"	20'

U. S. EXPERIMENTAL MODEL BASIN, NAVAL YARD,
WASHINGTON, D. C.

MODEL WAS TESTED WITH RUDDER AND SKEG IN 30-FT. BASIN

SPOTS	$\frac{V \text{ KTS.}}{\sqrt{D}}$	WATER DEPTH (D)
⊙	2.53	40'
⊙	2.576	27'
⊙	2.548	20'

IN 175' OF WATER

IN 40" OF WATER ①

IN 27' OF WATER

IN 20' OF WATER ③

② ④

SCALE FOR EFFECTIVE HORSE POWER

SCALE FOR SPEED IN KNOTS

Fig. 215. Shallow-water tests on a proposed 256-ft ferry. The contract for the construction of this ferry called for a continuous speed of 15 knots. As the average depth of the water in which this ferry was to run was only 27 ft, 13.5 knots was all that was indicated by the tests. As a consequence of these tests, one contractor disqualified the 15-knot guarantee, thus losing the contract; however, he saved himself an expensive lawsuit.

would be impractical), the whole picture would change, as has been mentioned previously.

OTHER FACTORS AFFECTING RESISTANCE

We have discussed how resistance may be measured and have mentioned some factors affecting the resistance of the hull, such as wave-making resistance, frictional resistance, fouling, and shallow water. There are several methods of reducing resistance which we have not mentioned previously and a general discussion may be in order.

The Bulbous Bow. Model tests indicate that the bulbous bow is effective in reducing wave-making resistance on vessels that travel at high speed-length ratios; *i.e.*, that travel at speeds which are high for the ship's length. Many tankers have very large bulbs; some bulbs are large enough to have a section area equal to 8 per cent of their midship section area. At the load water line, the stem of the vessel is made sharp to cut the surface of the water and to present a knife-edge to the action of large waves, and the maximum width of the bulb does not develop until this bulb area is well below the load water line (see Fig. 124). The flared-out portion toward the bottom of the stem is the bulb.

Riveted Shell Butts. Contrary to popular notion, if the shell-plating butts on a riveted ship are lapped forward, rather than aft, the total resistance of the vessel is reduced almost 3 per cent. This is due to the prevention of eddy formation at the after ends of the plating. Lapping the plating forward also prevents eddies from eating away and undercutting the after edges of the lapped plate. The forward edges of plates lapped forward should be well rounded.

Length. Increasing the length of a vessel reduces the speed-length ratio and, in general, reduces the wave-making resistance at a given speed. Added length also has a tendency to increase wetted surface, thereby increasing frictional resistance. If the first tendency is greater than the latter, and a vessel has her length increased by the addition of a longer bow or a new section amidship, the total resistance will decrease and her speed will increase, or less power may be used to maintain her old speed.

FORM COEFFICIENTS AND THEIR EFFECT ON RESISTANCE

Beam-draft Ratio. For definitions and derivations of these coefficients, see page 178.

Beam-draft ratio is expressed as follows:

$$\text{Beam-draft ratio} = \frac{B}{d}$$

and is usually equal to about 3. As the beam increases and the draft decreases, this ratio becomes larger and total resistance usually increases, but at a low rate. As the ratio becomes smaller, the resistance usually decreases slightly.

Prismatic Coefficient. Sometimes called the coefficient of fineness (see page 178). The prismatic coefficient of a rectangular barge is 1, that of a high-speed displacement yacht is about 0.60, and that of the average freighter is about 0.70. In general, the lower the prismatic coefficient, the more easily a vessel will drive.

Parallel Middle Body. The parallel middle body of a ship, best shown on the sectional-area curve, is the length of the curve that does not increase or decrease in height, or the distance along the hull over which the maximum section area remains constant. See Fig. 162 for a sectional-area curve of a vessel with zero parallel middle body and Fig. 152 for the sectional-area curve of a vessel with approximately 15 per cent parallel middle body. In general, for slow full vessels, a long parallel middle body is desirable, and for fast fine vessels, the parallel middle body is reduced or eliminated.

Displacement-length Ratio. As mentioned on page 177, the displacement-length ratio is sometimes called the "fatness" ratio and is used in determining the relative fatness of vessels. From the table on page 181, it will be seen that the displacement-length ratio for the tug *Huntington* is 489 while for the *S.S. America* it is only 106. In general, for fast fine vessels, the lower the displacement-length ratio, the easier the vessel will drive in proportion to her displacement.

In this brief discussion, it should be noted that the form coefficients and their relation to resistance, referred to above, are generalizations which are so entwined that a change in any one will change all of these dimensionless coefficients in some way, for any particular vessel. A study of the table on page 181 and of the vessels listed on page 359 will illustrate in a small way why ships are shaped as they are and why vessels for different trades have different characteristics. A quick review of Chap. XIV, particularly of the latter part, will be most helpful to the student at this point.

Summary

The preceding discussion gives an idea of how we may approximate horsepower required for a new design by working either from a model or from a previous ship whose resistance is known. The steps to be followed are summarized below:

1. Measure by test or know the total resistance of a previous similar ship or model.

2. Subtract the proper frictional resistance from the total resistance; the remainder thus obtained is the residual resistance.

3. Expand the residual resistance to the new size by making it vary as the displacement of the two vessels.

4. The expanded residual resistance will apply, not to the old speed of the comparable vessel, but to the new speed. Therefore, the following correction should be made:

Corresponding speed of new vessel = knots (old vessel) $\times \sqrt{\text{linear ratio}}$

5. From curves (Fig. 205) for frictional ehp per thousand sq ft of wetted surface, pick up ehp_f for the new size.

6. Add ehp_r and ehp_f at the various speeds to produce a curve of ehp_t (total ehp).

7. Increase the ehp_t to suit the propulsive coefficient expected. Add an additional 15 per cent margin for fouling, wind, and waves.

TAYLOR'S STANDARD SERIES

Quite often the naval architect is not in possession of results from either a model or a similar ship. However, he has one other recourse which is very accurate, Taylor's great work entitled "Speed and Power of Ships."

Admiral D. W. Taylor was in charge of the Washington model basin for years and during his tenure produced a parent model of a vessel.   From this parent model he produced a series of models by varying the prismatic and block coefficients (see page 178).

Fig. 216. Full-sized models, or "mock-ups," of parts of ships are also used.   This photograph shows a mock-up (full-sized) of the piping in No. 2 pump room of a supertanker.   These mock-ups are made in the shop where machines and tools are handy, and holes are drilled to fit; and the piping is bent and fitted.   The parts when taken to the vessel then present a simple assembly job which proceeds with great rapidity.   This method is especially valuable when a series of identical ships are to be built.

He towed a series of the models and plotted the results in *"residual resistance in pounds per ton of displacement."* This series is now known as "Taylor's Standard Series."   As Admiral Taylor gives an excellent description of the use of these curves, and as the student must have the numerous charts on hand, no further discussion is necessary.   Once residual resistance is obtained from Taylor's charts, it is expanded as previously discussed.

CHAPTER XXI

PROPULSION

We have discussed the power required to overcome resistance and the three types of resistances encountered by the vessel in passing through the water. In this chapter we shall discuss the methods used in transmitting power to the water thus moving the vessel.

Fig. 217. The *Thomas W. Lawson*, the world's largest sailing vessel. A seven-masted steel-hulled schooner, she was lost in a storm off southern England. The order beginning at the forward mast is: foremast, mainmast, mizzen, jigger, spanker driver, and pusher. However, the crew named them after the days of the week. Her demise ended competition between sail and power-propelled vessels.

METHODS OF MARINE POWER TRANSMISSION

There are several methods of transmitting power; namely: oars, sails, paddle wheels, jets (jet propulsion), propellers (numerous types), etc. We shall not attempt to discuss all of these methods but shall dwell only on standard propellers; however, a few words about the other methods should be of interest.

283

Oars. Oars impart power when they are forced through the water. This is an ancient method.

Sails. Sails are of several types. The older ships had square sails which were extremely advantageous when sailing before "the trades." ("Trades" are winds which blow almost constantly in one direction and arise due to the rotation of the earth.) Ships

Fig. 218. The American-cup defender *Ranger* in light air. Note the overlapping headsails which give a double "tunnel effect." The vessel is sailing to windward (towards the wind).

with square sails sail fairly efficiently with the wind abaft or on the beam but are of little value to windward. (Sailing in the direction from which the wind is blowing.)

To overcome this latter disadvantage, the fore-and-aft rig was developed. This rig was successful in driving a ship to windward and was primarily used as a gaff-headed schooner-type rig as shown on the *Thomas W. Lawson*, a seven-masted schooner (see Fig. 217).

Later the "leg-of-mutton," or "Marconi," rig was developed;

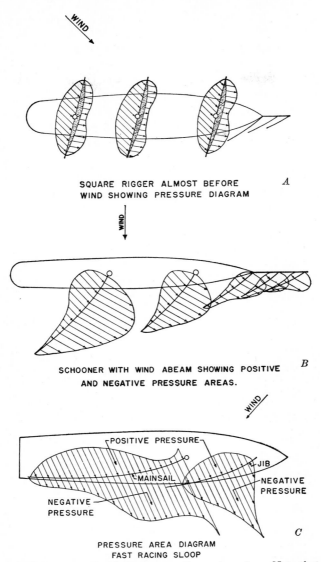

SQUARE RIGGER ALMOST BEFORE
WIND SHOWING PRESSURE DIAGRAM

A

SCHOONER WITH WIND ABEAM SHOWING POSITIVE
AND NEGATIVE PRESSURE AREAS.

B

PRESSURE AREA DIAGRAM
FAST RACING SLOOP

C

Fig. 219. Approximate sail-pressure diagrams for various rigs. Note that for fore-and-aft rigged vessels the maximum pressure, or lift, which is negative in this case, is forward of the sail. In aircraft work this negative pressure is known as lift and occurs on top of the wing. It is the force that keeps the plane afloat (in the air).

285

it resembles a true airfoil. A picture of the yacht *Ranger* shows the ultimate in this type of rig (see Fig. 218).

Fast-racing sailing yachts make their greatest speed under normal conditions when sailing with the wind abeam or slightly before the beam.

Effect of Direction of the Wind. When the wind is abaft the beam, the vessel is constantly sailing away from the wind. If the

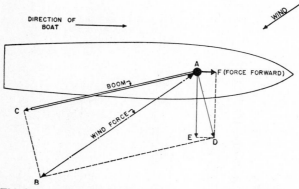

Fɪɢ. 220. This figure is a parallelogram of forces. It illustrates a single-masted vessel on the wind on a port tack. The line *AB* represents the direction of the wind, and its length represents the force of the wind. This force may be broken down into two forces, one parallel to and acting along the sail, which may be neglected as it produces only friction, and a smaller force *AD* acting at right angles to the sail. This smaller force is somewhat forward and may be broken into two components, the larger of which is *AE* and acts at right angles to the keel. The smaller force *AF* acts in the direction of travel of the boat.

Because of the resistance to sliding offered by the hull and keel, the motion sideways is small. As the resistance to forward motion is much less, the boat begins to move forward and its speed will be proportional to the component force *AF*. The sideways drift of a boat on the wind amounts to about 4 to 9 deg off its heading, depending on the contours of the underwater hull.

vessel is sailing before a twenty-knot wind at a speed of five knots, it is experiencing a push from the wind of only fifteen knots. When the vessel has a twenty-knot wind abeam, it is traveling in approximately a twenty-knot wind regardless of its speed.

Figure 220 shows a single-masted vessel on the wind on a port tack. The direction of line *AB* represents the direction of the wind and its length represents its force. According to the parallelogram of forces, this force may be broken into two forces, one parallel to and acting along the sail which may be neglected as it produces only friction, and a smaller force, AD, acting at right angles to the sail. This smaller force is somewhat forward and may be broken into two components: the larger one, AE, acts at right angles to the keel and the smaller acts in the direction the boat is intended to travel.

Because of the resistance to sliding offered by the hull and keel, the motion sideways is small. As the resistance to forward motion is small, the boat begins to move in that direction and its speed will be proportional to the component force AF. The drift sideways of a boat on the wind amounts to about 4 to 9 deg off its heading, depending on the contours of the underwater hull. If the vessel *is going against* the wind at an angle, the faster the vessel moves toward the wind the faster the wind blows past the sails. Figures 219A, B, and C illustrate the above circumstances, and the force diagram in Fig. 220 shows the force components which cause a sailing vessel to sail to windward.

It should be noted that the wind does very little pushing on a sailing vessel unless the vessel is sailing directly before the wind. When the vessel has wind abeam or is going into the wind, a low-pressure area forms on the back and at the leading edge of the sail and tapers to the after end of the sail. (Luff to leach.) The sails tend to move into the low-pressure area and, as they are attached to the boat, pull the vessel forward.

Since a sail acts as an airfoil, a typical example of which is an aeroplane wing, the closer the sail approaches the shape of a successful wing, the better will be the sail for pulling.

The deep keel, or centerboard, of a sailboat minimizes any tendency to slide sideways. If the wind is from any quarter except directly ahead, the easiest path for the vessel to travel to permit the sail to pass into the low-pressure area will be forward, with a little sliding sideways, called *leeway*. In general, the deeper the keel, or centerboard, the less the leeway. As the leading edge of the sail gives the most lift, the longer the edge, the greater the lift.

This is true of depth of the keel, so we find high narrow sails and deep narrow centerboards, or keels, on fast racing yachts.

The addition of a jib gives an amazing increase in pull to a mainsail. While the jib may be only 25 sq ft and the mainsail 100 sq ft, the addition of a jib, properly overlapping and cut, may increase the pull exerted by the two in combination as much as 50 to 75

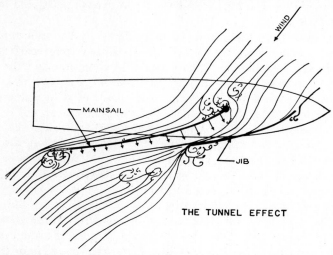

THE TUNNEL EFFECT

FIG. 221. "The tunnel effect." The jib catches a large volume of air and directs it through a narrow slot past the lee of the mainsail. Because of the pressure upon it while moving through the narrow slot, the wind increases its speed while the pressure on the back of the mainsail decreases. The addition of a jib also tends to decrease the formation of eddies on the back of the mainsail and thereby increase its efficiency.

per cent. This result is due principally to what is known aerodynamically as the *tunnel effect* and is shown in Fig. 221.

The jib channels the wind and, because of the slot between the jib and mainsail, forces the wind past the back of the mainsail at a high rate of speed. The high speed causes an increase of the low-pressure area, thus increasing the efficiency of the mainsail.

The poem "Sailing" (author unknown) illustrates somewhat the art of sailing and is quoted below:

Ships sail east and ships sail west
On the self same wind that blows,
But it's not the gales,
It's the set of the sails,
That determines the way she goes.

Paddle Wheels. Paddle wheels are not out-of-date and may be seen either at the side or on the stern of a vessel. Stern-wheelers can be shallower than most propeller boats and are extensively used on inland waterways. Both the stern- and side-wheelers must be used in relatively smooth water as large waves tend to damage the paddles and supporting structure. Also, their immersion varies greatly in a seaway because of the rolling and pitching of the vessel which adds to the damaging effect of the waves. To reduce draft and compete with paddle wheels, propeller designers have recessed the propeller in a tunnel at the stern which has proved very successful in extremely shallow water.

Cycloidal Propellers. These are vertical-axis feathering-blade propellers and have been widely used in Europe for shallow-draft vessels and to some extent on small craft for the United States Army and Navy. They have the advantage of having a high degree of maneuverability since pitch is adjusted from full ahead to full astern and the direction of thrust is adjustable over 360-deg arc, thus eliminating the need for a rudder. These propellers are known in Europe as the "Voith-Schneider" type. In this country the "Kirsten" type has been developed which has directional adjustment of thrust over 360-deg arc, but the pitch is fixed.

Jet Propulsion. This type of propulsion is relatively old. Because of its inefficiency in marine work, it has not been commercially successful. Most experiments with the jet type have been on the principle of a propeller located in a tunnel which is open at the bow and runs through to the stern. The recessed-propeller type, as noted above, is more efficient and is extensively used, particularly for push- or towboats, on the Mississippi River. The "Kort Nozzle," which is an annular ring fitted around, but not touching the tips of, the propeller blades, greatly increases the towing power of tug boats which operate at high rates of slip.

The Screw Propeller.   The screw propeller is the most important of all and is universally adopted.   We are not going into all the minute details necessary to someone who wishes to become a propeller expert; however we should know how to "talk the language."

In order to discuss this rather complicated subject, we must first define some of the terms that will be used:

Wake.   There are three types of wake, namely, *frictional, streamline,* and *wave-orbit wake.*   The frictional wake is produced

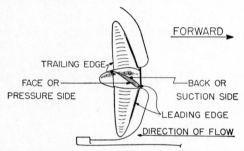

Fig. 222. Sketch showing location of face and back of propeller blades.   To determine whether a propeller is right- or left-handed, stand aft of the propeller and look forward; if the propeller turns to your right, it is a right-handed propeller.   The rotation of the machinery to turn this propeller will be to the left, as the rotation of machinery is taken looking aft.

by the layer of water which is dragged along by the skin friction of the ship (the friction belt) and is the largest of the three wake components.   The streamline wake is that due to the closing in of the streamline flow at the stern.   It is a greater portion of the total wake on twin-screw than on single-screw ships.   Wave-orbit wake is negligible except on high-speed vessels with pronounced wave systems.   The wave-orbit wake is positive if a wave crest is abreast of the propeller and negative if a trough is abreast of the propeller.

Wake Fraction.   So far as the propeller is concerned, the total wake is all that needs to be considered.   The total wake, in effect, reduces the velocity at which the propeller advances through

FIG. 223. One of the propellers for the *S.S. United States.* This propeller has been rough-machined, and a workman is marking the amount to be removed in thirty-seconds of an inch during the final machining. After finish machining the propeller will be dynamically balanced, and amounts of material removed until the propeller runs fair and smooth with no vibration. The developed-area ratio is about one, owing to the high thrust.

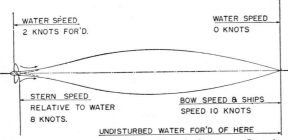

FIG. 224. The bow of the vessel enters undisturbed water. Ignoring the flow of water caused by currents or tidal movements, we may say that its speed is zero. The stern of the vessel is not passing through undisturbed water, but is passing through water that has been dragged along by the surface friction of the hull, and in this case the dragging amounts to a forward speed of two knots. In the above case we may say that the bow is traveling 10 knots and the stern 8 knots in relation to the undisturbed water.

the water.   If the total wake adds up to 30 per cent of the ship's
velocity, the propeller advances through the water at 70 per cent
of the ship's velocity.   This is a gain and is sometimes referred to as
wake gain.   The ratio of wake velocity to ship velocity is called

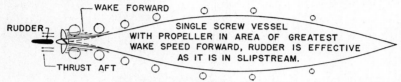

SINGLE SCREW ACTION
WAKE GAIN

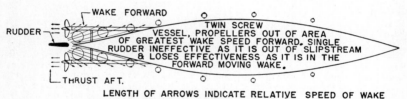

TWIN SCREW ACTION
WAKE GAIN

FIG. 225. The length of the arrows on the periphery of the circles rolling along the
hull are used to indicate the relative speed of the particles in the wake.   The diameter of the circles also indicates the strength and intensity of the wake at the various
distances from the hull.

wake fraction, *w*, and would be 0.30 in the case just cited.   The
speed of advance of the propeller would be

$$V_a = V(1 - w) = 0.70V$$

where V is the speed of the ship and V_a is the speed of advance
of the propeller.   Wake fraction on full-lined single-screw ships,
where the screw works largely in the friction belt, may exceed 0.35,
and values as high as 0.40 or even 0.50 are not unknown.   On the
other hand, the wake fraction on fine-lined twin-screw ships, where
the propellers are further removed from the friction belt, may be

0.10 or less. Destroyers have practically zero wake fraction. A table of wake fractions for various types of vessels is given later under propeller design.

On multiple-screw vessels there is danger of vibration if the clearance between propeller tips and hull is less than one-sixth propeller diameter, and on very high-powered ships a clearance of one-fourth diameter should be maintained if possible. Because

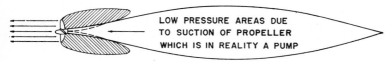

LOW PRESSURE AREAS DUE
TO SUCTION OF PROPELLER
WHICH IS IN REALITY A PUMP

PLAN VIEW OF LOW PRESSURE AREA

THRUST DEDUCTION

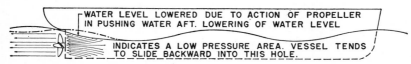

WATER LEVEL LOWERED DUE TO ACTION OF PROPELLER
IN PUSHING WATER AFT. LOWERING OF WATER LEVEL
INDICATES A LOW PRESSURE AREA. VESSEL TENDS
TO SLIDE BACKWARD INTO THIS HOLE.

ELEVATION OF WAVE PROFILE DUE TO PROPELLER ACTION

Fig. 226. Diagrammatic sketch. An idea of thrust-deductive forces.

of its extremely high speed, the tip clearance on the *S.S. United States* is about one-third the diameter of the propellers, and vibration from the propellers, which is the major source of vibration on a ship, is negligible.

Thrust Deduction. In order to drive the ship through the water there must be high pressure on the after side, or driving face, of the blades and low pressure on the forward side, or back, of the blades (see Fig. 226). The accelerated flow of water into this low-pressure area creates a suction on the stern of the ship thus requiring the propeller to exert more thrust to drive the ship ahead than the pull that would be required on a tow line if the ship were being towed at the same speed. The amount by which propeller thrust T exceeds towed resistance R is expressed as follows:

$$T = \frac{R}{(1 - t)} \qquad \text{or} \qquad R = T(1 - t)$$

where t = thrust deduction.

In addition to the suction caused by the propellers on the stern of the ship, there is another effect on single-screw vessels which adds to the towrope resistance. This effect is due to the drag of the rudder and rudderpost in the slipstream, or wash, from the propeller and is included in the thrust deduction. On old-style single-screw vessels with square stern and rudderposts, and plate rudders with rudderstock extending down to the shoe, the thrust deduction, t, may be as large as the wake fraction, w. Where attention has been given to efficient streamlining of sternpost, rudderpost, and rudder, t may be as low as $0.6w$ (see Fig. 202). On multiple-screw vessels t is usually about equal to, or slightly greater than, w.

Hull Efficiency. The foregoing discussion is of considerable importance in view of the effect of the relative values of wake fraction w and thrust deduction t. We have noted how the effective thrust of the propeller is diminished by the thrust deduction in the amount $(1 - t)$. However, since the propeller does not have to move as fast through water as the vessel is moving, the work it has to do is also diminished by the amount $1 - w$ (Fig. 227). The quantity $1 - w$ is called *wake gain*, the gain being similar to the help a man shoving a pushcart would receive by walking on a moving platform (like an escalator) advancing slowly in his direction. The combined effect of wake gain and thrust deduction is called *hull efficiency* and is expressed as follows:

$$\text{Hull efficiency} = \frac{(1 - t)}{(1 - w)}$$

It will be seen that a tanker whose wake fraction w is 0.40 and thrust deduction $t = 0.6w = 0.24$ will have a hull efficiency of

$$\frac{1 - 0.24}{1 - 0.40} = 1.27$$

This means, as will be shown later, that the over-all propulsive efficiency of the ship is 27 per cent higher than would be the case if propulsive efficiency were determined by propeller efficiency alone.

Speed of Advance of Propeller through the Water. The speed of advance of the propeller through the water in which it is working (see Fig. 224) is usually less than the speed of the ship through the

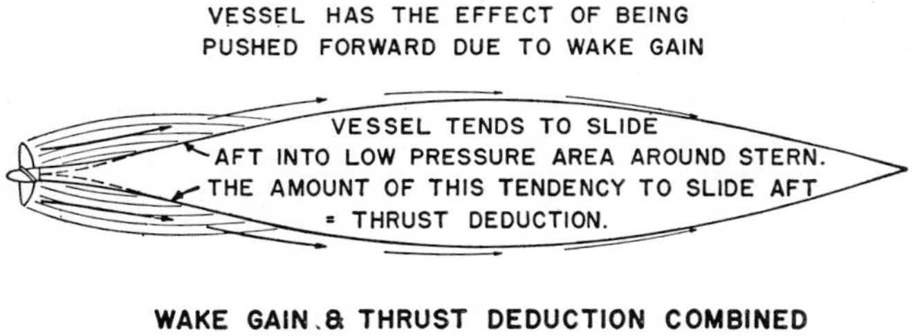

VESSEL HAS THE EFFECT OF BEING
PUSHED FORWARD DUE TO WAKE GAIN

VESSEL TENDS TO SLIDE
AFT INTO LOW PRESSURE AREA AROUND STERN.
THE AMOUNT OF THIS TENDENCY TO SLIDE AFT
= THRUST DEDUCTION.

WAKE GAIN & THRUST DEDUCTION COMBINED

Fig. 227. Diagrammatic sketch of thrust deduction and wake gain combined. Illustrative only.

undisturbed water. The amount of this difference is, of course, equal to the wake.

1. *Pitch.* This is the distance the propeller would travel, or advance, in one revolution if it were traveling in a so-called *nut.*

2. *Slip.* This is the difference between the actual speed of the ship and the speed of the propeller if it were working in a so-called *nut.* There are two types of slip:

a. Apparent Slip. This is based on the pitch speed of the propeller compared with the speed of the ship.

b. Real Slip. This is based on the pitch speed of the propeller compared with its actual speed through the wake of the ship. The actual, or real, slip must exert a sternward motion to the water, *i.e.*, it must have a positive value or the ship will not move forward (Fig. 227). It is possible for the apparent slip to be negative, that is, for the forward motion due to the wake to be slightly greater than the sternward motion of the water due to the push of the propeller. This can easily happen when we have a large propeller imparting a slow motion to a large mass of water and often occurs on single-screw vessels at light draft.

SLIP IS NECESSARY

WATER MUST BE MOVED AFT (CALLED *SLIP*) IN ORDER TO IMPART
THRUST TO PROPELLER AND MOVE VESSEL FORWARD.

A

VESSEL WITH PROPELLER OF ZERO PITCH (BLADES FLAT), NO
WATER MOVES AFT, FORWARD MOTION OF VESSEL ZERO.

B

VESSEL WITH PROPELLER OF NORMAL PITCH, SAY 100 PER CENT
OF DIAMETER (20 FT DIAM. 20 FT PITCH) TURNING AT 100 RPM.
SPEED OF BLADE PITCH = 100 × 20 = 2000 FPM
PROPELLER SPEED THRU WATER, SAY 15 KN. = 1520 FPM
DIFFERENCE = SPEED OF WATER AFT = SLIP = 480 FPM = 24%

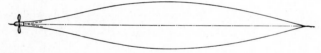

C

VESSEL WITH PROPELLER OF SLIGHT PITCH, SAY 50 PER CENT OF
DIAMETER (20 FT DIAM. 10 FT PITCH) TURNING AT 100 RPM.
SPEED OF BLADE PITCH = 100 × 10 = 1000 FPM
PROPELLER SPEED THRU WATER, SAY 7.5 KN. = 760 FPM
DIFFERENCE = SPEED OF WATER AFT = SLIP = 240 FPM = 24%

D

BLADES WITH INFINITE PITCH (AT RIGHT ANGLES TO WATER).
NO WATER MOVES AFT, FORWARD MOTION OF VESSEL ZERO.

FIG. 228. Without true slip there is no forward motion of the vessel derived from the
working of the propeller. Figures *A*, *B*, *C*, and *D* illustrate by means of sketches
the qualitative effect of the amount of slip and its effect on the motion of the hull.

As an illustration consider the following examples:

V = speed of ship = 16.85 knots (by observation)
w = wake fraction = 0.25
V_a = speed of advance of propeller in vessel's wake =
$\quad$ $V(1 - w)$ = 16.85 × 0.75 = 12.63 knots
p = pitch = 20 ft
N = rpm = 80

Propeller pitch speed, knots = $\dfrac{60pN}{6,080}$ = $\dfrac{pN}{101.33}$

$$= \frac{20 \times 80}{101.33} = 15.80 \text{ knots}$$

Apparent slip = $\dfrac{15.80 - 16.85}{15.80}$ = -0.0665 (negative)

$$= -6.65 \text{ per cent (negative)}$$

Real slip = $\dfrac{15.80 - 12.63}{15.80}$ = 0.20 = 20 per cent

It should be noted by the student that

$$\text{Apparent slip} = \frac{\text{propeller pitch speed} - \text{ship speed}}{\text{propeller pitch speed}}$$

and

$$\text{Real slip} = \frac{\text{propeller pitch speed} - \text{speed of propeller in wake}}{\text{propeller pitch speed}}$$

Most engineers on vessels, when figuring slip, use only apparent slip, and this practice is based on distance traveled rather than speed; thus

$$\text{Apparent slip} = \frac{\text{distance by propeller} - \text{distance by observation}}{\text{distance by propeller}}$$

where distance by observation equals distance between ports or distance run in a 24-hr period and

Distance by propeller =
$$\frac{\text{number of turns made by propeller in same period (taken from revolution counter)} \times \text{pitch in ft}}{6,080}$$

The previous example would indicate that the vessel is traveling faster than if the propeller were turning in a solid nut, and the apparent negative slip would be 1.05 knots, or 6.65 per cent. As mentioned before, the propeller must impart sternward motion to the water in order to push the vessel ahead. The real slip is still 20 per cent; it is the apparent slip that is negative in this case. The C-3 Maritime Commission vessels have 20-ft 8-in.-diameter propellers with an rpm of 77 at 16.5 knots, a real slip of 30 per cent and an apparent slip of zero; *i.e.*, the propeller acts as if it were being turned through a solid even though the vessel is traveling through a liquid.

Propeller Efficiency. The loss of energy in a propeller is in two main parts:

1. The loss due to the movement of the column of water aft which is dissipated as friction, and

2. The frictional drag of the blades through the water. The first loss is necessary, but it can be reduced by applying a slow movement to a large mass of water rather than a fast movement to a small mass of water. This effect is achieved by using as large a propeller as possible and turning it very slowly (say, at 70 to 80 rpm). This calls for slow-turning reciprocating engines or turbines with reduction devices. The most efficient large-diameter propellers will have efficiencies of only about 70 per cent because of the two energy losses mentioned above.

The second loss may be reduced by using narrow blades, but the ultimate extent to which this can be carried is limited by the thrust per square inch of blade area as discussed under "cavitation." In narrowing the blades and reducing drag, we may go to the multibladed propeller which reduces efficiency slightly. However, the most recent model basin reports indicate that there is little difference between 3- and 4-bladed propellers and that 5-bladed propellers are only slightly less efficient. The advantage of using 5- or more bladed propellers is mainly in reducing vibration. It is for this reason that two of the four propellers of the *S.S. United States* are 5-bladed.

Reduction Gears. The fact that the large slow-turning propeller is the most efficient brings us to consider the reason for installing speed-reducing devices between the power plant and the propeller.

Reciprocating engines turn at a very slow rate of speed and can be connected directly to the propeller.

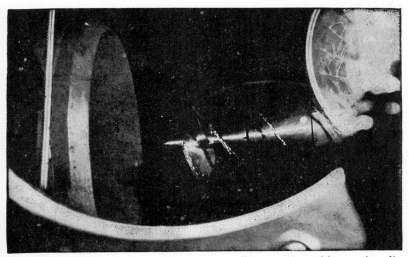

Fig. 229A. Stroboscopic photograph of a propeller operating with negative slip. The model propeller is rotating at a model speed of 55 rpm and simulates a ship's speed ahead of 17.5 knots. This photograph was taken through a watertight port at the propeller basin of the U.S. Navy at Cardarock, Md. As the tip of the blade travels faster through the water than any other part of the blade, cavitation will start at this point. The photograph shows the bubbles plainly. This effect accounts for the rapid erosion of blade tips on many propellers.

For a turbine to be efficient it must turn at a very high rate of speed, which is exactly the opposite of what we desire for our propeller. To overcome this difficulty, we install reducing mechanisms which may be reduction gears, electric, magnetic, or fluid couplings, torque converters, or belt drives between the turbine and the propeller. The friction loss in these drives is less than the gain due to increased propeller efficiency. The reduction gear is the most popular type of drive for large installations.

Cavitation. If a propeller turns so fast and develops so much thrust that the blades push the water aft faster than the water can flow into the back, or suction face, of the blades, bubbles or cavities will form on the back of the blades. These will be filled with

Fig. 229*B*. In this stroboscopic photograph the rotation of the blade has been reversed rapidly to include cavitation. The water has not had time to flow in its normal course, and air is beginning to break from the surface and flow to the propeller. At a moment of high thrust such as this, some bubbles are drawn from the water.

water vapor, if the propeller is sufficiently submerged, or perhaps with air, if the propeller is close enough to the surface for air to break through. This latter condition can cause the propeller to race and damage the machinery. What is ordinarily known as cavitation occurs when the propeller is well submerged and is illustrated in the series of photographs shown in Figs. 229*A*, *B*, and *C*. Actually there are numerous degrees of cavitation from zero to full, and various other factors play a part. The point at which bubbles, or vacuum pockets, begin to form on the back of the blades is known as the *cavitation point*. At speeds above this point, the propeller progressively loses thrust and efficiency. As a general rule we can say that, to prevent cavitation, we should keep the thrust on the face of the blades less than about 12 lb to the square inch of projected area and keep the tip speed below 10,000 ft per min. Increase in diameter or blade width will reduce pressure.

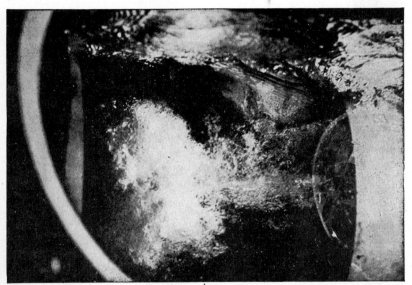

Fig. 229C. Here the air has broken through from the surface and has completely enveloped the propeller. The propeller is revolving in an envelope of air. Thrust approaches zero, and without governors the machinery would run wild. Cavitation is almost complete.

Since wide blades lead to loss in efficiency, it is better to increase diameter and pitch, thus providing more area and reducing rpm and tip speed. However, there may be physical limitations on both diameter and rpm and, like many other design problems in shipbuilding, compromise becomes necessary. It should be noted that many ships operate with a thrust load of greater than 12 lb per sq in. and a greater tip speed than 10,000 ft per min and yet do not cavitate. The above is only a guide.

TESTING PROPELLERS IN A MODEL BASIN

Propellers, as well as hulls, are tested in the model basin. Propellers are tested both in open water, no ship model ahead, and in place behind a ship model.

The model is fitted with the propeller, shafting, bossing, struts, etc., to simulate the ship and made to exact scale. A

FIG. 230. Preparing to lift a 1,200 hp Diesel engine to place it in a tug. These Diesel packaged power plants are excellent for small and some large installations. They reduce the number in the crew and obviate Coast Guard inspection of the power plant and auxiliaries.

small electric motor turns the propeller and also acts as a dynamometer, showing the exact horsepower and thrust being transmitted. A carriage-type tank is necessary to obtain accurate results from self-propelled tests so that the model may be controlled and accurate readings taken.

The model is affixed to the carriage through a towing arm and the current fed to the motor. The carriage proceeds down the tank at the desired speed and the current flow to the propeller motor is increased until the model releases its pressure on the towing arm, which indicates that the model is now self-propelled. Accurate readings of horsepower required are now taken. These, when expanded, will give the horsepower required for the full-scale propeller and a ship. On most naval and some merchant designs, several shapes, types, and sizes are tried, and slight variations are made in each until the one which has the greatest number of desirable characteristics is found. The dimensions of this model propeller are then expanded to full size for use on the vessel when built.

During these runs, the effects of the design of appendages such as bossings, struts, rudder, injection scoops, and line of bilge keels are studied and modified in order to give the best over-all efficiency from all standpoints (see page 146).

This discussion should give the student an idea of the importance of model-basin research in keeping this country's flag on the high seas.

Summary

In general, we may make the following statements relative to propellers and propulsion. These statements may be erroneous in certain specific cases and, therefore, should be treated as generalizations.

1. Propulsion is the power that moves the vessel forward.

2. Propellers are the most successful means of propelling a vessel economically.

3. Propellers should have as slow a rate of revolution and as large a diameter as the ship's structure and the tip speed permit.

4. To reduce vibration to a minimum, the hull clearance from the propeller tip should be at least one-sixth the diameter of the propeller, and for high speeds and correspondingly large powers, clearances up to one-third diameter are desirable.

5. The most economical submerged-blade shape is long, thin, and pointed, cavitation permitting.

6. If the propeller is to run partly submerged at times, such as when the vessel is light, the blades should be broad and the tips

rounded.   This reduces racing in a seaway as the degree of immersion changes, because the pressure per square inch is less for each blade.

7. Tugboats have wide blades with the maximum width often near the tip of the blades.   Since these propellers operate at a high slip, the blades are made wide to reduce load per square inch and thus reduce the tendency to cavitate.

Fig. 231. A turbine rotor with the upper half of the casing removed.   The steam impinging on the multitudinous blades causes the rotor to revolve, and through reduction gears this rotary movement drives the propeller.

8. Propeller design has been scientifically approached for half a century since Admiral Taylor ran his standard series of propellers in the old towing tank at the Washington Navy Yard.   Some refinements in blade shape and pitch distribution have been made in recent years, but the basic variables—rpm, diameter, pitch, and area—can still be derived from Taylor's tests.   The method of selecting the best combination of these variables is explained in Chap. XXII.   For average conditions, the square propeller (pitch = diameter, or pitch ratio = 1.0) fits fairly well.

9. Propellers on the center line gain more from wake than off-center propellers, such as are found in twin- and quadruple-screw installations.

10. In high-powered vessels, say 20,000 shp and above, it becomes necessary to break up the individual power loads transmitted by a propeller into two or more propellers because of the structure of the ship and the loading of the blades. Many small tankers have twin-screw installations as a single small propeller may cavitate.

11. For maneuvering purposes, it is desirable in multiscrew installations to have the rudders somewhat in line with the propellers so they may benefit from the propeller race. This is particularly true in vessels which must have high maneuverability for survival, such as naval vessels and vessels traveling in constricted waters.

The above points are for the student's guidance and should be treated as generalizations. Students desiring to pursue this subject further are referred to the texts listed in the back of this book. Particularly recommended is Taylor's "Speed and Power of Ships."

Questions and Problems

1. What are trade winds?

2. Why does the modern sailing-yacht enthusiast usually dislike to sail directly before the wind?

3. Describe in your own words how a modern sailing vessel may be made to go to windward.

4. What is wake?

5. A freighter is traveling at 15 knots. Approximately what would be the speed of her wake? (See pages 290 and 311.)

6. Why does the designer of an ocean-going vessel prefer the single-screw installation for low powers?

7. Thrust deduction is a loss. How does it compare with the wake gain?

8. A propeller must have real slip or apparent slip in order to propel a vessel. Which one, and why?

9. If a vessel has negative slip, it means that the propeller apparently is traveling faster than the ship. Does this mean that the propeller would arrive in port prior to the ship?

10. About what efficiency would you expect from a normal merchant-vessel propeller?

11. What are the evil effects of cavitation?

12. At what tip speed and what top loading is the usual-shaped propeller safe from cavitation?

13. Describe how a self-propelled model is tested.

14. To keep propeller vibration to a minimum, give the least distance from the tip of the blade to the nearest hull point for an 18-ft diameter propeller *a.* for a merchant vessel; *b.* for a 35-knot ocean liner.

15. If you are designing a propeller for a vessel, such as a collier, which travels half her time light, what should be the shape of her blades?

16. What is a square wheel?

CHAPTER XXII

PROPELLER DESIGN[1]

The design of a ship's propeller is thought by many to be especially difficult, primarily because of the mathematics involved. The method presented here requires that the student be able to extract the square root of a number and be somewhat familiar with powers and roots of numbers.

Summary of Powers and Roots of Numbers. For those who may not have studied powers and roots of numbers, and as a memory refresher for those who have, the following summary is presented:

1. To square a number, we multiply this number by itself:

$$2^2 = 2 \times 2 = 4$$

2. To extract the square root of a number, we find two like numbers which, when multiplied together, will equal the number whose square root is desired.

For example, find the square root of a number N, say 4, which may be written $\sqrt{4}$:

$$\sqrt{4} = 2; \quad \text{for } 2 \times 2 = 4$$

3. To cube a number (N^3), we multiply it by itself 3 times; to raise it to the fourth power (N^4), we multiply it by itself 4 times; and to raise it to the fifth power (N^5), we multiply it by itself 5 times; etc.

4. Conversely, to find the fifth root $(\sqrt[5]{N})$ of a number, we find a number which when multiplied by itself 5 times will equal the number of which the fifth root is desired.

For example, find the fifth root of 32 which would be written $\sqrt[5]{32}$.

[1] In collaboration with Mr. E. F. Hewins, Engine Technical Division, Newport News Shipbuilding and Dry Dock Company.

Thus,

$$\sqrt[5]{32} = 2; \text{ for } 2 \times 2 \times 2 \times 2 \times 2 = 32$$

5. This reasoning also applies to the fourth root $\sqrt[4]{N}$ and the cube root $\sqrt[3]{N}$.

6. Quite often, to save making the extraction, or root sign $\sqrt{}$, and for other reasons, a fractional power is used.

$$\sqrt[2]{N} \text{ may be written } N^{\frac{1}{2}}$$
$$\sqrt[3]{N} \text{ may be written } N^{\frac{1}{3}}$$
$$\sqrt[4]{N} \text{ may be written } N^{\frac{1}{4}}$$
$$\sqrt[5]{N} \text{ may be written } N^{\frac{1}{5}}$$

7. In dealing with propeller design and many other engineering problems, not only must we raise a number (N) to a power (N^2) or extract a root $(\sqrt{N})$, we sometimes must extract a root $(\sqrt{N})$ of a power (N^3).

As an example of extracting a root of a power, assume that we wish to extract the square root of 4 cubed, or 4^3. This is written $\sqrt[2]{4^3}$. It also may be written $4^{\frac{3}{2}}$, from which it may be seen that, when we omit the root sign $(\sqrt{})$, we simply invert the roots and powers and draw a divisional line between them. As an illustration, the square root of N cubed may be written $\sqrt{N^3}$, or what is the same thing, $N^{\frac{3}{2}}$. Thus, the square root of 4 cubed may be written

$$4^{\frac{3}{2}} = \sqrt{4^3} = \sqrt{4 \times 4 \times 4} = \sqrt{64} = 8$$

The numbers used above as illustrations have been chosen for their simplicity. The student who expects to advance in ship-building engineering is advised to become familiar with logarithms by which he may extract roots or raise a number to a power very easily.

Even without a knowledge of logarithms, and with only the simple ideas of roots and powers presented above, the student should be able to follow through intelligently examples illustrating this method of propeller design.

The curves (Fig. 232) and tables presented in this chapter are based on tests made on modern airfoil 4-bladed propellers of 40 per cent developed-area ratio by Prof. Laurens Troost, formerly Superintendent of the Wageningen Model Basin in Holland and now head of the Department of Naval Architecture, M.I.T. The tables and curves also closely approximate results on 3- and 5-bladed propellers.

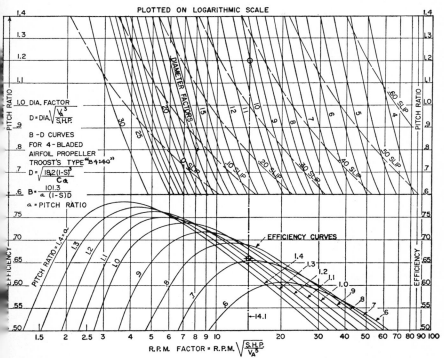

Fig. 232. Propeller design curves. These curves are based on the work of Dr. Laurens Troost and are a replot of Troost's type, altered in form for simplicity of presentation. Actually, the student may use the values in the table on page 311, *Pitch-ratio Relations*, because these values were taken from the above curves.

Summary of Formulas and Symbols.

As a ready reference, the formulas and symbols which will be used in this chapter are summarized below. These formulas and symbols are more fully explained in the preceding chapter.

$$a = \frac{\text{pitch}}{\text{diameter}} = \frac{p}{d} = \text{pitch ratio}$$

$$D = \frac{dV_a^{3/2}}{P^{1/2}} = \text{diameter factor} = \text{diameter} \sqrt{\frac{V_a^3}{\text{shp}}}$$

$$B = \frac{NP^{1/2}}{V_a^{5/2}} = \text{rpm factor} = \text{rpm} \sqrt{\frac{\text{shp}}{V_a^5}}$$

$$N = \text{rpm} = \frac{BV_a^{5/2}}{P^{1/2}}$$

shp = shaft horsepower = P

P = shp

$$d = \text{diameter of propeller} = \frac{DP^{1/2}}{V_a^{3/2}}$$

p = pitch = ad

V = ship's speed, knots

V_a = speed of advance of propeller through wake = $V(1 - w)$

$$w = \text{wake fraction} = \frac{\text{wake velocity}}{\text{ship's velocity}}$$

Wake gain = $(1 - w)$

$D.A.R.$ = developed-area ratio

$$= \frac{\text{area of blades if flattened out}}{\text{area of a circle whose diameter is equal to the diameter of the propeller}}$$

T = thrust or push of propeller

$$T = \frac{\text{ft-lb of work per min} \times e \times P}{\dfrac{6080 \text{ ft} \times V_a}{60 \text{ min}}} = \frac{33,000 \times eP}{101.3 \times V_a}$$

t = thrust deduction

$$\frac{\text{ehp}}{\text{shp}} = \text{propulsive coefficient} = e\,\frac{1 - t}{1 - w}\,e_{rr}$$

e = propeller efficiency

$$\frac{1 - t}{1 - w} = \text{hull efficiency}$$

e_{rr} = relative rotative efficiency

The relation between the speed and power of a ship, on the one hand, and the propeller diameter, rpm, and efficiency, may be determined from the following table, which represents the best combination of diameter and rpm for each even pitch ratio p/d.

PITCH-RATIO RELATIONS
Best combinations

Combination*	Pitch-diameter ratio $a = \dfrac{p}{d}$	Diameter factor $D = \dfrac{dV_a^{3/5}}{P^{1/2}}$	RPM factor $B = \dfrac{NP^{1/2}}{V_a^{5/2}}$	Efficiency e
1	1.4	19.3	4.5	0.78
2	1.3	17.4	5.5	0.765
3	1.2	16.0	6.5	0.75
4	1.1	14.5	8.0	0.735
5	1.0	13.0	10.0	0.72
6	0.9	11.4	13.0	0.695
7	0.8	9.0	20.0	0.65
8	0.7	6.8	33.0	0.59
9	0.6	4.9	60.0	0.51

* It should be noted that the above values are the best combinations, and are those to be used if circumstances permit. As this table covers a wide range of possibilities, it will suffice in the design of most propellers. See curves of propeller design for innumerable other combinations (Fig. 232).

Approximate values of wake fraction w may be taken from the following table:

WAKE-FRACTION TABLE

Type of vessel	1 propeller	2 or 4 propellers
Tankers and slow cargo vessels	0.35	0.20
Passenger and fast cargo vessels	0.30	0.15
Yachts and bay steamers	0.25	0.10
Scout cruisers and tugs	0.20	0.05
Destroyers and motor boats	0.15	0

From the above tables, it is possible to determine the propeller most suitable for a given set of conditions. Two items must be known: the shp, P, which is expected to power the vessel (determined from model or other comparison) and the desired speed, V. If diameter d is fixed by the draft of the vessel or other considerations, determine $D = \dfrac{dV_a^{3/2}}{P^{1/2}}$. The corresponding values of B, a, and e may be read from the table. If revolutions N are fixed by the type of machinery or other considerations, determine $B = \dfrac{NP^{1/2}}{V_a^{5/2}}$. The corresponding values of D, a, and e may be read from the table as before.

Examples Illustrating a Method of Propeller Design. In order to illustrate the foregoing paragraph, we shall design three propellers for a bay steamer: first, with the diameter limited; second, with the rpm limited; and, finally, with rpm and diameter limited. In the first two examples, we shall use the table of pitch-ratio relations on page 311, and in Ex. 3 we shall use Fig. 232, propeller chart, directly to illustrate how they may be used to solve many propeller problems.

Example 1: *Limited Diameter.* Design a suitable single-screw propeller for a bay steamer with the following characteristics:

$$\text{Diameter} = 10 \text{ ft } 10 \text{ in. (limited by draft)}$$
$$\text{Speed} = 16 \text{ knots}$$
$$\text{shp} = 2{,}500 = P$$
$$\text{Wake, } w = 0.25 \text{ (from wake-fraction table on page 311)}$$

a. Solve for the speed of advance of the propeller through the wake of the ship.

$$V_a = V(1 - w) = 16(1 - 0.25) = 12 \text{ knots}$$

b. Solve for the three variables as noted below which will be substituted in the equations for D and rpm.

(1) $$V_a^{3/2} = \sqrt{V_a^3} = V_a \sqrt{V_a}$$

We have now reduced the equation to a simple square-root extraction; we may substitute $V_a = 12$ knots and solve:

$$V_a \sqrt{V} = 12 \sqrt{12} = 12 \times 3.46 = 41.5$$

(2)
$$V_a{}^{5/2} = \sqrt{V_a{}^5} = V_a \sqrt{V_a{}^3}$$

This is again a square-root extraction; so, substituting

$$V_a \sqrt{V_a{}^3} = 12 \sqrt{12^3}$$
$$= 12 \sqrt{1,728}$$
$$= 12 \times 41.5$$
$$= 498$$

(3)
$$P^{1/2} = \sqrt{P} = \sqrt{2,500} = 50$$

c. The above values may be used in the next two examples and need not be recalculated. Substituting, we obtain

$$D = \frac{dV^{3/2}}{P^{1/2}} = \frac{10.83 \times 41.5}{50} = 9.0$$

d. Referring to our pitch-ratio table, we find that $D = 9.0$ in line 7 and the best B value is just opposite the D value of 9.0 in the same line. This is found to be 20.0, and we may substitute and solve:

$$\text{rpm} = \frac{BV_a{}^{5/2}}{P^{1/2}} = \frac{20 \times 498}{50} = 200$$

e. We may now pick up the value $a = 0.8$ in line 7 and substitute to determine pitch.

$$\text{Pitch} = ad = 0.8 \times 10.83 \text{ ft} = 8.67 \text{ ft} = 8 \text{ ft } 8 \text{ in.}$$

The efficiency to be expected may also be picked up from line 7.

$$\text{Efficiency, } e = 0.65$$

Summarizing our propeller design we would have

$$\text{shp} = 2,500$$
$$\text{rpm} = 200$$
$$\text{Pitch} = 8 \text{ ft } 8 \text{ in.}$$
$$\text{Diameter} = 10 \text{ ft } 10 \text{ in.}$$
$$\text{Efficiency} = 0.65 \text{ or } 65 \text{ per cent}$$

Example 2: *Limited rpm.*   Design a propeller for the same bay steamer; however, the rpm is limited by the machinery to 129.

$$\text{rpm} = N = 129$$
$$\text{shp} = 2,500 = P$$
$$\text{Speed} = 16 \text{ knots}$$
$$\text{Wake, } w = 0.25$$

In the previous example, as the diameter was limited and was known, we solved for D. In this example, as the diameter is unknown, we solve for B since we know the rpm.

$$B = \frac{NP^{\frac{1}{2}}}{V_a{}^{\frac{5}{2}}}$$
$$N = \text{rpm} = 129$$
$$P^{\frac{1}{2}} = \sqrt[2]{P} = \sqrt[2]{\text{shp}} = \sqrt[2]{2500} = 50$$
$$V_a{}^{\frac{5}{2}} = 498 \text{ (from Ex. } b(2)\text{)}$$

Substituting

$$B = \frac{129 \times 50}{498} = 13.0$$

In the pitch-ratio relation table we find a B value of 13 in line 6, and in the same line we find a corresponding D value of 11.4. Therefore

$$d = \frac{DP^{\frac{1}{2}}}{V_a{}^{\frac{3}{2}}} = \frac{11.4 \times 50}{41.5}$$
$$= 13.75 \text{ ft} = 13 \text{ ft } 9 \text{ in.}$$

Line 6 also gives an a value of 0.9 and an e value of 0.695, so pitch, $p = ad = 0.9 \times 13.75 \text{ ft} = 12.33 \text{ ft} = 12 \text{ ft } 4 \text{ in.}$ Efficiency of this propeller would be efficiency, $e = 0.695$.

Summarizing we would have

$$\text{rpm} = 129$$
$$\text{shp} = 2,500$$
$$\text{Diameter} = 13 \text{ ft } 9 \text{ in.}$$
$$\text{Pitch} = 12 \text{ ft } 4 \text{ in.}$$
$$\text{Efficiency} = 0.695$$

This second example illustrates the point brought out in the chapter on propulsion that *a larger diameter and slower rpm gives better efficiency.* If the smaller diameter cannot be avoided, the corresponding rpm indicated by the table should be used if possible. Sometimes, however, both rpm and diameter will be limited and this condition must be solved by using curves based on Troost's tests, Fig. 232.

Example 3: *Limited rpm and Diameter.* Design a propeller for a single-screw bay steamer with the following characteristics known

$$\text{rpm} = N = 140 \text{ (limited by machinery)}$$
$$\text{shp} = P = 2{,}500$$
$$\text{Diameter} = d = 11 \text{ ft } 6 \text{ in. (limited by draft)}$$
$$\text{Wake} = w = 0.25$$

In this case we solve for both B and D. From Ex. 1

$$P^{\frac{1}{2}} = 50$$
$$V^{\frac{5}{2}} = 498$$
$$V^{\frac{3}{2}} = 41.5$$

Finding B (rpm) factor and D (diameter) factor

$$B = \frac{NP^{\frac{1}{2}}}{V_a^{\frac{5}{2}}} = \frac{140 \times 50}{498} = 14.1$$
$$D = \frac{dV_a^{\frac{3}{2}}}{P^{\frac{1}{2}}} = \frac{11.5 \text{ ft} \times 41.5}{50} = 9.5$$

As these B and D values fall between lines 6 and 7 in our pitch-ratio relation table, we refer directly to Fig. 232.

B values (or rpm factors) are given across the bottom of the figure and a heavy vertical dot-dash line has been drawn upward until it intersects the D factor (diameter factor) value of 9.5 which we have just determined. Reading across to the left, we pick up a pitch ratio, a of 1.2. This will determine our optimum pitch as follows:

$$\text{Pitch} = ad = 1.2 \times 11.5 \text{ ft} = 13.75 \text{ ft} = 13 \text{ ft } 9 \text{ in.}$$

We may read the efficiency to be expected directly from the efficiency curves at the bottom of the page where the heavy vertical dot-dash line crosses the efficiency curve for a pitch ratio, *a*, of 1.2. Reading from this curve, we obtain an expected efficiency of 0.658.

It will be noted that this is about 3 per cent below the maximum efficiency that could have been obtained by holding the *B* factor (rpm factor) at 14.1 and using a larger diameter and less pitch. A pitch ratio, *a*, of 0.8 would have given an efficiency of 0.68, as will be observed by inspecting the efficiency curves.

Summarizing

$$
\begin{aligned}
\text{rpm} &= 140 \\
\text{shp} &= 2{,}500 \\
\text{Diameter} &= 11 \text{ ft } 6 \text{ in.} \\
\text{Pitch} &= 13 \text{ ft } 9 \text{ in.} \\
\text{Efficiency} &= 0.658
\end{aligned}
$$

Developed-area Ratio. Ordinarily, when diameter and pitch have been determined, it is sufficient to use a developed-area ratio of about 40 per cent. *Developed area* is the area of the blades of the propeller. *Developed-area ratio* is the area of the blades of the propeller compared to the area of a solid disk of the same diameter as the propeller.

$$
\text{Developed area} = 0.40(d)^2 \times \frac{4}{\pi}
$$

where d = diameter of propeller in feet.

$$
\text{Developed-area ratio} = \frac{\text{developed area of blades}}{\text{area of a circle the diameter of the propeller}}
$$

There is little gain in using a developed-area ratio of less than 40 per cent. The thrust per square inch of developed area should be checked, and if the thrust approaches 10 lb per sq in., the developed-area ratio should be increased by increasing the width of the blades to prevent cavitation. In high-powered vessels similar to the *S.S. United States*, this developed-area ratio may approach 1.0 (see Fig. 223).

The formula for thrust is

$$T = \frac{33,000eP}{101.3V_a} \quad \text{(see summary of formulas)}$$

For Ex. 1, page 313, the thrust on the blades would be

$$T = \frac{33,000 \times 0.65 \times 2,500}{101.3 \times 12} = 44,000 \text{ lb}$$

and the thrust per square inch with 40 per cent D.A.R. would be

$$T \text{ per sq in.} = \frac{44,000}{0.40(10.83 \times 12)^2} \times \frac{4}{\pi} = 8.3 \text{ lb per sq in.}$$

For Ex. 2, page 314, the thrust per sq in. would be

$$T = \frac{33,000 \times 0.695 \times 2,500}{101.3 \times 12} = 47,000 \text{ lb}$$

and with 40 per cent D.A.R.

$$T \text{ per sq in.} = \frac{47,000}{0.40(13.75 \text{ ft} \times 12)^2} \times \frac{4}{\pi} = 5.5 \text{ lb per sq in.}$$

In our design, the 40 per cent developed-area ratio (D.A.R.) is safe, in so far as cavitation is concerned, as it is below 10 lb per sq in. An increase in area beyond 40 per cent developed-area ratio is accompanied by a loss in efficiency, approximately indicated below:

D.A.R. (developed-area ratio)	Efficiency loss
0.40	0
0.50	0.007
0.60	0.016
0.70	0.031
0.80	0.050
0.90	0.073
1.00	0.098

If effective, or towrope horsepower, ehp, of the ship is known, it is now possible to check the shp. Assume that the ehp of the bay steamer used in the above example is 1,600 at 16 knots and that the ship is provided with modern streamlined sternpost, rudderpost, and rudder. Thrust deduction may be taken as

$$0.6w = 0.6 \times 0.25 = 0.15$$

Then $(1 - t)/(1 - w) = 0.85/0.75 = 1.13$. This correction is then applied to the propeller efficiency obtained above in order to get the over-all propulsion coefficient, ehp/shp.

In Ex. 1

$$\frac{ehp}{shp} = 1.13 \times 0.65 = 0.735$$

and the ideal shp will be

$$\frac{eph}{0.735} = \frac{1,600}{0.735} = 2,180 \text{ shp}$$

Thus, the designed horsepower of 2,500 provides about 15 per cent margin for fouling and other service conditions which retard the speed of the vessel. If the large propeller of Ex. 2 had been used, ehp/shp would have been $1.13 \times 0.695 = 0.785$. The ideal shp would be

$$\frac{1,600}{785} = 2,040$$

and 2,500 shp in this case provides a margin of about 22.5 per cent. If 15 per cent margin is considered sufficient, the power plant could be reduced to $2,040 = 1.15 = 2,350$ shp, or, if preferred, the original power of 2,500 could be retained to provide speed in excess of 16 knots.

Relative Rotative Efficiency. The shp as obtained in the foregoing paragraph represents, fairly closely, model tank results with a self-propelled model. However, even when the propeller efficiency, wake, and thrust deduction are determined in such a test, ehp/shp for single-screw models is usually greater than

$$\frac{(1 - t)}{(1 - w)} \times (\text{propeller efficiency})$$

This requires the introduction of another factor called *relative rotative efficiency*.

Then

$$\frac{\text{ehp}}{\text{shp}} = \frac{(1 - t)}{(1 - w)} \times e \times e_{rr}$$

where e_{rr} is the relative rotative efficiency.

Actually, relative rotative efficiency does not derive from, is not dependent upon, and has no relation to the design of the propeller but is entirely dependent upon the appendages aft of the propeller and, in a few cases, the shape of the propeller post forward of the propeller (see Fig. 132). However, as it is a factor in the over-all characteristics of propeller design, we shall discuss it here.

A revolving propeller imparts a push on the water behind it and, at the same time, imparts a rotary or twisting movement to the water in the race of the propeller. If this twist can be removed from the race and made to impart a forward thrust, the ship will either gain speed or require less power to maintain the same speed.

Scientists have worked on this last problem for years and many patents have been awarded on the solutions they proposed. The Goldschmidt patent is probably the most familiar application of this principle. Figure 132 shows the effect of the rotative race being straightened and illustrates, by a force diagram, how it operates to increase propulsive efficiency.

A twin-screw propeller installation with a single centerline rudder has no appendage aft of the propeller and therefore cannot benefit from the untwisting of the race. The relative rotative efficiency would in this case be unity (one). Some single-screw self-propelled models have had relative rotative efficiencies as high as 10 per cent (1.10).

In estimating trial performance of a new design, it is probably unsafe to count on more than a relative rotative efficiency of 1.03, regardless of the type of appendages behind or before the propeller.

Shallow-water Effect. Ship trials in deep water when the ship's bottom is clean and coated with smooth antifouling paint usually follow model test results very closely (see Fig. 234). However, if the trials are run in shallow water, the increased resistance due to shallowness becomes noticeable (*i.e.*, exceeds 10 per cent) unless the following limits are observed. See Fig. 215 and the following table:

SHALLOW-WATER LIMITATIONS

If the $\dfrac{\text{speed, knots}}{\sqrt{\text{depth of water, ft}}}$ equals 1.2 1.5 1.8 2.1 2.4 2.7

Then $\dfrac{\text{depth of water, ft}}{\text{draft of vessel, ft}}$ must exceed 2.0 2.4 3.1 4.5 7.0 10.0

NOTE: The above table is based on J. M. Voith's data and has been found to give good agreement with results of ship trials. For other methods see section on "Requirements of a Trial Course," p. 328.

Service Margin. A service margin is usually provided to allow for shallow water, rough sea, and fouling. The service margin of 15 per cent allowed in the propeller examples previously presented is probably sufficient for bay steamers (which seldom encounter rough seas), if there is no shallow-water effect. Ocean-going vessels usually allow 25 per cent for rough sea and fouling. (In this case there should be no shallow water effect except in harbors at the ends of the voyage.) Great Lakes vessels, whose length is sufficient to avoid any appreciable effect on resistance from rough sea, often have no service margin at all (other than the 10 per cent overload capacity of the machinery), since fouling in fresh water is very slight. Also, Great Lakes runs are short enough so that speed is not so important a factor as in the case of ocean-going vessels, where voyages may last months.

Variable-pitch Propellers. In early days, propellers were of the *true pitch* type, which usually meant that the blade had the same pitch from the root to the tip of the blade. Modern propeller theory indicates that some gain in efficiency may be obtained by varying the pitch from root to tip. Propellers with varying pitch are called *variable-pitch propellers* and are largely in use today.

Variable-pitch propellers usually have a low pitch at the hub, where the rotative speed through the water is low, and higher pitch at the tip, where the rotative speed through the water is higher. Sometimes, in order to delay tip cavitation, pitch is reduced at the tip and increased at the hub. The mean average pitch of the variable-pitch propeller is usually taken at 0.7 diameter.

The variable-pitch propeller mentioned here has fixed blades and should not be confused with the *reversible-pitch propeller*, whose pitch may be made zero or even negative through a mechanism in the propeller controlled from the pilot house.

Automatic-pitch propellers, which adjust themselves to suit the rpm and blade loading by means of gyroscopic action on weights in the hub, are also not variable-pitch propellers in our sense of the word.

Propeller Manufacture. After pitch, diameter, developed-area ratio, and efficiency of the propeller have been determined, this information is turned over to the drawing room and the propeller is laid out, using the principles of descriptive geometry.

After the draftsman has developed the propeller lines, he makes a drawing which is sent to the pattern shop. From this drawing the patternmaker makes a pattern, usually of soft white pine. The pattern is made slightly oversized to leave some material on the casting for machining.

This pattern is then taken to the foundry where it is placed in a special cement from which a mold is made (Fig. 28, page 31). The pattern is removed from the mold after the cement has hardened, and molten bronze is poured into the cement mold, thus forming the rough propeller casting.

This casting, after cooling, is sent to the machine shop where it is bored, keyed, machined, balanced, and polished into the finished product. In finishing propellers, it is highly important that the shop (1) remove all humps and hollows from the blade surface and (2) check the shape of the blade sections of leading and trailing edges with templates. Failure to remove humps and hollows in the blade may lead to cavitation and resulting erosion (page 291).

Example 1: The original Liberty-ship propeller was designed to develop 2,500 ihp at 76 rpm. Owing to torsional vibration troubles, some Liberty ships had their rpm reduced to 66. To find what propeller would hold the same engine down to 66 rpm, assume that the 2,500 ihp is reduced $^{66}/_{76}$, *i.e.*, to about 2,200 ihp or 2,000 shp. The stern arrangements of Liberty ships limit the propeller diameter to 18 ft 6 in. The sea speed of these vessels may be taken as 11 knots and the wake fraction as 0.25. Find the pitch.

Given:

$$V = 11 \text{ knots}$$
$$w = 0.25 \quad (\text{NOTE: These ships had much less wake than would have been normally expected. See table on page 311.})$$
$$V_a = V(1 - w) = 11 \times 0.75 = 8.25$$
$$P = \text{shp} = 2,000$$
$$d = \text{diameter} = 18.5$$
$$N = \text{rpm} = 66$$

then D = diameter factor

$$= d \sqrt{\frac{V_a{}^3}{P}} = \frac{18.5 \times 8.25 \sqrt{8.25}}{\sqrt{2,000}}$$

$$= \frac{438}{44.8} = 9.8$$

and B = rpm factor

$$= N \sqrt{\frac{P}{V_a{}^5}} = \frac{66 \times \sqrt{2,000}}{8.25 \times 8.25 \sqrt{8.25}}$$

$$= \frac{2,960}{195} = 15.2$$

Referring to Fig. 232, when $D = 9.8$ and $B = 15.2$ pitch ratio = 0.95. Therefore, pitch = $0.95 \times 18.5 = 17.5$ ft.

Example 2: *Small-craft Propeller.*   A 40-ft cruiser is powered with an engine rated 100 hp at 2,000 rpm, and fitted with a 2 to 1 reduction gear. Speed desired is 12 statute miles per hour. Find the best diameter and pitch for the above conditions.

Assume wake fraction $w = 0.15$

Given:

$$V = 12 \text{ mph} \times \frac{5{,}280 \text{ ft}}{6{,}080 \text{ ft}} = 10.4 \text{ knots}$$

$w = 0.15$
$V_a = V(1 - w) = 8.85$
$P = 100$
$N = 1{,}000$ (because of the 2 to 1 reduction gear)

$$B = N \sqrt{\frac{P}{V_a{}^5}} = \frac{1{,}000 \times \sqrt{100}}{8.85 \times 8.85 \times \sqrt{8.85}}$$
$$= \frac{1{,}000}{234} = 43$$

Refer to the efficiency curves at the bottom of Fig. 232 and observe that, if we select a pitch ratio of 0.6 when $B = 43$, the efficiency is 0.554; at pitch ratio of 0.7, the efficiency is 0.552; at pitch ratio of 0.8, the efficiency is 0.545; and at pitch ratio of 0.9, the efficiency is 0.529.

Now refer to the curves at the top of Fig. 232. Remembering that $B = 43$, D will equal 6.1 at 0.6 pitch ratio; 5.7 at 0.7 pitch ratio; 5.45 at 0.8 pitch ratio, and 5.2 at 0.9 pitch ratio.

This information may be tabulated and diameter and pitch worked out as follows:

The equation for determining diameter is

$$\text{Diameter} = \frac{D \sqrt{P}}{V_a \sqrt{V_a}} = \frac{D \sqrt{100}}{8.85 \sqrt{8.85}} = 0.38D$$

As D in the first column below is 6.1,

$$\text{Diameter} = 0.38D = 0.38 \times 6.1 = 2.32 \text{ ft} = 28 \text{ in.}$$

The equation for determining pitch is

$$p = \text{diameter} \times \text{pitch ratio}$$
$$p = 28 \text{ in.} \times 0.6 = 17 \text{ in.}$$

In the above problems, we worked out only the pitch and diameter for the first column of the following table. It is suggested that the student check the figures in the other columns.

PROPELLERS TO DELIVER 100 HP AT 1,000 RPM WITH $B = 43$

P/D	0.6	0.7	0.8	0.9
Efficiency	0.554	0.552	0.545	0.529
D	6.1	5.7	5.45	5.2
Diameter	2.32 ft	2.16 ft	2.07 ft	1.98 ft
Diameter, in	28 in.	26 in.	25 in.	24 in.
Pitch, in	17 in.	18 in.	20 in.	21 in.

From inspection of the above table, the most efficient propeller would be 28-in. diameter × 17-in. pitch; however, the 26-in. diameter × 18-in. pitch is almost as efficient, and the loss would be but 1 per cent if the 25-in. diameter and 20-in. pitch propeller is used. The 24- by 21-in. propeller would show a considerable loss in efficiency and would not be recommended.

Small-craft propellers, up to about 3 ft in diameter, are calculated only to the nearest inch to suit propeller manufacturers' standard sizes.

CHAPTER XXIII

TESTING THE SHIP ON TRIALS

Almost every man in a shipyard hopes some day to be aboard during the trial trip of a new ship. This interest is heightened as the worker observes the ship undergoing dock trials a few days prior to the sea trials. This dock trial is held while the ship is tied to the builder's pier for the purpose of making certain that all machinery installations are in an operating condition. It is

Fig. 233. This is the vessel whose progress we shall follow over the trial course near Rockland, Me., to see how such a trial is conducted. We shall see how she is kept ballasted to a certain line, what tests she must pass, her travel on the speed runs, her rpm, shp, maneuverability, and auxiliary machinery performance.

usually held at about half power, and the main propulsion units and auxiliaries are checked for defects.

While the sea trial is, for most of the personnel, both work and pleasure, very few aboard ship actually understand all the purposes of the trial or the interesting things that are going on around them. In this chapter we shall discuss briefly some of the more outstanding features relating to the specialized equipment required for measurements and to the requirements of trial courses. We shall also touch on the standardization runs and tests that are held during the trial. Throughout this chapter the official trial trip of the passenger liner *S.S. America,* as run on the measured mile at Rockland, Me., in June, 1940, will be used as an example. At the end of the chapter the trial trip of the *S.S. United States* will be presented for comparison.

THE PURPOSE OF THE TRIAL TRIP

During the preliminary design stages of a ship, the naval architect develops the lines (shape) of the hull that will suit the speed and displacement required. A 20-ft model is usually made from these lines and is run, self-propelled, in the Taylor Model Basin at Cardarock, Md., or some other model basin, in order to determine the horsepower and revolutions of the propellers required for various speeds. From the results of such tests, a calculation is made for the full-sized ship. Figure 234 shows how closely the model basin can predict the actual trial results for a full-sized ship from the results obtained from a 20-ft model. The curve for the actual ship has not been corrected for the effect of the wind. In fact, some naval architects feel that careful predictions based on model tests are probably more accurate than the horsepower measured on most trial trips.

As the ability of the ship to develop her power and the efficiency of the machinery in developing this power are extremely important, it is usually stipulated in the contract between the builder and the owner that she must develop a certain power and operate at a certain efficiency in developing this power. Another usual stipulation in the contract provides that if the terms of the contract are not met a certain amount will be deducted from the contract price of the vessel. On the other hand, if the guaranteed performance is better than stipulated in the contract, the builder is to receive a bonus. As an illustration, in the contract of the *S.S. America* there was no limitation on the amount the shipyard could be penalized for not meeting the guarantees, but the maximum fuel-economy bonus allowed was to be $50,000.

To determine the speed of a ship at a particular displacement in the open sea where the economy trials are run, we first must know the rpm of the propellers that will give a certain speed. To determine this relation we run the ship over a measured-mile course at various speeds and record simultaneously the rpm, speed, and horsepower. When these three factors have been determined, we

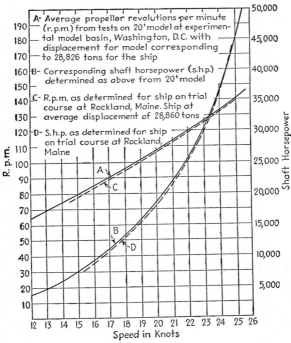

Fig. 234. Horsepower and rpm curves, *S.S. America*.

can plot results as in Fig. 234 and then proceed to the open sea for the 4-hr economy runs and other tests.

Besides giving the above information, these trials also give the engineering personnel an opportunity to check their preliminary calculations on the performance of the ship and the machinery in the operating condition and also to gather information that is invaluable when making up future designs. The data thus obtained are studied and analyzed after the trial is completed.   Great advances in marine engineering have resulted from the study of such data. Preceding the official trial trip of the ship an unofficial *builder's trial* is run for most large vessels to make sure that all the machinery is in proper working condition.   It is of short duration and need not include measured-mile runs.

After the builder's trial has been run, the official trial is conducted. For naval vessels a third trial called the *final-acceptance trial* is run during the 6-month period in which the shipbuilder has to guarantee the performance of the vessel.   If the final-acceptance trial is satisfactory, at the end of the 6-month guarantee period the contract is considered discharged and the builder is paid the contract price in full.

REQUIREMENTS OF A TRIAL COURSE

1. Depth of Water.   If the water in which a ship is operating is shallow in relation to the draft of the ship, the over-all resistance of the ship and the horsepower required to drive the ship at a given speed are ordinarily increased.   This phenomenon is due to interference between the bottom of the bay or ocean and the wave system set up by the ship and necessitates that the trial course be laid out in deep water.   Admiral Taylor, in his "Speed and Power of Ships,"[1] gives the following formula for the least depth of water required to overcome this interference:

$$\text{Least depth} = 10 \times \text{ship's draft in feet} \times \frac{\text{speed in knots}}{\sqrt{\text{length of ship in feet}}}$$

This is another way of saying that the depth required is proportional to the speed-length ratio of the ship if the draft is constant.   However, it should be noted here that John P. Comstock and C. H. Hancock in a paper "The Effect of Size of Towing Tank on Model Resistance" read before the Society of Naval Architects in 1942, pointed out that, from their experiments, the depth of water required is not proportional to the speed-length ratio $V/\sqrt{L}$ but that for speed-length ratios of less than 1 ($V/\sqrt{L}$ for *S.S. America* = 0.89) the depth of water should be about 75 per cent of the length of the

[1] U.S. Maritime Administration, Washington, D.C.

ship. Later in the chapter we shall use both these formulas for calculating the least depth required on our trial course.

2. Closeness to Shore. The course must be close to some shore line, for it must be possible to sight on fixed markers (beacons) set up on shore. The distance between these markers is accurately surveyed. There are very few places in this country where there is sufficient depth close enough to the shore line to permit the markers to be seen. About 1 mile is the maximum distance for good visibility.

3. Tides and Currents. Ideally the course should be free of tides and currents. This, of course, is impossible; but if conditions permit, the course should be such that the tides and currents will be small and will run nearly parallel to it.

4. Direction of the Course. An east-west course with the range beacons to the north is more desirable than a north-south course. With the latter it is necessary during some part of the day to pick up the markers against the sun.

5. Weather. The course should be in a locality that is not affected too often by fogs and strong prevailing winds.

6. Sea Protection. The course should be protected from large waves.

7. Right of Way. The course should not be located across a much-used trade lane, for traffic might interfere with the trial.

To be able to locate a course to meet all the above requirements would be indeed fortunate. All courses now used are deficient in one or more of these particulars. There are five deepwater courses now in general use for vessels built in the United States. They are

1. Rockland, Me., in Penobscot Bay (see Fig. 235) for surface ships.

2. Provincetown, Mass., for submarines.

3. San Pedro, Calif., for surface ships.

4. San Diego, Calif., for submarines.

5. Guantánamo Bay, off the coast of Cuba, for surface ships.

We shall discuss only one of the above courses, that at Rockland, Me. This is considered by the United States Navy to be the best all-round deepwater course in the country. The most important drawbacks of the Rockland course are the great distance from some of the shipyards, the fog, and the extremely cold weather in winter.

LAYOUT OF THE COURSE

The trial course at Rockland is laid out as shown in Fig. 235 and runs approximately north and south. There are six large can buoys on the course, painted white. The total run between extreme buoys is 7 miles. There is a 3-mile approach at either end for high-speed runs and a 1-mile approach for slow-speed runs. The depth of water on the course averages about 400 ft. Substituting the characteristics of the *S.S. America* in the Taylor formula for minimum depth of water gives

$$\text{Minimum depth} = \frac{10d \times \text{speed}}{\sqrt{L \text{ ft}}} = \frac{10 \times 28 \text{ ft} \times 23 \text{ knots}}{\sqrt{666 \text{ ft}}} = 250 \text{ ft}$$

And substituting this in the formula given by Comstock and Hancock,

$$0.75 \times 666 \text{ ft} = 500 \text{ ft}$$

The depth of water is ample by Taylor's formula but is not quite sufficient by Comstock and Hancock's.

Traveling south on the course the observers line up the marker beacons, which can be seen in Fig. 235. When the three beacons are in line, the ship is "on the mile" (a nautical mile of 6,080 ft). When the second set of beacons are lined up, the ship is "off the mile" and after a short run turns as indicated by the arrows and retraces her run. Note that the turn is always made so as to get a long straight approach to allow time for accelerating.

The beacons are constructed on structural steel bases and have a tubular "transit" pole affixed to the top of the structure. For added visibility in light fogs and at night, the rear beacons have 500-watt electric reflecting lights affixed to their tops.

The course is in Penobscot Bay; therefore, heavy seas are seldom encountered. The tide over the course sets practically parallel with the course and usually averages less than $\frac{1}{2}$ knot.

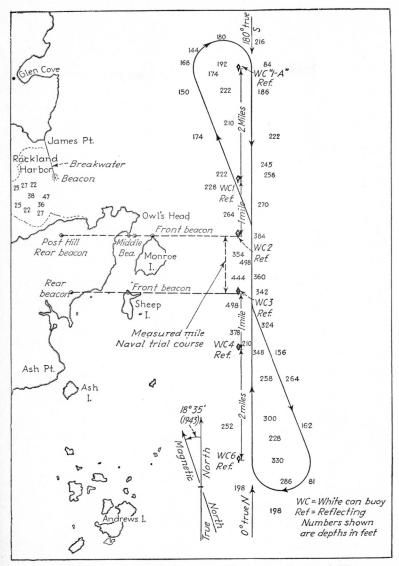

FIG. 235. The United States Navy trial course at Rockland, Me.

331

FACTORS AFFECTING THE TRIAL

The Standardization Runs.   To plot the curves shown in Fig. 234, we must make a series of runs over the measured mile and while the ship is under way measure accurately the revolutions of the propellers, the speed, and the horsepower developed.   We usually make three runs over the mile at each speed, one in one direction and two in the other.   For the full-power runs, the ship usually traverses the mile five times.

Timing.   We cannot use an average of the ship's time over the mile to obtain the average speed, for the answer might be seriously in error.   This may be simply illustrated by the following:

Example: Assume that a man is rowing in a river that has a downstream current of 2 knots.   *He is able to row the boat at the speed of 4 knots.*   Therefore, going upstream he is able to make a speed over the ground of 2 knots; downstream, a speed of 6 knots.   Should the average speed be obtained by averaging time or by averaging speed?

Solution: The time to row 1 mile upstream would be

$$\frac{1 \text{ mile}}{2 \text{ knots}} = 0.5 \text{ hr or } 30 \text{ min}$$

The time to row 1 mile downstream would be

$$\frac{1 \text{ mile}}{6 \text{ knots}} = 0.166 \text{ hr or } 10 \text{ min}$$

As a comparison, we average both time and speed and see which is correct.

Direction	Time, min	Speed, knots
Upstream...............	30	2
Downstream............	10	6
Total.................	40	8

The average time of the run would be

$$\frac{40 \text{ min}}{2} = 20 \text{ min or } 0.33 \text{ hr}$$

So average knots based on averaging time would be

$$\text{Speed} = \frac{\text{distance}}{\text{time}} = \frac{1 \text{ mile}}{0.33 \text{ hr}} = 3 \text{ knots}$$

Now, averaging the speeds we should have

$$\frac{8 \text{ knots}}{2} = 4 \text{ knots}$$

which is the actual speed assumed. Averaging the speeds agrees with the original assumption of a rowing speed of 4 knots. Had we averaged time instead of speed we should have obtained 3 knots, which would be in error by

$$4 \text{ knots} - 3 \text{ knots} = 1 \text{ knot}$$

In ship timing the tide and the wind seriously affect the results. The tide is compensated by taking a mean of means of the runs, which is simply an average of more than two runs. The wind effect is calculated later. This mean of means (or averaging of the runs) is not correct unless the trial speeds during each run are very nearly constant both ways. Admiral Taylor in his "Speed and Power of Ships" brings out this fact clearly.

Omitting details, to obtain this mean of means we attach twice as much importance to the second run as we do to the first and third. Giving twice as much weight to the second run as we do to the first and third helps to eliminate the tide effect. To illustrate this procedure, assume that we make three runs at the following speeds and that the tide is decreasing 0.2 knots each run. Then, as shown in the table below, we should obtain the correct average speed of 15 knots:

Direction	Speed on mile, knots	First mean, knots	Second mean, knots
Run north.........	15.5	15.1	
Run south.........	14.7		15
Run north.........	15.1	14.9	

If we had added the speeds of the above three runs and then divided the sum by 3, we should have obtained 15.1 knots, which

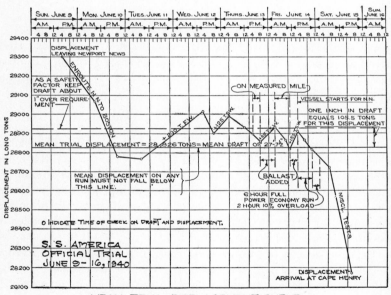

MEAN TRIAL DISPLACEMENT CURVE

Fig. 236.

would have been in error by $\frac{1}{10}$ knot. The use of "Raydist," mentioned later, obviates the necessity of using the mean of means as the buoy is floating in the same tide, current, and wind as the ship.

Displacement. As the displacement, or the weight of the ship, has a great effect on the power required, a standard trial displacement is written into the contract. It is very important that the mean trial displacement be reached at the middle of the full-power runs. If the ship falls much below the mean trial displacement (weight), the runs should be voided and run over.

Figure 236 shows a graph of the displacement of the *S.S. America* from the time she left Newport News until she arrived off Cape Henry (Virginia Capes) on her return. It will be noted from the figure that the ship left Newport News at 4 P.M., Sunday, June 9, with a displacement of 29,300 tons. At 6 P.M. she had passed the Capes.

ADJUSTING THE MAGNETIC COMPASSES (SWINGING SHIP)

As soon as the *S.S. America* was at sea a few miles east of the Virginia Capes, a professional compass adjuster compensated the ship's magnetic compasses. There are usually three magnetic compasses aboard an ocean liner (not including those in the lifeboats): one in the pilothouse, the standard compass on top of the pilothouse, and one at the after steering station. Although gyroscopic compasses are now standard equipment on all large American vessels, magnetic compasses are nevertheless fitted as a precaution in case the gyrocompass should fail and also as a check on the latter.

As magnetic compasses are directed by the earth's magnetic field and as the steel in the vessel may deflect that magnetic field locally, it is necessary to correct the compasses to eliminate all, or nearly all, the deviation. (Deviation is the deflection of the compass needle away from the actual magnetic north.)

Because the strength of a magnetic field varies inversely as the square of the distance from the point of affectation, it is possible to use a group of relatively small round bar magnets located in the binnacle below the compass to counteract the ship's local effect on the earth's magnetic field. The two large round iron balls on either side of the compass are also used in this connection.

The compass adjuster has the ship headed for a short run on such courses as magnetic north, south, east, and west and then northeast and northwest. While at each of these headings, he changes the magnets and iron balls until the deviation is eliminated as much as possible. At the same time, an observer uses a pelorus to obtain the exact heading of the vessel from a shadow from the sun and depends upon this for his work. After the deviation has been corrected as much as possible by these means, the ship is again slowly turned through 360 deg and the remaining uncorrected deviation is recorded every 15 deg. The deviation, after compensation has been completed, is ordinarily not over a degree or two and frequently is zero for most headings. The navigator must take any existing deviation into account in his work at sea; therefore the remaining deviation is marked on a card, and a correction is made for this when the ship is being navigated by magnetic compass.

FURTHER CHECKING

On the trial run of the *S.S. America*, after the compasses were adjusted the ship started for Boston for dry-docking and bottom cleaning. On June 10, a preliminary full-power dress-rehearsal run was made en route. This was completed at 4 P.M. At 8 P.M. that night the ship anchored in Boston Harbor. The displacement at that time was 28,780 tons. This figure was obtained by reading internal-draft gauges, which are affixed forward, amidships, and aft. With the average draft known, the displacement is read from the displacement curve. (A small correction must be made for hog, or sag, and for the density of the water. See page 193 for a memory refresher.) The vessel was placed in dry dock on June 11, at 7:45 A.M., and the crew given shore leave.

At 1:15 P.M. on June 12, the ship was clear of the dry dock and proceeding to Rockland, Me. It will be noted that 230 tons of fresh water had been added at Boston, which increased the displacement to 29,010 tons. This is somewhat above the 28,820 required for trial. At 5:15 P.M., the *S.S. America* had arrived off Monhegan Island, south of Rockland and was hove to because of fog. The displacement was checked; as it was too low owing to consumption while anchored, 125 tons of salt-water ballast was added. On June

13, at 10:30 A.M., the ship was still anchored off Monhegan Island, owing to the fog.

In order to utilize this time it was decided to hold the *anchor-windlass test*. This test is a working trial of the anchor windlass under specified conditions. It must be held in 30 fathoms or more of water (a fathom is 6 ft). The windlasses must raise both anchors and their chains simultaneously at the rate of at least 6 fathoms per min.

The anchors are then let go and their braking apparatus must be able to stop the anchor and 30 fathoms of chain within a distance of 2 fathoms. Sometimes brakes fail to hold; therefore, it is best to clear the deck before the test, for the bitter end of the anchor chain may lash out of the chain locker and sweep the deck with great speed and violence.

At 12:16 P.M. the fog had cleared, and the ship proceeded toward Rockland. At 3:36 P.M., June 13, the ship was on the measured mile. At this point we shall consider the apparatus used to determine speed, horsepower, and rpm.

TRIAL EQUIPMENT

The United States Navy and the Maritime Commission provide complete sets of special equipment for use aboard ships during trial. This equipment is placed aboard the ship sometime before the trial and is distributed about as shown in Fig. 237. This figure should be consulted during the following discussion.

1. The Smith-Cummings Mechanical Revolution Counter. The Smith-Cummings revolution counter is attached to each shaft at some point in the shaft alley. An observer stationed at the counter copies the readings on a special data pad and sends them by messenger to the computing room, where they are tabulated. This counter is in reality two counters, one of them running only while on the measured mile and the other running at all other times. When the midship deck observer (see Figs. 237 and 238) clicks the key upon sighting the two beacons in line, he starts one of the counters and stops the other. At the end of the mile he again presses the key, which stops one counter and starts the other.   The reading from this counter is used only if the Taylor counter fails.

2. The Taylor Electric Printing Revolution Counter. One of these Taylor counters is attached to each shaft at a point in the shaft alley.   The counting mechanism is operated by a worm drive directly from the shaft.   Both the forward and aft observers

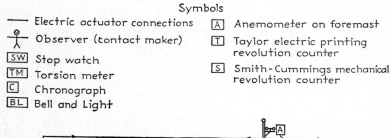

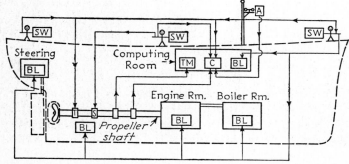

Fig. 237. Schematic diagram showing arrangement of instruments throughout the ship for making observations on the measured mile, *S.S. America.*

operate this counter so that two sets of readings are obtained. These are printed on a tape, which is torn off and sent to the computing room.

Both the Taylor and Smith-Cummings counters are started simultaneously with the chronograph, which is located in the computing room.

3. The Chronograph. This is a special instrument made at the model basin in Washington especially for trial trips. A chronometer is attached to the chronograph that, by means of an electric make-and-break circuit, scratches a ½-sec broken line on waxed paper fed through the machine. These ½-sec interval marks make it possible to count the time interval between the marks on the waxed paper made when the deck observers click the contact makers. The anemometer (wind-gauge) readings and

Photograph by Wythe W. Holt

Fig. 238. Sighting the beacons on the measured mile. The author as midship deck observer on the official trial of the *S.S. America*. The beacons are located on the shore line, which is barely visible in the background. The stop watch attached to the top of the contact-making device may be seen in the observer's right hand. Pressure on the contact maker starts the stop watch and through an electrical connection starts one Smith-Cummings counter in the shaft alley, stops the other, and makes a mark on the chronograph tape in the computing room.

revolutions of the shaft are also recorded on this waxed tape, a picture or record of the entire operation being thus created.

4. The Electric Torsion Meter. The electric torsion meter is placed on each shaft to record the twist of the shaft in a certain length. As this twist is small, it is magnified mechanically, electrically, or optically. The Ford torsion meters used on the *S.S. America* were of the electric type. This measured twist is proportional to the torque developed.

The shaft horsepower, shp, developed is found by the following formula:

$$shp = \frac{rpm \times torsion\text{-}meter\ reading}{c}$$

The constant c in the formula is obtained by multiplying a rigidity factor for the particular propeller shaft by the torsion-meter factor that is inherent in the instrument used or by calibrating the shafts in the shop before installation by applying a known torque and measuring the twist.

To obtain a zero reading for the torsion meter, we allow the propellers to idle. This is done by getting the ship under way at a speed of at least 5 knots and then shutting off the steam. The propeller shafts rapidly slow down until the idling speed of the propeller is reached. From this point on, the propeller revolutions drop very slowly, and the twist in the shaft most nearly approaches zero. In order to obtain a good zero reading, we attempt to read the zero for the torsion meter right at the transition point between the rapidly decelerating and the slowly decelerating propeller. The zero reading is noted, and the steam is again allowed to pass into the turbines. Any reading above this zero reading just obtained is proportional to the torque in the shaft.

While the ship is on the measured mile, the torsion meters are read about every 10 sec. The results are averaged and combined with the rpm of the shafts to obtain an average horsepower over the mile.

5. The Contact Makers. Each of the three deck observers has one contact maker in his hand. This is a squeeze-type electric contact device connected electrically to the chronograph and to one of the counters in the shaft alley. A stop watch is attached at the top of the squeezing device (see observer's right hand, Fig. 238). When the contact is made by any of the observers, it makes a record on the chronograph in the computing room. If actuated at either the forward or after observation post, it starts the Taylor counter in the shaft alley. If actuated at the midship post, it starts the Smith-Cummings counter, also located in the shaft alley. The act of contact making also starts or stops a stop watch attached to the contact-making squeezing device. A record of the elapsed time over the mile as recorded by the stop watch is marked down on a slip of paper and sent to the computing room. The stop-watch timing marked on the paper is not used unless the electric chronograph fails.

6. The Bell-and-light System. Bells and lights are located about as shown in Fig. 237. The forward-deck observer operates this system and gives a double bell-light warning 30 sec before the measured mile is reached and a single bell light at the beginning and end of the mile for the information of the engine-room and data-taking personnel.

7. Control Panel. The electric control panel for controlling the trial equipment is located in the trial-board room.

8. Anemometer. The anemometer is located on a bracket on the mast or on the signal yard and is electrically connected to the chronograph. The wind speed at each instant is recorded on the waxed tape.

9. Fuel-oil Meters. Always one and very frequently two fuel-oil meters are connected in series to each fuel-oil line. These meters are accurately calibrated before and after the trial. During the trial, they show the amount of fuel oil used during any interval.

CREW AND SPECIAL PERSONNEL

The crew operating the ship is made up of the personnel of the shipyard that constructed the vessel. Besides the regular operating crew, there are

1. *The management's representative.* He is in charge of the vessel for the shipyard.

2. *The trial board* is in charge of conducting the actual trials. The board maintains its own staff of experts, who go from ship to ship conducting trials.

3. *Navigating crew*, consisting of a captain and usually three mates. A captain is chosen who is familiar with the trials of ships and particularly with the trial course chosen.

4. *Representatives of the hull and engine departments.* Usually represented by the naval architect and the chief engineer.

5. *Owner's representatives* (for merchant vessels) *and supervisory prospective crew members.*

6. *Sub-contractor's representatives.* As some of the auxiliary machinery of a vessel is subcontracted, the subcontractors are represented by experts on the various pieces of machinery that they have supplied. They observe the operation of their machines and stand by to give any aid they can should their particular installation give trouble.

7. *Data takers.* These men read the various gauges, thermometers, revolution counters, torsion meters, fuel meters, etc., and serve as contact makers and computers.

The total persons aboard the *S.S. America* numbered 799, very few of whom were not actually engaged in necessary duties.

Usually on the way to the trial course the ship's company and data takers will have several dress rehersals to familiarize the personnel with their duties. The trial board sometimes goes to the course with the ship but more often boards the vessel just before she goes on the measured mile. The trial board brings its own special instruments, forms, data books, and chronograph.

Just before the trial is about to start, the data takers are called together and given final instructions. Then they proceed to their appointed stations.

Activity in the Engine and Boiler Rooms. While not directly connected with the timing of the trials, the engine- and boiler-room personnel have important functions. Steam pressures and temperatures, fuel-oil pressures and temperatures, bearing temperatures, forced-draft pressures, noise levels, reduction-gear noises, and many other items are all recorded to show that the machinery is meeting the requirements of the specifications. During the economy trials every effort is made to avoid wasteful use of lights, pumps, galley equipment, ventilation, fans, etc., for this adds to the fuel consumption and decreases economy.

THE MEASURED MILE

As previously mentioned, the object of running the measured mile is to ascertain the relationship between rpm and speed as well as the maximum speed obtainable. The trials on the mile are therefore run at progressive speeds. An attempt was made to run the *S.S. America* over the mile at speeds of 10, 15, 18, 21, and 22.5 knots and at full power. To obtain these speeds (which would give a good spread of spots on the rpm-speed curve, Fig. 234) the number of rpm to give the speeds required was estimated in advance from the model-basin curves shown in Fig. 234.

The estimated information on the rpm to give the required progressive speeds is given to the engine-room supervisors. With all observers in place, the ship is ready to enter the measured mile. The forward-deck observer has a contact maker, which he presses 30 sec before the ship enters the mile. This 30-sec notice is indicated by two bells and lights at the spaces noted in Fig. 237. Also, over the ship's loudspeaker system comes the warning, "We are now coming on the range—we are now coming on the range—we are now on the range." As the ship crosses the line of the markers, the following events take place:

1. The forward observer upon getting the two shore beacons in his line of sight presses the bell-light contact once and also presses the contact maker, thus tripping the Taylor counter in the shaft alley and making a mark on the chronograph tape in the computing room. The stop watch in the contact maker is also started by squeezing the contact maker.

2. A few seconds later, the shore beacons line up with the line of sight of the midship observer (Fig. 238), and he presses the contact maker. This starts the stop watch, starts one of the Smith-Cummings counters and stops the other, and makes a record on the chronograph tape.

3. The shore beacons then come into the line of sight of the aft observer, and he presses the contact maker, which starts a stop watch, again trips the Taylor counter, and makes a record on the chronograph.

At the bell-light signal, flashed by the forward observer, the data takers take readings of oil temperatures, bearing temperatures, etc. At the end of the mile, the three observers press their contacts as the markers come in line.

Immediately after the ship leaves the mile, the computers in the computing room start to work from the collected data. They must calculate the rpm and shaft horsepower so that they may send these data to the engine room before the ship turns and enters the measured mile again.

It is highly important that any one set of runs over the measured mile be made at a constant speed. This is difficult to do in practice. If the runs are too erratic the results of the means of the runs is doubtful.

Note the precautions taken to prevent the loss of a run over the course.

1. If either the forward or the aft observer fails the other observer will trip the Taylor counter and mark the tape on the chronograph.

2. The midship observer is independent of both the other observers, for he operates the Smith-Cummings counter and makes his own mark on the chronograph tape.

3. If all three observers fail to mark the chronograph tape, the timings may be taken from the stop watches.

If the time recorded by the three observers varies by 0.3 sec (naval vessels), the run is usually thrown out.

The Backing Standardization Run. The ship is usually backed over the measured mile to obtain rpm-speed at about 90 per cent of full-power backing. This is to get rpm for the astern test.

After making all runs at the progressive speeds previously indicated and the backing run, we plot the results of the runs on a curve as shown in Fig. 234 and are ready to proceed to sea for the endurance and economy runs.

Note here from Fig. 236 that the displacement of the vessel has been kept to an average of about 28,870 tons. As the tons per inch immersion of the *S.S. America* at this draft was about 105 tons, she averaged about 27 ft 8 in. draft, which gave a ½-in. draft to spare.

Endurance and Economy Runs. During endurance and economy runs, signals are given from the forward deck observer station every 30 min so that data takers may take simultaneous readings. Sometimes these signals are only 15 min apart. The torsion meters are read at more frequent intervals.

Full-power Four-hour Endurance and Economy Run. This run is made at full power to measure the fuel oil burned per shaft horsepower and to test the reliability of the machinery and boilers. Often no bonus is paid for overpower, but a deduction is usually specified in the contract for underpower. For the *S.S. America*, the 8-hr run described below was substituted for this run.

Eight-hour Endurance and Economy Trial. As the contract on the *S.S. America* for fuel oil consumed was based on speed and not on horsepower developed, speed was used as a criterion of these runs. (Quite often fuel-oil consumption is based on horsepower developed.) Such endurance and economy trials are held in deep water, and the ship is so ballasted that she reaches her mean trial displacement at the middle of the run. Note from Fig. 236 that the *S.S. America* was within ¼ in. of this required draft. The run consisted of 6 hr of full power plus a 2-hr run with boilers at 10 per cent overload. Half of the run was made with the wind and half against the wind so as to minimize the wind effect.

MISCELLANEOUS TESTS

There are several miscellaneous tests that are usually made on the way home.

The log of the *S.S. America* on trial follows:

June 14, 4:15 A.M., start dragging shafts for torsion-meter zeros.
    4:28 A.M. Finish dragging shafts for torsion-meter zeros.
    5:00 A.M. Start first 18-knot standardization run.

10:16 A.M.   Finish last full-power standardization run; proceeding to New-
         port News.
2:30 P.M.   Start 6-hr full-power economy trial.
8:30 P.M.   Finish above trial.
8:30 P.M.   Start 2-hr 10 per cent boiler overload run.
10:30 P.M.   Finish above run.
June 15, 8:00 A.M.   Start ahead steering tests.

Steering tests consist of several maneuvers, which were as follows for the *S.S. America:*

1. *Steering-gear and rudder test.* The rudder is put hard over to hard over. This test is a modification of the old figure 8 maneuver. Most landlubbers get quite a thrill from it. The angle of heel is very seldom over 18 deg but appears to be much greater. During this test it is best to remove dishes, etc., from the tables and to stop galley operations. This test is primarily for the steering gear and rudder.

2. *The Z maneuver.* This is a test of maneuvering ability. The rudder is put over to 20 deg at full power (also at half power) and held there until the ship is at 20 deg to its original course. When the angle is reached, the helm is put over 20 deg to the opposite side and held until the ship is 20 deg to the other side of her original course. The rudder is then put over to the opposite side and held until the vessel is back on the original course. The total time elapsed between the beginning and the end of the maneuver indicates the maneuvering ability of the ship.

3. *Astern steering tests.* The rudder is put hard over to hard over while under full-power astern. The oil pressure in the steering engine should not exceed the design pressure. The time required for hard over to hard over is noted.

4. *Turning diameter.* This is determined by a turning test at normal horsepower. A floating object is thrown overboard, and the turning diameter is observed at intervals through a small range finder as the vessel completes the turn. A small navigational range finder is adequate. From these data the tactical turning diameter is obtained.

5. *Crash-backing test.* This consists of a change-over from full

power ahead to full power astern. The time required and distance traveled from full power ahead to dead in the water are noted.

Besides the above tests the trial board or owner's representatives check on

1. Unfinished work.
2. Proposed alterations.
3. Rolling period of ship.
4. Auxiliary-machinery operation.
5. Angle of squat at various speeds (for high-speed ships).

The ship is also given a general inspection.

By this time the ship is in sight of her birthplace, and a broom is usually seen tied at her masthead to denote that she has made a clean sweep of all trials. Most of the crew members aboard are only too glad to get home for some much-needed sleep. The ship is tied up to the pier and after a few minor adjustments and changes is ready to be delivered.

Figure 233 shows the *S.S. America* after the trials as she left the yard to go to New York for delivery to her owners, the United States Lines.

BUILDER'S TRIAL

S.S. UNITED STATES

A new distance-measuring device, known as *Raydist*, altered the location of the trial trip for the *S.S. United States* and saved a considerable amount of money. Loran was used as a check on the Raydist system during the trials, and since the Raydist proved successful, it has become unnecessary to travel great distances to find suitable courses for trials. As the tests used were approximately the same as those that would have been used had the ship gone to a regular trial course, no further description of the tests are given, as they are covered in the discussion of the trial trip of the *S.S. America*.

A rough log of the trial trip of the *S.S. United States* and an explanation of the Raydist system follows:

The builder's trials for the *S.S. United States* were held about 100 to 150 miles in the Atlantic Ocean, east of the Virginia Capes. The

United States left the plant at 9 A.M. on May 14 and returned at 5 P.M. on May 16.

Ordinarily the builder's trials of a vessel are of shorter duration than official trials and they are held to satisfy the builders that the ship is in operating condition for her official tests. However, in the case of the *United States*, many of the official tests, including standardization, were held on the builder's trials. This was brought

FIG. 239. The *S.S. United States* on trial 150 miles east of the Virginia Capes. The use of Raydist made this deep-water trial possible. Wind speed at the time this photo was taken was 36 knots. The motion of the vessel caused by this heavy sea was imperceptible to persons aboard.

about by the decision to use the Raydist instruments to determine distance traveled rather than using an actual measured mile with beacons located on shore.

A ship's measurement of speed is computed by the revolutions of the propeller shafts per minute. There are no speedometers that indicate miles per hour, or knots, unless the rpm versus distance has first been obtained over a known distance and from this, speed can be calculated as time is known. The standardization tests over a known mile are held to determine how fast the ship travels at a given number of revolutions of the shaft. There are only two measured-mile deep-water courses used by large vessels on the East coast of this country; one is off Rockland, Me., the other off Guantánamo, Cuba. The water on the Rockland course is not deep enough and the approaches are too hazardous for a ship the size and speed of the *United States*. Had the Raydist not been available, it would have been necessary for the vessel to travel to Guantánamo, Cuba, which would have taken a period of at least five or six days. The trials would have been considerably more costly and, as it developed, not so accurate.

It was, therefore, decided that, if the Raydist proved workable in lieu of a measured mile, and as the trial board would be on the *United States*, the runs of the mile on the builder's trial would become the official standardization tests. Inasmuch as the Raydist did prove successful, even under the most difficult weather conditions, the vessel was standardized and the necessity for additional standardization runs was eliminated.

The following are the details of the builder's trials:

Wednesday, May 14, 1952

9:00 A.M. Left the shipyard.

9:45 A.M. The vessel passed Old Point Comfort and the Distilling Plant tests were started.

10:45 A.M. The vessel passed Cape Henry, at which point the first steam rate tests were started. These tests determine the efficiency of the turbines by measuring the pounds of steam per horsepower in an hour. This involves computation of readings from a water meter in the condensate flow and a torsion meter on the shaft. The tests were made using various numbers of nozzles in the turbines.

12:00 M. The vessel arrived at Chesapeake Lightship.

1:30 P.M. The compass and radio direction-finder operations were completed. The compass adjustments were made by sighting the sun with a pelorus to determine the sun's hour angle. The resulting direction, as shown in the azimuth book, was then checked with that on the compass. If the sun is not visible, sights are made on objects in known positions on shore. The radio calibration was made by checking the bearings of the finder with the known position of the signal sender, which in this case was the Light vessel. The vessel then proceeded to sea, building up to cruising shaft horsepower.

4:00 P.M. The *United States* started her first builder's economy trial. This trial is held to measure the fuel consumption in pounds per shaft horsepower-hour.

5:00 P.M. The vessel arrived at the Raydist buoy and checked the functioning of the Raydist and Loran systems The Raydist system was developed by the Hastings Instrument Co., Hampton, Va., and was used for the purpose of determining speed of a large vessel for the first time on a more or less experimental basis. The system operates by placing a small buoy with its Raydist equipment in the water. The buoy equipment sends out impulses which are received on another set of apparatus installed on the ship. The ship may then move in any direction from the buoy and a measurement, possibly as accurate as one part in 5,000, can be made of a given distance. To guard against power failure, a second, or stand-by, buoy with its equipment was also placed in the water. This system may replace the old method of sighting objects on land to measure the speed. The word Loran means long-range navigation. Loran was used as a check by keeping the ship in a course parallel to the Hatteras-Nantucket Loran base line. In this way, it was not necessary to obtain a "fix" to determine the ship's speed. Measurements were obtained with a special recorder recently developed by the United States Coast Guard.

6:10 P.M. The *United States* started her official economy trials.

12:00 P.M. The official economy trials were sufficiently completed in accordance with the specifications and the ship started increasing power to normal horsepower. During the balance of the night, the *United States* cruised at normal speeds.

Thursday, May 15, 1952

4:00 A.M. The *United States* completed cruising and started drag-shaft operations. Contact was made with the United States Coast Guard tender *Conifer* to place the Raydist buoys in the trial-course area. Because of high winds and seas, considerable difficulty was experienced in placing the buoys. As a result, the first speed runs were delayed more than three hours.

8:10 A.M. The *United States* started her 15-knot speed runs. Other runs continued at speeds up to 32 knots until 4 P.M. At this point, it was determined that some of the bearings in the gears were showing a tendency to heat, and additional speed runs were postponed until the official trials.

4:00 P.M. The vessel cruised at normal speeds for the remainder of the night.

Friday, May 16, 1952

3:00 A.M. The *United States* arrived at the 60-fathom line to prepare for a windlass test. At 5 A.M., the windlass test was begun with each anchor being lowered by the hand brake in 15-fathom shots up to 60 fathoms and then heaved in. Each anchor was also let out to 100 fathoms and heaved in, completing all windlass tests.

8:30 A.M. The *United States* started slow-speed steering tests, including emergency steering, on a single ram of the steering gear.

9:00 A.M. All tests were completed, and the *United States* headed for Newport News. At 5 P.M., the ship was docked.

Later, on her first passage, this vessel operating at a cruising speed of 35.59 knots took the blue ribbon for North Atlantic passages for the eastern run. The highest speed recorded for any one day was 36.17 knots.

Questions

1. What is the purpose of the trial trip?

2. What is meant by swinging the ship?

3. Why is it necessary to run a self-propelled model of a large ship in the model basin before we take the ship to the measured mile?

4. What are some of the usual guarantees that have to be made by a shipbuilder?

5. Where are economy trials run?

6. What is the difference between a builder's trial, an official trial, and a preliminary-acceptance trial?

7. List six requirements of a trial course.

8. Name two trial courses for submarines.

9. Why is it not possible to average the time over a measured course in order to determine the average speed?

10. How much excess draft is usually allowed as a safety factor on the measured mile and the economy trials?

11. Describe the anchor-windlass test.

12. Who furnishes the trial equipment?

13. How many revolution-counting machines are used on the measured mile?

14. Describe what happens when the midship observer clicks his contact maker.

15. How is the recording done on the chronograph?

16. Why are shafts dragged?

17. Describe what happens as the ship crosses the line of the first beacons.

18. What is the purpose of the economy run?

19. What precautions should be taken during this run?

20. Describe the *Z* maneuver.

21. What is the purpose of the steering test?

22. Describe a crash backing test.

23. What does a broom at the masthead signify?

Bibliography

TAYLOR, ADM. D. W.: "Speed and Power of Ships," U.S. Maritime Administration, Washington, D.C.

Data on Official Trials of the *S.S. America*, from files of Engine and Hull Technical Divisions, Newport News Shipbuilding and Dry Dock Company.

CHAPTER XXIV

MARITIME ADMINISTRATION VESSELS

For this nation to survive, it has always been necessary for our government to produce merchant and other vessels with great rapidity, during emergencies. Prior to the outbreak of hostilities in the Far East and Europe, it again became apparent that this nation would need many merchant vessels for troop transports and materiel. At that time, the merchant marine was very small, and ships then operating were, in most cases, out of date.

Because of this anticipated demand for ships, Congress authorized the formation of the United States Maritime Commission, now the Maritime Administration, a division of the Department of Commerce. The Commission was given fairly broad powers and immediately set about its task of building a merchant marine. Many outstanding experts and designers in all phases of shipping and shipbuilding were added to its staff. From their design boards, from the boards of many private naval architects and marine engineers, and from the design departments of many shipyards emerged the gigantic shipbuilding program which was to play a major part in winning the Second World War.

Many vessels were designed but never built; however, a discussion of the types actually built would fill a fair-sized book. It is not our purpose here to discuss all the types built but, rather, to give a simple sketch and the principal characteristics of the designs used as prototypes from which the largest number of vessels were produced so that the student may become somewhat familiar with the vessels we are to live with for many years. A simple inboard-profile sketch of the more frequently met types of United States Maritime Commission cargo vessels is shown in Figs. 240 to 251.

Tables of the principal characteristics of 27 United States

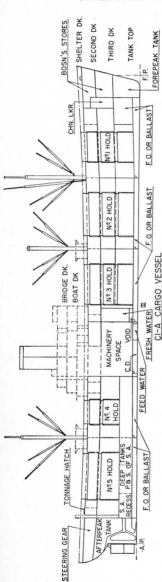

BOSN'S. STORES
SHELTER DK.
SECOND DK
THIRD DK.
TANK TOP
F.P.
FOREPEAK TANK
CHN. LKR
No. 1 HOLD
F.O. OR BALLAST
No. 2 HOLD
F.O. OR BALLAST
No. 3 HOLD
BRIDGE DK.
BOAT DK
F.O. OR BALLAST
MACHINERY SPACE
C.D. VOID
FEED WATER
FRESH WATER
No. 4 HOLD
TONNAGE HATCH
No. 5 HOLD
S.A. DEEP TANKS
RECESS P & S. OF S.A.
F.O. OR BALLAST
STEERING GEAR
AFTERPEAK TANK
A.P.

C1-A CARGO VESSEL

L.O.A.-412'-3". MOULDED DIMENSIONS-L.B.P.-390'-0", BEAM-60'-0", DEPTH Ⅲ.-28-5⅜" TO SECOND DK.

FIG. 240. C-1A. A shelter-deck vessel for light bulky cargoes.

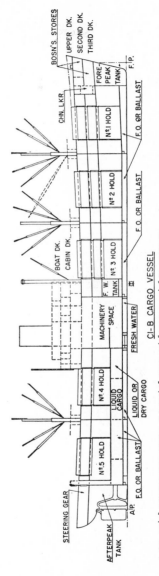

BOSN'S. STORES
UPPER DK.
SECOND DK.
THIRD DK.
FORE PEAK TANK
F.P.
CHN. LKR
No. 1 HOLD
F.O. OR BALLAST
No. 2 HOLD
F.O. OR BALLAST
No. 3 HOLD
BOAT DK.
CABIN DK.
F.W. TANK
MACHINERY SPACE
FRESH WATER
No. 4 HOLD
LIQUID CARGO
LIQUID OR DRY CARGO
No. 5 HOLD
F.O. OR BALLAST
STEERING GEAR
AFTERPEAK TANK
A.P.

C1-B CARGO VESSEL

L.O.A.-417'-9". MOULDED DIMENSIONS-L.B.P.-395'-0", BEAM-60'-0", DEPTH Ⅲ.-37'-6" TO UPPER DK.

FIG. 241. C-1B. A full-scantling vessel for dense cargoes. Compare depth to freeboard deck with C-1A.

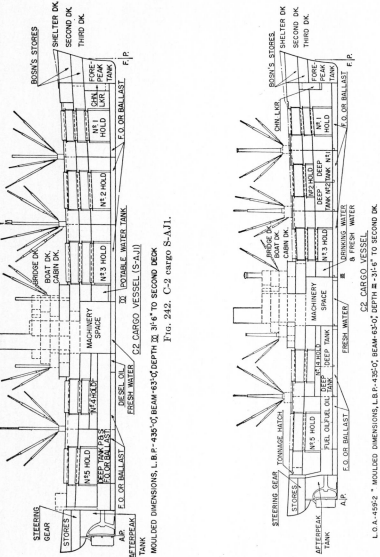

STEERING GEAR
AFTERPEAK TANK
A.P.
STORES
N⁰ 5 HOLD
DEEP TANK P&S
F.O. OR BALLAST
F.O. OR BALLAST
N⁰ 4 HOLD
DIESEL OIL
FRESH WATER
MACHINERY SPACE
BRIDGE DK.
BOAT DK.
CABIN DK.
N⁰ 3 HOLD
POTABLE WATER TANK
⊠ 3'-6" TO SECOND DECK
BOSN'S STORES
SHELTER DK.
SECOND DK.
THIRD DK.
N⁰ 2 HOLD
N⁰ 1 HOLD
CHN. LKR.
FORE-PEAK TANK
F.O. OR BALLAST
F.P.

C2 CARGO VESSEL (S-AJ)

MOULDED DIMENSIONS, L.B.P.-435'-0", BEAM-63'-0", DEPTH ⊠ 3'-6" TO SECOND DECK

FIG. 242. C-2 cargo S-AJ1.

STEERING GEAR
AFTERPEAK TANK
A.P.
STORES
TONNAGE HATCH
N⁰ 5 HOLD
FUEL OIL
FUEL OIL TANK
DEEP TANK
N⁰ 4 HOLD
FRESH WATER
MACHINERY SPACE
BRIDGE DK.
BOAT DK.
CABIN DK.
N⁰ 3 HOLD
DRINKING WATER & FRESH WATER
DEEP TANK N⁰ 2
DEEP TANK N⁰ 1
N⁰ 2 HOLD
N⁰ 1 HOLD
CHN. LKR.
BOSN'S STORES
SHELTER DK.
SECOND DK.
THIRD DK.
FORE-PEAK TANK
F.O. OR BALLAST
F.P.
F.O. OR BALLAST

C2 CARGO VESSEL

L.O.A.-459'-2 " MOULDED DIMENSIONS, L.B.P.-435'-0", BEAM-63'-0", DEPTH ⊠ 3'-6" TO SECOND DK.

FIG. 243. C-2-S-B1. Cargo vessel. Note deep tanks.

MOULDED DIMENSIONS, L.B.P.-465'-0", BEAM-69'-6, DEPTH 33'-6" TO SECOND DECK

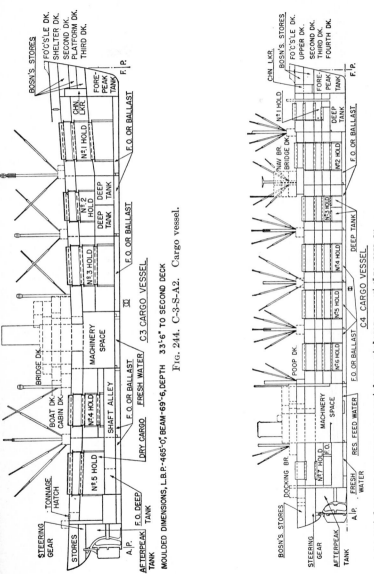

FIG. 244. C-3-S-A2. Cargo vessel.

L.O.A.-520'-0". MOULDED DIMENSIONS-L.B.P.-496'-8", BEAM-71'-6", DEPTH -43'-6" TO UPPER DK

FIG. 245. C-4-S-B5. Cargo vessel.

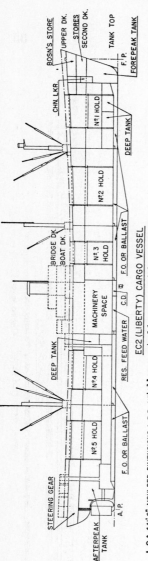

EC2 (LIBERTY) CARGO VESSEL

L. O. A.-441'-6". MOULDED DIMENSIONS-L. B. P.-417'-8¾", BEAM-56'-10¾", DEPTH Ⅲ. 37'-4" TO UPPER DK.

Fig. 246.   The Liberty cargo vessel.

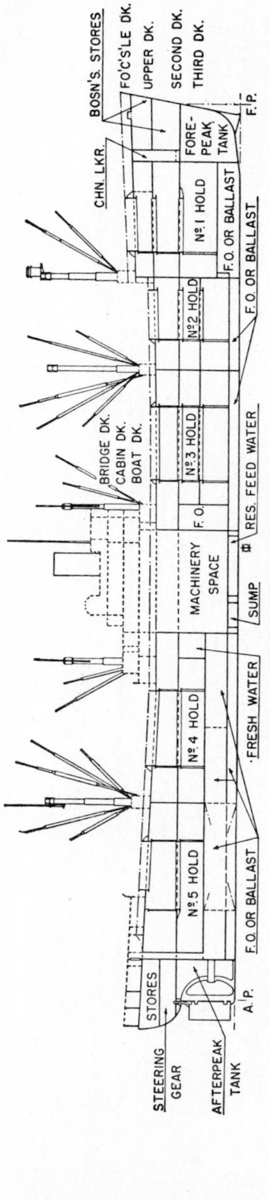

VC2 (VICTORY) CARGO VESSEL

L. O. A.-455'-3". MOULDED DIMENSIONS-L. B. P.-436'-6", BEAM-62'-0", DEPTH Ⅲ - 38'-0" TO UPPER DK.

Fig. 247.   VC-2.   The Victory cargo vessel.

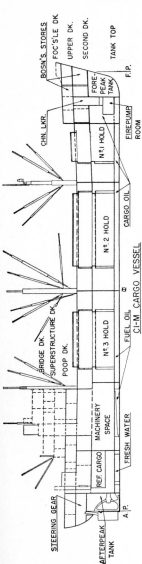

FIG. 248. C1-M-AV1. Coastal cargo vessel.

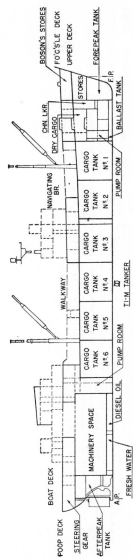

FIG. 249. T1-M-BT2. Coastal tanker.

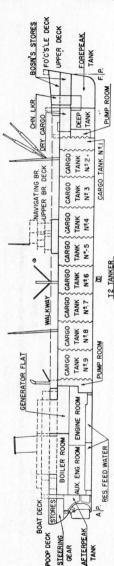

I2 TANKER

L.O.A.-523'-6". MOULDED DIMENSIONS-L.B.P.-503'-0", BEAM-68'-0", DEPTH IX -39'-3" TO UPPER DECK

Fig. 250. T2-SE-A1, and T2-SE-A2 tanker.

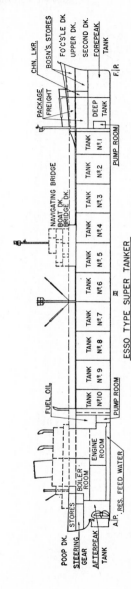

ESSO TYPE SUPER TANKER

L.O.A.-628'-0". MOULDED DIMENSIONS-L.B.P.-601'-2", BEAM-82'-6", DEPTH-MOULDED-42'-6".

Fig. 251. Esso-type supertanker. (Not a USMC design.)

CHARACTERISTICS OF SOME LARGER VESSELS

	Length, over-all	Length, B.P.	Beam	Depth	Draft	Displacement (load)	Deadweight (tons)	Gross tons	Net tons	Type propulsion	Shaft horsepower	Speed (knots)	Passengers	Crew	Year	Bale cubic capacity	Cruising distance (nautical miles)	See Fig.
S.S. America	723' 0"	662' 7"	93' 3"	55' 8"	32' 9"	35,440	14,331	26,314	13,536	Turbine	34,000	22	1,202	643	1940			239
S.S. United States	990' 0"	905' 3"	101' 6"	74' 3"	31'			53,329	29,474	Turbine	200,000	36	2,000	1,000	1952			2
S.S. Queen Mary	1018' 0"	975.2'	118' 6"	68' 5"	38' 9"	76,378		81,237	33,238	Turbine	200,000	32	2,141	1,101	1936			
Mariner class cargo	560' 0"		76' 0"	35' 6"	29' 10"	21,093	13,388			Turbine	19,250	24	12		1952			251
Supertankers																		
Esso	601' 0"		82' 6"	42' 6"	31' 11"	34,640	26,759	17,061	10,486	Turbine	13,750	17			1948			
Bulkoil	615' 0"		84' 0"	43' 9"	33' 5"	37,833	29,950	15,586	13,042	Turbine	17,600	18			1947			
Atlantic Refining	652' 0"		85' 0"	45'	34' 3"	39,644	30,155	19,498	11,929	Turbine	18,000	18			1950			
S.S. Wilfred Sykes (ore carrier)	678' 0"		70' 0"	37'	25' 8"	28,330	21,700	12,730	7,875	Turbine	7,000	14			1951			
S.S. President Jackson (combined passenger)	536' 0"		73' 0"	(Taken over by Navy)		19,600	11,800			Turbine	13,750	19	204		1951			
S.S. Independence (passenger)	683' 0"		89' 0"	52' 11"	30' 2"	30,090	10,600	23,719	11,166	Turbine	55,000	25	1,000		1950	446,100	21,000	240
C1A (M) or (S) (cargo)	412' 3"		60' 0"	37' 6"	23' 6"	11,086	7,400	5,100	2,900	Diesel or Turbine	4,000	14	8					
C1B (S) or (M) (cargo)	417' 9"		60' 0"	37' 6"	27' 6"	12,875	9,100	6,700	3,900	Diesel or Turbine	4,000	14	8-12			433,975	15,700	241
C2-AJ1 (cargo)	459' 1"		63' 0"	40' 0"	27' 7"	14,945	10,800	8,300	4,800	Turbine	6,000	15½	8			528,000	16,200	242
C2-S-B1 (cargo)	459' 0"		63' 0"	40' 6"	25' 9"	13,789	9,200	6,200	3,500	Turbine	6,000	15½	8			546,188	13,900	243
C2-SU (refrigerated)	474' 1"		63' 0"	40' 6"	26' 6"	15,025	7,700	8,600	5,050	Diesel	7,500	16	12			375,700	18,100	
R2-S-BV1 (refrigerated cargo)	495' 2½"		63' 0"	40' 6"	25' 9"	13,860	9,200	6,200	3,500	Turbine	6,000	15½	8			348,200	16,550	244
C3-S-A2 (cargo)	492' 0"		69' 6"	42' 6"	28' 6"	17,615	12,300	7,900	4,600	Turbine	8,500	16½	12			730,549	12,000	
C4-S-A4 (cargo)	522' 10½"		71' 6"	43' 6"	32' 9"	22,000	15,540	10,680	7,490	Turbine	9,000	16½	4			672,200	14,600	
C4-S-B5 (cargo)	520' 0"		71' 6"	43' 6"	32' 9"	19,958	15,570	10,780	7,530	Turbine	9,000	16½	12			440,000	14,500	245
EC2-S-C1 (liberty cargo)	441 6"		56' 10¾"	37' 4"	27' 8"	14,243	10,800	7,170	4,380	Reciprocating	2,500	11				500,245	10,000	246

CHARACTERISTICS OF MARITIME ADMINISTRATION STANDARD VESSELS

	Length, over-all	Length, B.P.	Beam	Depth	Draft	Displacement (load)	Deadweight (tons)	Gross tons	Net tons	Type propulsion	Shaft horse-power	Speed (knots)	Passengers	Crew	Year	Bale cubic capacity	Cruising distance (nautical miles)	See Fig.
EC2-S-AW1 (liberty collier)	441' 6"	..	56' 10¾"	37' 4"	28' 7"	14,730	11,040	6,640	3,740	Reciprocating	2,500	11	..	..	..	472,800	9,000	
Z-ET1-S-C3 (liberty tanker)	441' 6"	..	56' 10¾"	37' 4"	27' 8"	14,245	10,600	7,240	4,380	Reciprocating	2,500	11	..	..	..	64,800*	10,000	
Z-EC2-S-C5 (boxed air transport)	441' 6"	..	56' 10¾"	37' 4"	27' 8"	14,245	10,600	7,200	4,300	Reciprocating	2,500	11	..	..	..	492,000	10,000	
VC2-S-AP2 (victory)	455' 0"	..	62' 0"	38' 0"	28' 6"	15,199	10,800	7,600	4,600	Turbine	6,000	15.3	8	..	..	453,200	23,500	247
VC2-S-AP3 (victory)	455' 3"	..	62' 0"	38' 0"	28' 6"	15,199	10,800	7,600	4,600	Turbine	8,500	17	8	..	..	453,210	20,500	247
VC2-M-AP4 (victory)	455' 0"	..	62' 0"	38' 0"	28' 6"	15,199	10,280	7,600	4,600	Diesel	6,000	15	8	..	..	452,300	34,200	
P2-SE2-R3 (passenger cargo)	590' 0"	..	75' 6"	52' 6"	30' 0"	23,515	11,815	15,100	8,450	Turbo-electric	18,000	19	563	..	..	274,843	15,500	
S8-S2-BP1 (cable ship)	349' 0"	..	47' 0"	33' 9"	25' 0"	7,900	4,280	3,943	1,693	Reciprocating	4,000	14	..	..	..	49,640	8,250	
C1-M-AV1 (cargo)	338' 8½"	..	50' 0"	29' 0"	21' 0"	7,430	5,100	3,800	2,100	Diesel	1,700	10½	..	..	..	227,930	14,500	248
C1-MT-BU1 (lumber freighter)	319' 0"	..	49' 0"	26' 0"	21' 6½"	6,740	4,950	3,130	1,900	Diesel	2,400	12	..	..	..	185,200	9,130	
C1-S-D1 (concrete cargo)	386' 4"	..	54' 0"	35' 0"	27' 3"	11,370	5,310	4,820	3,400	Reciprocating	1,300	7	..	..	..	227,910	7,000	27
N3-S-A2 (coastal cargo)	259' 9½"	..	42' 1"	20' 5"	17' 11¾"	4,040	2,760	1,900	1,000	Reciprocating	1,300	11	..	..	..	121,300	5,200	
T1-M-BT2 (tanker)	325' 4"	..	48' 2"	21' 9"	19' 0"	5,980	4,189	3,260	1,680	Diesel	1,400	10	..	..	..	31,000*	8,630	249
T2-SE-A1 (tanker)	523' 6"	..	68' 0"	39' 3"	30' 2"	21,880	16,760	10,200	6,100	Turbo-electric	6,000	14½	..	..	..	152,030*	12,600	250
T2-SE-A2 (tanker)	523' 6"	..	68' 0"	39' 3"	30' 2"	21,880	16,580	10,460	7,340	Turbo-electric	10,000	16	..	..	..	141,000*	8,300	250
T3-S-A1 (tanker)	501' 8"	..	68' 0"	37' 0"	29' 11½"	21,530	16,500	9,900	5,900	Turbine	7,000	15½	..	..	..	24,722	11,850	
T3-M-AZ1 (tanker)	547' 3¾"	..	70' 0"	40' 0"	30' 1"	24,110	17,910	11,400	6,900	Diesel	7,500	15½	..	..	..	152,600*	14,000	

* Figures marked with an asterisk are in barrels (42 cu ft to the ton). All other bale capacity figures are in cubic feet.

Maritime Commission vessels are given for the student's information. A thorough study of these tables, making comparisons along the line, will illustrate some of the points emphasized in this text about the relation of length to beam, of length, beam, and draft to cubic capacity, of shaft horsepower to speed based on displacement, and of numerous other relationships. A thorough study of these tables will also give the student a "bird's-eye view" of ships which will greatly increase his understanding of the subject as a whole.

COST OF MARITIME COMMISSION WAR-BUILT MERCHANT VESSELS

The Merchant Marine Ship Sales Act of 1946 set up a sales program for the vast fleet of merchant vessels built during the war. The basis used for determining selling price was the domestic war cost of all of the vessels of a certain class divided by the number of vessels in that class. An estimated cost of these vessels was made with the estimate based on prewar figures. A statutory sales price was then calculated from the estimated 1941 price and for dry-cargo vessels this was determined to be 50 per cent of the estimated 1941 cost, and for tankers $87\frac{1}{2}$ per cent of the 1941 estimated cost. The floor price (least price for selling) was set up at 35 per cent of the domestic war cost for dry-cargo vessels and 50 per cent of the domestic war cost for tankers.

The act also provided that a down payment of 25 per cent was the least amount acceptable, the balance to be paid in 20 years (the expected life of the vessel) in annual installments, and with interest of $3\frac{1}{2}$ per cent per year on the unpaid balance. The act further stipulated that, if a vessel was traded in for a newer United States Maritime Commission vessel, the amount received by the owner on the trade-in could be allowed only on the unpaid balance and not on the down payment.

The following table lists prices based on the Merchant Marine Ship Sales Act of 1946. It should be noted that present prices for the construction of a single new vessel would be approximately 65 per cent greater than the domestic war cost.

PRICES FOR STANDARD MARITIME COMMISSION VESSELS IN ACCORDANCE WITH
THE MERCHANT SHIP SALES ACT OF 1946

Type of vessel	Estimated cost as of Jan. 1, 1941	Domestic war cost	Statutory sales price (unadjusted) 50% of 1941 cost	Floor price 35% of war cost
Dry cargo				
C1-MT-BU1..........	$1,063,000	$1,396,813	$ 531,500	$ 488,885
C1...................	1,940,000	2,608,168	970,000	912,859
C2...................	2,100,000	2,736,624	1,050,000	957,818
C4...................	3,300,000	4,420,965	1,650,000	1,547,338
VC2-S-AP2 (15K).....	1,958,000	2,511,877	979,000	879,157
VC2-S-AP3 (17K).....	2,130,000	2,872,659	1,065,000	1,005,431
N3..................	760,000	1,339,477	380,000*	468,817
C1-M-AV1...........	1,280,000	1,982,464	640,000*	693,862
C3.................	2,460,000	3,659,228	1,230,000*	1,280,730
				31½%, of war cost
Liberty Ship (All designs)..............	1,278,000	1,728,590	639,000	544,506
Tankers			87½% of 1941 cost	50% of war cost
T2-SE-A1 (14K).......	2,316,000	3,010,703	2,026,500	1,505,352
T3-S-A1 (15K)........	2,175,000	2,970,029	1,093,125	1,485,015
T1-M-BT.............	994,000	1,774,033	869,750*	887,019

* This price is inapplicable since under the terms of the Ship Sales Act of 1946 no dry-cargo vessel, except a Liberty-type vessel, may be sold at less than 35 per cent of the domestic war cost and no tanker may be sold at less than 50 per cent of the domestic war cost.

POSTWAR VESSELS (1945 TO 1951)

Besides the vessels built during the war, numerous vessels have been built since the war for special trades. Some of the more noteworthy of these are shown in sketches and their characteristics are shown in tabular form. While very few of these vessels are Maritime Commission sponsored, they are presented here because of the changing trend they denote.

The President Jackson-class Liners. There are three ships of this class, namely the *President Jackson*, the *President Adams*, and the *President Hayes*, all built for the American President Lines. These ships, which were designed by George G. Sharp, were built in 1951 by the New York Shipbuilding Company at Camden, N.J. They are designed for round-the-world service. Their paying capacity is 250 passengers or 2,500 troops. The living quarters, as well as spaces for 181 members of the crew, are air-conditioned. The cost of each of these President vessels, as designed, was approximately $12,000,000. The Navy has now taken over these vessels and they are to be completed as troop transports instead of passenger liners.

The Independence-class Vessels.   There are two vessels of this class, the *S.S. Independence* and the *S.S. Constitution*, both built in 1950. They were designed and built by the Bethlehem Steel Company at its Quincy, Mass., plant for the American Export Lines. These vessels are designed for a crew of 578 officers and men and a passenger list of 1,000. In war time, they may be converted quickly to carry 5,000 troops. These ships are unusual in that they are completely air-conditioned, being designed for the relatively warm climate found in the United States to Mediterranean service. The air-conditioning system will supply 184,000 cu ft of cooled air per minute. The cost of each of these vessels was approximately $25,000,000.

Great Lakes Ore Carriers.   The Great Lakes ore-carrying fleet, although operating on inland waters, is a very important part of our merchant marine. At present, there are over 260 large ore-carrying vessels, varying in deadweight capacity from 6,000 to 21,000 tons. The total combined ore-carrying capacity of this fleet is approximately 84,000,000 tons annually. One of the more recent additions to this fleet is the ore carrier *S.S. Wilfred Sykes* built in 1950 by the American Shipbuilding Company at its Lorain, Ohio, plant. It should be noted that as these vessels operate in fresh and comparatively smooth water, the designer of these vessels faces a somewhat different problem than does the designer of ocean-going vessels. As an illustration, one of these differences is that the vessels operating in this fresh water are dry-docked only every two years or so, while the ocean-going vessel should be dry-docked every year for sea-valve inspection. Most owners dry-dock every six months for cleaning and painting the underwater hull.

The Supertanker.   Beginning in 1948 a series of supertankers began to appear on the oceans that in size began to approach the superliners in both displacement and length.   The first of the group, launched by the Universe Tankships, Incorporated, a subsidiary of the National Bulk Carriers, was built at Welding Shipyards in Norfolk, Va., in the remarkably short time of five and one-half months from the date of keel laying.   Five ships of this class were built, the last of the series being known as the *S.S. Bulktrader*.   As their names begin with *Bulk*, they have become popularly known as the *Bulk-Ships*.   The Esso Shipping Corporation, after the launching of the second Bulk-Ship, began to construct a series of supertankers only slightly smaller than the Bulk-Ship known as the *Esso Bermuda Class*.   As if in response to this challenge, the Atlantic Refining Company started building a series of supertankers of the *Atlantic Seamen* class and these are the largest of the supertankers.   Between 1948 and 1953 a total of sixty supertankers of the three above classes were completed.   A glance at the adjoining table will show their particulars.   The Texas Company and Standard Oil of California are now building tankers which compare in size to the supertankers.   The cost of supertankers is between $5,000,000 and $6,000,000 each.

SUBSIDIES

For American vessels to compete in most foreign trade, it is necessary that a subsidy be paid to the operator and owners of vessels which are in direct competition with foreign vessels.   This subsidy, which is known as the *Building and Operation Differential*, is based on the difference in cost of construction between American and foreign yards, the difference in operational costs due to the numerous safety factors built into American ships which are not found in foreign ships, and the higher wages paid to American crews.   Where special defense features are incorporated in the vessel, the Government pays the excess cost for the construction and operation of these features.

Vessels operating coastwise, such as colliers, ore carriers, tankers, inland-waterway vessels, and others which do not come into foreign competition, are allowed no formal subsidy.   (NOTE: A foreign vessel may not carry a cargo from one port to another port in the United States, if the cargo originated in the United States.)

The question of which vessels are to receive and which are not to receive subsidies is a ponderous one; however, the general rules outlined above are basic, although in some cases they may vary slightly.

GLOSSARY OF SHIPBUILDING DEFINITIONS

1. **Access hole.** Opening in any part of the ship's plating used as a passage way while ship is under construction.
2. **Accommodation ladder.** A portable set of steps suspended over the ship's side for the accommodation of people boarding from small boats or a pier.
3. **Aft.** Toward, at, or near the stern. (Adverb.)
4. **After.** Toward, at, or near the stern. (Adjective.)
5. **Afterpeak.** The compartment in the narrow part of the stern, aft of the last watertight bulkhead.
6. **Afterpeak bulkhead.** Watertight bulkhead farthest aft.
7. **After perpendicular.** A line perpendicular to the base line, intersecting the after edge of the sternpost at the designed water line on fantail stern ships. On ships with a cruiser stern, it is usually taken at the end of the waterline. This also applies to merchant cruiser sterns. The after perpendicular usually passes through center of rudder stock when vessel does not have a sternpost.
8. **Air-escape hole.** An aperture cut in the top of floors or in tanks to prevent air lock from inhibiting the free flow of a liquid.
9. **Air port.** A circular window with hinged glass in the ship's side or deckhouse, for light or ventilation; also called *porthole.*
10. **Amidships.** In the vicinity of the middle portion of a ship, as distinguished from the ends.
11. **Angle clip.** A short piece of angle bar used for attachment.
12. **Anneal.** To relieve locked-up stresses by heating and gradual cooling.
13. **Aperture.** The space provided between rudderpost and propeller post for the propeller.
14. **Assemble.** To put together sections of the ship's structure on the skids, in advance of erection on the ways.
15. **Athwartship.** Across the ship, at right angles to the fore-and-aft center line of a vessel.
16. **Auxiliaries.** Various winches, pumps, motors, and other small engines required on a ship.
17. **Backing angle.** A short piece of angle for reinforcing the butt joint or splice of two angles, placed behind the angles joined.
18. **Ballast.** Any weight or weights used to keep the ship from becoming top-heavy or to increase its draft or trim. In some designs which may be too

NOTE: See Fig. 253 for use with Glossary.

367

stable and therefore ride too hard when light, ballast may be placed high in the vessel to reduce stiffness.

19. Ballast tank. Watertight compartment to hold water ballast.

20. Base line. A fore-and-aft datum line from which vertical heights are measured. On riveted hulls it is usually parallel to the top edge of the garboard strakes. On welded hulls it is usually parallel to the top edge of the flat plate keel. However, as the location of this reference line is a designer's option, the lines plan should be checked to determine its exact location.

21. Beam. An athwartship horizontal member supporting a deck or flat. Also, the extreme width of the ship.

22. Beam bracket. A triangular flat plate welded or riveted to the shell frame and the deck beam where they terminate.

23. Beam knee. End of steel deck beam that is split, having one portion turned down and a piece of plate fitted between the split portions, forming a bracket for riveted connection to side frame. (Now obsolete.)

24. Below. Below a deck or decks (corresponding to *downstairs*).

25. Bending rolls. A machine in which power-driven steel rollers are used to give cylindrical curvature to plates.

26. Bending slabs. Heavy cast-iron perforated slabs arranged to form a large floor on which frames, etc., are bent, after heating in a furnace.

27. Berth. A place where a ship is docked or tied up; a place to sleep; a bunk.

28. Between decks. The space between any two continuous decks; also called *'tween decks*.

29. Bevel. The angle between the flanges of a frame or other member. (Greater than right angle, open bevel; less, closed bevel.)

30. Bilge. Curved section between the bottom and the side of a ship; the recess into which all water drains.

31. Bilge bracket. A flat plate welded or riveted to the tank top or margin plate and to the frame in the area of the bilge, sometimes called *margin bracket*.

32. Bilge keel. A fin fitted on the bottom of a ship at the turn of the bilge to reduce rolling. It commonly consists of a plate running fore and aft and attached to the shell plating by welding or by angle bars. It helps materially in steadying a ship and does not add much to the resistance to propulsion if fitted in the streamline flow. Sometimes called *rolling chocks*.

33. Bilge pump. Pump for removing bilge water.

34. Bilge strake. Course of plates at the bilge.

35. Bilge water. Water collecting in the bottom of a ship owing to leaks, sweat, etc.

36. Binnacle. A stand or box for holding and illuminating a compass so that it may be conveniently observed by the steersman.

FIG. 252. Standing on the forecastle deck looking aft. This is the same vessel shown in Fig. 253.

37. Brow plate.   Any ramped sloping plate around an access opening which facilitates the handling of cargo over an obstruction.

38. Bitt.   Tie post for making lines fast on deck.

39. Bitumastic.   An elastic bituminous cement used in place of paint to protect steel.

40. Block.   An encased roller revolving on a pin.   Sometimes called a *pulley*.

41. Boat deck. Deck on which lifeboats are kept.

42. Boiler chock. Stay brace to prevent fore-and-aft movement of boilers; also called *ramming chock*.

43. Boiler saddle. Support for scotch boilers.

44. Booby hatch. Watertight covering over an opening on deck of a ship for a stairway or ladder.

45. Boom. A long, round, heavy spar pivoted at one end, ordinarily used for hoisting cargo.

46. Bosom piece. A short piece of angle riveted inside a butt joint of two angles; butt strap for angle bars; splice piece.

47. Boss. The curved swelling portion of the ship's hull around the propeller shaft.

48. Boss frame. Hull frame that is bent for clearing propeller-shaft tube.

49. Boss plate. Shell plate covering curved portion of hull where propeller shaft passes outboard.

50. Bow. The forward end of a ship.

51. Bracket. A triangular plate used to connect rigidly two or more parts, such as deck beam to frame or frame to margin plate.

52. Braze. To join certain metals by the use of a hard solder.

53. Breasthook. A flanged plate bracket joining port and starboard side stringers at their forward end at the point of the stem.

54. Bridge. Platform extending athwartship at pilothouse; also, an amidships superstructure.

55. Bridge deck. Deck at top of bridge superstructure.

56. Building slip. Place where the ship is built before launching.

57. Bulb angle. Angle shape reinforced at one toe.

58. Bulb plate. Narrow plate reinforced on one edge.

59. Bulb tee. T bar with toe of web reinforced.

60. Bulkhead. A vertical steel partition corresponding to the wall of a room, extending either athwartship or fore and aft.

61. Bulwark. The strake of shell plating above a weather deck. It helps to keep the deck dry and also serves as a guard against losing deck cargo or men overboard.

62. Bunker. A compartment used for the stowage of coal or other fuel.

63. Buoyancy. Ability to float; upward force of water pressure. It is equal to the weight of the displaced liquid.

64. Buoyancy, reserve. The additional buoyancy that would result if that part of the vessel's hull which is above the load water line were immersed.

65. Butt. The joint formed when two parts are placed edge to edge; the end joint between two plates.

66. Buttock. The intersection of a fore-and-aft vertical plane with the molded form of the ship.

67. **Butt strap.** A strip or strap that overlaps both pieces, serving as a connecting strap between the butted ends of plating.
68. **Camber.** The rise or crown of a deck, athwartship.
69. **Cant frame.** A frame not square to the center line, usually at the counter of the vessel.
70. **Capstan.** A revolving device with axis vertical, used for heaving-in mooring lines.
71. **Cargo.** The freight carried by a ship.
72. **Cargo batten.** Strip of wood used to keep cargo away from steel hull.
73. **Cargo boom.** Heavy boom used in loading cargo.
74. **Cargo hatch.** Large opening in a deck to permit loading of cargo into holds.
75. **Cargo port.** Opening in a ship's side for loading and unloading cargo.
76. **Carling** (also called *carlines*). Fore-and-aft member at side of hatch, extending across ends of beams where cut to form hatch, also placed between beams to stiffen areas under points of great stress such as under winches.
77. **Casing.** Bulkheads enclosing portion of vessel such as engine or boiler casing. Also, covering for parts of machinery, such as engine-cylinder casing.
78. **Casting.** An object made by pouring molten metal into a mold and allowing it to cool.
79. **Caulk (calk).** To make a joint watertight.
80. **Center line.** The fore-and-aft middle line of the ship, from stem to stern.
81. **Ceiling.** A surface, usually of wood, placed over the tank top for protection.
82. **Chafing plate.** Bent plate for minimizing chafing of ropes, as at hatches.
83. **Chain locker.** Compartment in forward lower portion of ship in which anchor chain is stowed.
84. **Chain pipe.** Pipe for passage of chain from windlass to chain locker.
85. **Chart house.** Small room adjacent to steering wheel for charts and navigational instruments.
86. **Chock.** A heavy fitting through which ropes or hawsers may be led. Saddle or seat of wood or metal.
87. **Chock, roller.** A chock with a sheave to prevent chafing of rope.
88. **Classification society.** An institution that supervises the construction of vessels under established rules, witnesses all tests on materials for hulls, machinery, and boilers, proof-tests all anchors and chains, and issues a certificate of classification. The major institutions are American Bureau of Shipping (ABS), United States; Lloyd's Register (LR), Great Britain; British Corporation (BC) Scotland; and Norwegian Veritas (NV), Norway. Numerous other smaller societies exist.

89. Cleat. A fitting having two arms or horns around which ropes may be made fast. A clip on the frames of a ship to hold the cargo battens in place.

90. Coaming. The vertical boundary of a hatch or skylight.

91. Cofferdam. Narrow empty space between two bulkheads that prevents leakage into adjoining compartments.

92. Collision bulkhead. First watertight bulkhead from bow of ship.

93. Companion way. An access hatchway in a deck, with a ladder leading below, generally for the crew's use.

94. Compartment. A subdivision of space or room in a ship.

95. Compass. A device for indicating the magnetic north, by means of a magnetized bar or needle, or the true north, through the action of a gyroscope.

96. Compression. Stress caused by pushing.

97. Contraguide. A trade name usually referring to the Goldschmidt patented contraguide rudder, rudderpost and stern frame "from which the vessel receives a forward push from the rotation of the water in the propeller race which is lost energy unless the contraguides are fitted." (Words in quotations are claimed.) See Figs. 131 and 132.

98. Counter. Overhang of stern of a ship.

99. Countersink. The taper of a rivet hole for a flush rivet.

100. Cowl. Hood-shaped top of ventilator pipe.

101. Crack arrestor. A slot cut or hole bored near an area of probable high stress to stop a crack should one start in the stressed area. The theory being that the intense stresses in the apex of a crack will lessen when the apex becomes a slot or circular hole.

102. Cradle. (*a*) A form on which furnaced plates are shaped (Fig. 81). (*b*) The support in which a ship lies during launching, called *launching cradle*.

103. Crow's-nest. An elevated lookout station on a ship, usually attached to forward side of foremast.

104. Davit. A crane arm for handling anchors, lifeboats, stores, etc.

105. Dead flat. The portion of a ship's form or structure that has the same transverse shape or the same area as the midship section.

106. Dead rise. Rise or slant up athwartship of the bottom of a ship from the keel to the bilge.

107. Deadweight. The total weight of cargo, fuel, water, stores, passengers and crew, and their effects, that a ship can carry.

108. Deck. The deck on a ship, corresponding to the floor in a building.

109. Deck beam. Athwartship support of deck.

110. Deck, bulkhead. The uppermost continuous deck to which all the main transverse watertight bulkheads are carried. This deck should be watertight to prevent any compartment that is open to the sea from flooding the one adjacent to it.

111. Deck, freeboard. (*a*) Deck to which freeboard is measured. (*b*) Deck above which bulkheads need not be watertight. (*c*) The watertight deck. Also called *bulkhead deck.*

112. Deck house. Shelter built on deck, not extending to the sides.

113. Deck, main. The principal deck, usually the freeboard deck.

114. Deck, orlop. A partial deck in the hold.

115. Deck, shelter. A complete weather deck above the freeboard deck. The space directly below the shelter deck is suitable for carrying cargo, although it is exempt from tonnage measurements since the deck is theoretically nonwatertight. Since this is the uppermost through deck, it is sometimes the strength deck.

116. Deck stringer. The strake of plating that runs along the outer edge of a deck.

117. Deck, weather. Full deck with no overhead protection, watertight except in case of a shelter deck.

118. Deflection. The amount of bending.

119. Derrick. A device for hoisting heavy weights, cargo, etc.

120. Die. (*a*) A tool having several cutting edges, used for cutting threads. (*b*) In drop-forging work, a template tool used to stamp out a piece of work in one operation.

121. Displacement. The total weight of the ship when afloat, including everything on board, equals weight of water displaced. Displacement may be expressed in either cubic feet or long tons. A cubic foot of sea water weighs 64 lb and one of fresh water 62.5 lb; consequently, one long ton is equal to 35 cu ft of sea water or 35.9 cu ft of fresh water. One long ton equals 2,240 lb.

122. Docking keel. Keel on each side, and in plane of regular keel, used to distribute the weight in dry dock in the case of large ships. (Seldom used except on largest naval ships and now almost extinct.)

123. Dog. (*a*) A small metal fitting used to hold doors, hatch covers, manhole covers, etc., closed. (*b*) A bent bar of round iron used for holding shapes on the bending slab.

124. Double bottom. Compartments at bottom of a ship between inner and outer bottoms, used for ballast tanks, oil, water, fuel, etc.

125. Doubling plate. A plate fitted outside or inside of and faying (touching) against another to give extra strength or stiffness.

126. Draft. The depth of the lowest point of the ship below the surface of the water when she is afloat.

127. Draft marks. The numbers painted at the bow and stern of a vessel to indicate how much water she draws. These marks are 6 in. high and spaced 12 in. from the bottom of one number to the bottom of the next number.

128. Drift pin. A small tapered tool driven through rivet holes and used to draw adjoining plates or bars into alignment with each other.

129. Drop strake. A strake that is terminated before it reaches the bow or stern. The number of strakes dropped depends on the reduction of girth between the midship section and the ends (Fig. 83).

130. Dry dock. A dock in which a ship's hull may be kept out of water during construction or repair. Three types are used: (*a*) the graving dock, a basin excavated near a waterway, with a gate to exclude the water after pumping out; (*b*) the floating dock, a hollow structure of wood or steel, which is sunk to receive the ship to be docked and is pumped out to lift it from the water; (*c*) the marine railway, a cradle of wood or steel on which the ship may be hauled out of water along inclined tracks leading up the bank of a waterway.

131. Dutchman. Any piece used to connect two or more pieces or a piece to fill in the gap between members.

132. Ensign staff. A flagstaff at stern of vessel from which the national ensign may be flown.

133. Erect. To hoist into place and bolt up on the ways fabricated and assembled parts of a ship's hull, preparatory to riveting or welding.

134. Escape trunk. A vertical trunk usually located in the after end of the shaft alley to permit the engine room personnel or anyone trapped in the shaft alley a means of escape.

135. Even keel. A ship is said to be on an even keel when the keel is level or parallel to the surface of the water and the hull is not listed, or tipped, sideways.

136. Expansion trunk. Upper portion of a tank on an oil tanker, used to allow for the expansion of oil when the temperature rises, and for contraction upon cooling without permitting a large area of free surface.

137. Eyebrow. A plate shaped around the top of an opening to prevent drainage from above entering the opening.

138. Fabricate. To process hull material in the shops prior to assembly or erection. In hull work fabrication consists in shearing, shaping, punching, drilling, countersinking, scarfing, rabbeting, beveling, etc.

139. Fair (fair up). (*a*) To correct or fair up a ship's lines on mold-loft floor; (*b*) to assemble the parts of a ship so that they will be fair, *i.e.*, without kinks, bumps, or waves; (*c*) to bring rivet holes into alignment.

140. Fairlead. Any ringbolt, eye, loop, or sheave which guides a rope in the required direction.

141. Fantail. (*a*) Fan-shaped plate on center line of ship on overhanging stern. (*b*) Plates forming overhang at stern (Fig. 133).

142. Fathom. A measure of length, equivalent to 6 linear feet, used for depths of water and lengths of rope or chain.

143. Faying surface. The surface between two adjoining parts.

144. Fender. Heavy strip of wood or steel attached to the side of the vessel, running fore and aft, at the water line, for the purpose of preventing rubbing or chafing of the hull.

145. Fidley hatch. Hatch around smokestack and uptake for ventilating the boiler room.

146. Fixed light. Circular window with fixed glass in side of ship, door, skylight cover, etc.

147. Flagstaff. A light spar or pole from which a flag may be displayed.

148. Flange. Portion of a plate or shape at, or nearly at, right angles to main portion; to flange is to bend over to form such an angle.

149. Floor. A plate placed vertically in the bottom of a ship, usually on every frame, and running athwartship from bilge to bilge (see Figs. 63, 64, 64*A*, and 65).

150. Floor plate. Vertical plate in bottom (see *Floor*).

151. Fore and aft. In line with the length of the ship; longitudinal.

152. Forecastle. The forward upper portion of the hull, usually used for rope, paint, and boatswain's stores.

153. Forefoot. The part of the stem that curves aft to meet the keel.

154. Forepeak. A narrow compartment, or tank, at the bow in the lower part of the ship forward of the collision bulkhead.

155. Forging. A piece of metal hammered, bent, or pressed to shape while heated white-hot (Fig. 28).

156. Forward. Near, at, or toward the bow of the ship.

157. Forward perpendicular. A line perpendicular to the base line, intersecting the forward edge of the stem at the designed water line.

158. Foundations, main. Supports for boilers and engines.

159. Foundations, auxiliary. Supports for small machinery such as winches, condensers, heaters, etc.

160. Frame. One of the ribs forming the skeleton of a ship.

161. Frame spacing. The fore-and-aft distance between heel and heel of adjacent transverse frames along the center line.

162. Frame, web. Heavy side or continuous frame, made with web plate between its members.

163. Freeboard. The distance from the water line to the top of freeboard deck at side.

164. Freeing port. An opening in the bulwarks, close to the deck and fitted with a flap cover which opens outboard, or with rods, to allow water shipped upon the deck to free itself from the vessel rapidly but without carrying any crew members with it.

165. Funnel. Smokestack of a vessel.

166. Furnace. Heater or large forge for heating plates or shapes for bending. To furnace is to bend after heating in a furnace.

167. Galley. A cookroom or kitchen on a ship.

168. Galvanizing. Coating metal parts with zinc for protection against rust.

169. Gangway. A passageway, ladder, or other means of boarding a ship.

170. Gasket. Flexible material used to pack joints in machinery, piping, doors, hatches, etc., to prevent leakage of liquids or gases.

171. Girder. A continuous member running in a fore-and-aft direction under the deck for the purpose of supporting the deck beams and deck. The girder is generally supported by widely spaced pillars.

172. Girth. Distance around a vessel's shell from gunwale to bilges, to keel, to bilge to gunwale.

173. Grating. A structure built out of wooden strips or metal bars, to form a walkway across a deck or opening without interference with light, drainage, or ventilation.

174. Gross tonnage. A figure obtained by dividing the total volume of the ship, in cubic feet, by 100, after the omission of all spaces exempted from measurement by law (Chap. XVIII).

175. Ground ways. Timbers fixed to the ground, under the hull on each side of the keel, on which ship slides during launching.

176. Gudgeons. Bosses on sternpost drilled for pins (pintles) for rudder to swing on (Fig. 125).

177. Gunwale. Junction of deck and shell at top of sheer strake.

178. Gunwale bar. Angle bar that connects deck stringer plate and shell plates at weather deck.

179. Gusset plate. Triangular plate that connects members or braces.

180. Hatch. Opening in deck for passage of cargo, etc.

181. Hatch beam. Portable beam across the hatch to support covers.

182. Hawse pipe. Casting extending through deck and side of ship for passage of anchor chain, for stowage of anchor in most cases.

183. Header. A member added for local strength which is not parallel to the main strength members of the vessel. Usually used to deliver the load from some strength member which has been cut to other strength members in the area.

184. Heeling. Tipping of a vessel to one side; also called *listing*.

185. Helm. A term used to designate the rudder's position as controlled by the tiller, wheel, or steering gear.

186. Hogging. Straining of the ship that tends to make the bow and stern lower than the middle portion (see *Sagging*.)

187. Hold. (*a*) The spaces below deck allotted for the stowage of cargo; (*b*) the lowermost cargo space.

188. Hold beams. Beams in a hold, similar to deck beams, but having no plating or planking on them; now obsolete.

189. Horseshoe plate.   Small horseshoe-shaped plate around rudderstock on shell of ship, for the purpose of preventing water from backing up into the rudder trunk.

190. Hull.   The body of a ship, including shell plating, framing, decks, and bulkheads.

191. Inboard.   Inside the ship; toward the center line.

192. Inner bottom.   Plating forming the top of the double bottom. Also called *tank top.*

193. Intercostal.   Made in separate parts, between successive frames or beams.; the opposite of *continuous.*

194. Inverted angle.   An angle with the toe welded to a plate, thus, in effect, in conjunction with a portion of the plate adjacent to the toe, forming a channel.

195. Jack staff.   A flagpole at bow of vessel, from which the union jack may be displayed.

196. Joggle.   To offset a plate or shape to save the use of liners.

197. Keel.   The principal fore-and-aft member of a ship's frame, which runs along the bottom and connects the stem and stern and to which is attached the frames of the ship. The backbone of the ship's frame.

198. Keel, bar.   A keel that protrudes through the bottom.

199. Keel blocks.   Heavy blocks on which ship rests during construction.

200. Keel, flat.   A fore-and-aft row of flat plates end to end on the center line, running along the bottom of the ship from stem to stern, the forward and after plates being dished up into a U shape to fit the stem and stern castings.

201. Keelson side.   Fore-and-aft member placed on each side of the center vertical keel.

202. Keel, vertical.   Vertical plate on center line, used as reinforcement for longitudinal flat keel; sometimes called *center keelson.*

203. King post.   A stub mast, outboard from center line, to carry cargo booms; also called *Samson post.*

204. Knot.   A speed measurement of 1 nautical mile per hour, a nautical mile being about $1\frac{1}{4}$ land miles (6,080 ft or $\frac{1}{60}$ deg at the equator).

205. Knuckle.   A sharp bend in a plate or shape.

206. Knuckle plate.   A plate bent to form a knuckle.

207. Ladder.   Vertical or inclined steps aboard ship, taking the place of stairs.

208. Lap.   A joint in which one part overlaps the other, the use of a butt strap being thus avoided.

209. Laminated plate.   A rolled piece of steel which looks more sandwichlike than solid when viewed edgewise. Laminated steel is invariably condemned.

210. Launching.   The operation of placing the hull in the water by allowing it to slide down the launching ways. During launching the weight of the hull is borne by the cradle and sliding ways, which are temporarily attached to the hull and slide with it down the ground ways.

211. **Laying off.**   Marking plates, shapes, etc., for fabrication.

212. **Length between perpendiculars.**   The length of a ship measured from the forward perpendicular to the after perpendicular.

213. **Length over all.**   The length of a ship measured from the forwardmost point of the stem to the aftermost point of the stern.

214. **Lift.**   To *lift* a template is to make it from measurements taken from the job.

215. **Lightening hole.**   A hole cut in a structural member to reduce its weight.

216. **Limber hole.**   A hole of a few inches diameter cut in a floor plate near the bottom to allow water to drain to lowest point of tank.

217. **Liner.**   A flat or tapered strip placed under a plate or shape to bring it in line with another part that it overlaps; a filler.

218. **Lines.**   The plans of a ship that show its form.

219. **Listing.**   See *Heeling.*

220. **Load water line.**   Line of surface of water on a ship when loaded to maximum allowance in salt water in the summertime.

221. **Longitudinal.**   A fore-and-aft structural member running parallel or nearly parallel to the center vertical keel, along the inner bottom, shell, or deck.

222. **Main deck.**   See *Deck, main.*

223. **Manhole.**   A round or oval-shaped hole cut in a ship's divisional plating, large enough for a man to pass through.

224. **Manifold.**   A box casting containing several valves, to which pipe lines are led to or from various compartments and pumps on a ship, thus allowing any tank to be connected to one or more pumps.

225. **Margin.**   Usually a plate or a shape attached to an outer edge.   Also an allowance for error plus or minus.

226. **Margin angle.**   Angle bar connecting margin plate to shell.

227. **Margin bracket.**   A bracket connecting the frame to the margin plates. Sometimes called *bilge bracket* or *wing bracket.*

228. **Margin plate.**   Any one of the outer row of plates of the inner bottom, connecting with the shell plating at the bilge (Figs. 63 and 64).

229. **Mast.**   A large long spar, placed nearly vertical on the center line of a ship.

230. **Mess room.**   Dining room for crew.

231. **Midship.**   Center of ship, located at the mid point between the forward and after perpendiculars.

232. **Midship section.**   A plan showing a cross section of the ship through the middle, or amidships.   This plan shows sizes of frames, beams, brackets, etc., and thicknesses of plating.

233. **Mold.**   A light pattern of a part of a ship, usually made of thin wood or paper; also called a *template.*

234. Mold loft. A building with a large smooth floor for laying down the lines of a vessel to actual size to be used for making templates from them for the structural work entering the hull (Fig. 147).

235. Mooring. Securing a ship in position by several lines or cables so that she cannot move or swing.

236. Mooring ring. A round or oval casting inserted in the bulwark plating of a ship, through which the mooring lines, or hawsers, are passed.

237. Net tonnage. A figure obtained by making deduction from the gross tonnage for space not available for carrying cargo or passengers.

238. Oiltight. Riveted, caulked, or welded to prevent oil leakage.

239. Outboard. Away from the center line, toward the side of a ship.

240. Overboard. Outside, over the side of a ship, in the water.

241. Overhang. Portion of the hull over and unsupported by the water.

242. Oxter plate. A bent shell plate that fits around upper part of sternpost; also called *tuck plate*. Now practically obsolete.

243. Packing. (*a*) Material put between plates or shapes to make them watertight. (*b*) Wooden blocks and wedges supporting ship on sliding ways.

244. Panting. The in-and-out movements of the frames and shell plating due to variation of wave pressure, most noticeable in the bow and stern.

245. Paravane. An object shaped like a small airplane. When two paravanes attached to steel cables are lowered into position on the paravane skeg one port and one starboard, they trail out at 45-deg angles. When the anchoring cable of a mine strikes the paravane cable, the mine travels to the paravane where it is cut loose.

246. Paravane skeg. A finlike protuberance at the bottom of the stem which allows the paravane crotch to ride at the lowest point of the stem.

247. Peak. The space at the extreme lower bow or stern.

248. Pillar. Vertical member or column giving support to a deck girder. Also called *stanchion*.

249. Pilothouse. Deckhouse containing steering wheel, compass, charts, etc., used for navigation of a ship. It is generally placed forward, near navigating bridge.

250. Pintles. The pins or bolts that hinge the rudder to the gudgeons on the sternpost.

251. Pipe tunnel. A longitudinal or transverse metal box through which pipes are run.

252. Planking. Wood covering for decks, etc.

253. Platen. Skids plated over, on which structural welded parts are assembled.

254. Platform. A flat deck, without camber or sheer.

255. Plating. The plates of a hull, a deck, a bulkhead, etc.

256. Plimsoll mark. A mark scribed and painted on the side of a vessel, designating the depth to which the ship may be loaded.

257. Poop. The after upper portion of the hull, usually containing the steering gear.

258. Port. (*a*) The left-hand side of a ship looking toward the bow. (*b*) An opening in the side of a ship for loading cargo, etc.

259. Porthole. A circular opening in the ship's side. See *Air port.*

260. Profile. Side elevation or fore-and-aft center-line section of a ship's form or structure.

261. Propeller. A revolving device that drives the ship through the water, consisting of three, four or more blades, resembling in shape those of an electric fan. Sometimes called a *screw* or *wheel.*

262. Propeller post. Forward post of stern frame, through which propeller shaft passes.

263. Quadrant. A casting, forging, or built-up frame on the rudderhead, to which the steering chains are attached.

264. Quarter deck. That portion of the weather deck nearest the stern.

265. Quarters. Living or sleeping rooms.

266. Rabbet. A depression or offset of parallel depth designed to take some other adjoining part, as, for example, the rabbet in the stem to take the shell plating.

267. Racking. Straining of a ship that tends to make the decks and bottom no longer square with the sides.

268. Rail. The rounded section at the upper edge of the bulwarks, or a horizontal pipe forming part of a railing fitted instead of a bulwark.

269. Reaming. Enlarging a rivet hole by means of a revolving cylindrical, slightly tapered, tool with cutting edges along its sides.

270. Reverse frame. An angle bar or other shape riveted to the inner edge of a transverse frame for reinforcement (almost obsolete).

271. Ribband. (*a*) A fore-and-aft wooden strip or heavy batten used to support the transverse frames temporarily after erection and to keep them in a fair line; (*b*) any similar batten for fairing a ship's structure.

272. Rigging. Ropes, wire ropes, lashings, etc., used to support masts, spars, booms, etc., and also for handling and placing cargo on board ship.

273. Rivet. A short, round metal connection used to fasten two or more members together by clinching after heating red-hot. Certain alloys of aluminum rivets are driven ice-cold.

274. Roller chock. See *Chock, roller.*

275. Rose box. A galvanized iron box with the sides perforated by small holes, the combined areas of which equal at least twice the area of the bilge suction pipe. The purpose is to prevent refuse from clogging the pumps when pumping bilge water.

276. Rough bolt. To bolt a plate or frame temporarily in place until it can be faired for reaming.

277. Rudder. A large heavy fitting hinged to the stern frame used for steering the ship.

278. Rudder lug. A projection cast or fitted to the forward edge of the rudder frame for the purpose of taking the pintle.

279. Rudderpost. After post of stern frame to which rudder is hung. Also called *sternpost*.

280. Rudderstock. Shaft of rudder, which extends through counter of ship.

281. Rudder stop. Lug on stern frame or a stanchion at each side of quadrant, to limit the swing of the rudder to approximately 34 deg port or starboard.

282. Sagging. Straining of the ship that tends to make the middle portion lower than the bow and stern (see *Hogging*).

283. Samson post. A heavy vertical post that supports cargo booms; also called *king post*.

284. Scantlings. The dimensions of the frames, girders, plating, etc., that go into a ship's structure. For merchant ships these dimensions are taken from the classification-society rules.

285. Scarf. A connection made between two pieces by tapering their ends so that they will mortise together in a joint of the same breadth and depth as the pieces connected. It is used on bar keels, stem and stern frames, and other parts.

286. Screen bulkhead. A bulkhead, dust-tight but not watertight, usually placed between engine and boiler rooms.

287. Scupper. Drain from weather decks to carry off sea and rain water. Usually called *drains* when it evacuates water from enclosed spaces.

288. Scupper pipe. Pipe that drains free moisture from scuppers through side of a ship, or to the bilges.

289. Scuttle. A small opening, usually circular, generally fitted in decks to provide access or to serve as a manhole or opening for stowing fuel, water, and small stores.

290. Scuttlebutt. (*a*) A drinking fountain aboard ship. (*b*) The Navy term for rumors aboard ship.

291. Sea chest. A casting fitted to shell of a vessel for the purpose of supplying water from the sea to the condenser and pumps.

292. Seam. Fore-and-aft joint of shell plating, deck and tank-top plating, or lengthwise side joint of any plating.

293. Seam strap. Strap connecting plates to form a flush seam.

294. Serrated member. A rolled section in which the web has been cut alternately long and short. The longer web pieces are welded to the plating leaving the shorter section clear of the plating for drainage. By the serrated cutting of a 12-in. I beam, two 7-in. tees are produced (see Fig. 95).

295. Shaft. Long, round, heavy forging connecting engine and propeller, or other rotating machinery to its parts.

296. Shaft alley (shaft tunnel). A watertight casing covering propeller shaft, large enough to walk in, extending from engine room to afterpeak bulkhead, to provide access and protection to shaft in way of after cargo holds.

297. Shape. Bar of constant cross section throughout its entire length, such as a channel, T bar, or angle bar.

298. Shear. A stress that tends to cause the adjacent parts of a body to slide over each other.

299. Shear line. Line to shear or cut to.

300. Shears. Large machine for cutting plates and shapes.

301. Sheave. A grooved roller revolving on a pin. When encased complete with a shackle is called a *block*.

302. Sheer. Fore-and-aft curvature of a deck.

303. Sheer plan. Side elevation of ship's form; a profile.

304. Sheer strake. Top full course of shell plates at strength deck level.

305. Shell expansion. A plan showing details of all plates of the shell.

306. Shell landings. Points on the frames showing where the edges of shell plates come.

307. Shell plating. The plates forming the outer skin of the hull.

308. Shelter deck. See *Deck, shelter.*

309. Shore. A brace or prop.

310. Skeg. A deep finlike projection on the bottom of a vessel usually toward the stern, installed (*a*) to support the lower edge of the rudder, (*b*) to support the propeller shaft, (*c*) for strength, (*d*) to prevent erratic steering in seaway.

311. Skids. A skeleton framework used to hold assemblies off ground to permit riveting or welding. See *Platen.*

312. Skylight. An opening in a deck to give light and air to the compartment below, usually fitted with hinged covers having fixed lights.

313. Sliding ways. See *Launching.*

314. Slop chute. Chute for dumping garbage overboard.

315. Smokestack. A metal chimney or passage through which the smoke and gases are led from the boiler uptakes to the open air.

316. Sounding pipe. Pipe in oil or water tank used to measure depth of liquid in tank.

317. Spar. A long, round, wooden timber used to carry rigging.

318. Spar deck. A light upper deck. (Now obsolete.) In lake freighters the strength deck.

319. Split frame. A channel or Z bar frame split at the bilge so that one flange may connect to the shell plating and the other to the tank top.

320. Stability. Tendency of a ship to return to her original position when inclined away from that position.

321. Stanchion. A pillar or upright post; a vertical rail post.

322. Staple angle. A piece of angle bent in the shape of a staple or other irregular shape.

323. Stapling. Collars, forged of angle bars, to fit around continuous members passing through bulkheads for watertightness; now obsolete.

324. Starboard. Right side of a ship looking forward.

325. Stay. A guy line.

326. Stealer. A plate extending into an adjoining strake in the case of a drop strake. Stealer plates are located in the bow and stern, where the narrowing girth compels a reduction in the number of strakes (Fig. 83).

327. Steering gear. Apparatus for controlling the rudder.

328. Steering wheel. Wooden or metal wheel having its spokes extended through the rim for handholds and used to control rudder by rope leads, or otherwise, through steering engine.

329. Stem. Forging, casting, or rounded plate forming extreme bow of ship, extending from keel to forecastle deck.

330. Step. To set in place, as applied to a mast.

331. Stern. After end of a ship.

332. Stern frame. Large casting or forging attached to after end of keel to form ship's stern. Includes rudderpost, propeller post, and aperture for propeller.

333. Sternpost. After part of stern frame to which rudder is attached; also called *rudderpost.*

334. Stern tube. Tube through stern through which propeller shaft passes.

335. Stiffener. An angle bar, T bar, channel, built-up section, etc., used to stiffen plating of a bulkhead, etc.

336. Stopwater. Canvas soaked in red lead or other material, fitted between two metal parts to make a watertight joint.

337. Storm valve. A check valve in a pipe opening above water line on a ship.

338. Stow. To put away.

339. Stowage. Equipment for support and fastening of articles to be stowed, as anchor or boat stowage.

340. Strain. Alteration in shape or dimensions resulting from stress.

341. Strake. A course, or row, of shell or other plating.

342. Stress. Force per unit area.

343. Stringer. A fore-and-aft member used to give longitudinal strength to shell plating. According to location stringers are called *hold stringers, bilge stringers, side stringers,* etc.

344. Stringer plate. (*a*) Deck plate at outboard edge of deck, connected to the shell of a ship by welding or with an angle; (*b*) Web of built-up side stringers.

345. Strongback. (*a*) Portable supporting girders for hatch covers; (*b*) a rig used in straightening bent plates; (*c*) a bar for locking cargo ports, (*d*) a central girder to support covers of wood, metal, or canvas.

346. Strum box. The enlarged terminal on the suction end of a pipe and forming a strainer that prevents the entrance of material likely to choke the pipe. See *Rose box.*

347. Strut. Outboard support for ·propeller tail shaft, used on ships with more than one propeller.

348. Superstructure. A structure extending across the ship, built immediately above the uppermost complete deck.

349. Swash plate. Baffle plate in tank to prevent excessive movement of the contained liquid.

350. Sweat batten. A plank attached to the inboard surface of the frames to prevent cargo touching the shell which may be damp due to the difference in temperature of the water outside and the air in the hold.

351. Tail shaft. Short section of propeller shaft extending through stern tube and carrying propeller.

352. Tangency bracket. A bracket whose inner face is curved rather than straight to distribute the stress over the face of the bracket rather than concentrate it in the corners (Fig. 93).

353. Tank. Compartment for liquid or gas, either built into ship's structure or independent of it and supported by an auxiliary foundation.

354. Tank top. The inner-bottom plating.

355. Template. A mold or pattern made to the exact size of a piece of work that is to be laid out or formed and on which such information as the position of rivet holes and size of laps is indicated. Common types are made of paper or thin boards.

356. Tension. Stress caused by pulling.

357. Thrust. Push or driving force.

358. Thrust bearing. Bearing on propeller line shaft, which relieves the engine from the driving force of the propeller and transfers this force to the structure of the ship.

359. Tie plank. The fastening which keeps the ship from sliding down the ways; also called *solepiece.*

360. Tie plate. A single fore-and-aft course of plating attached to deck beams under a wood deck to give extra strength.

361. Tiller. Arm attached to rudderhead for operating the rudder.

362. Transom. The aftermost transverse frame.

363. Transverse. Athwartship; at right angles to the keel.

364. Transverse frames. Athwartship members forming the ship's "ribs."

365. Trim. To shift ballast to make a ship change its position in the water. The trim is the excess of draft forward or aft.

366. Tripping bracket. A small piece of steel placed beside a plate or shape to prevent its collapsing or folding over. A more correct name would be *antitripping bracket.*

367. Trunk. Steel casing passing through deck and forming an enclosure for ladders or cargo hatches.

368. Tumble home. Slant inboard of a ship's side above the bilge.

369. 'Tween decks. The space between any two continuous decks; also called *between decks*.

370. Uptake. A metal casing connecting the boiler smokebox with the base of the smokestack. It conveys the smoke and hot gases from the boiler to the stack.

371. Ventilator. A device for furnishing fresh air to compartments below deck.

372. Vertical keel. Row of vertical plates extending along center of flat plate keel. Sometimes called *center keelson*.

373. Voice tube. Large speaking tube.

374. Warping bridge. Bridge at after end of hull, used while docking a ship; also called *docking bridge*.

375. Water line. The line of the water's edge when the ship is afloat; technically, the intersection of any horizontal plane with the molded form of the ship.

376. Watertight. So constructed as to prevent the passage of water.

377. Watertight flat. Short section of watertight deck, forming a step in a bulkhead or the top of a watertight compartment or water tank.

378. Waterway. A narrow passage along the edge of the deck for the drainage of the deck. A gutter.

379. Ways. Structure on which a ship is built and launched.

380. Weather deck. See *Deck, weather*.

381. Web. The vertical portion of a beam, the athwartship portion of a frame, etc.

382. Web frame. A built-up member consisting of a web plate, to the edges of which are attached single or double bars if riveted, or a face plate, if welded.

383. Welding. Making a joint of two metal parts by fusing the metal in between them or by forging together at welding heat.

384. Well. Space in bottom of a ship to which bilge water runs so that it may be pumped out.

385. Wheel. (*a*) Nickname for propeller; (*b*) steering-gear control.

386. Winch. A small hoisting engine, usually used in connection with the cargo gear.

387. Windlass. The machine used to hoist the anchors.

388. Wind sail. A tubular canvas ventilator open at the bottom and with a slot at the top. At each side of the slot are two large canvas flaps which direct the wind into the slot and down into the space to be ventilated.

389. Wind scoop. A device used to divert air into a compartment of a ship through an air port.

BOOKS RECOMMENDED FOR ADVANCED STUDY

The list below by no means covers the advanced field. There are numerous valuable books not listed here. The following texts have been carefully reviewed and are recommended to the ambitious student.

Naval Architecture and Strength of Materials

COMSTOCK, J. P.: "Introduction to Naval Architecture," Simmons-Boardman Publishing Corporation, New York. An excellent text for the beginner in naval architecture whether a high-school graduate or a transfer from some other branch of engineering. Combines the theoretical and the practical considerations of ship design. Very clearly written.

ATTWOOD and PENGELLY: "Theoretical Naval Architecture," Longmans, Green and Company, New York. A standard work on naval architecture. More advanced than Comstock's book above. Well written and up to date. Numerous practical problems add to its value.

TAYLOR, ADM. D. W.: "The Speed and Power of Ships," U.S. Maritime Administration, Washington, D.C. A classical work on speed, power, and propulsion. The curves given in the back of the book are invaluable to the naval architect and marine engineer. Highly recommended.

"Principles of Naval Architecture," 2 vols., Society of Naval Architects and Marine Engineers, New York. Written by a group of professionals and edited by Russell and Chapman. This book is more a reference book than a textbook. Highly technical. No problems. Not recommended for the beginner, but an excellent book for more advanced students.

MURRAY, A. J.: "Strength of Ships," Longmans, Green and Company, New York. Now out of print but still available in some bookstores. The age of the book limits its value, but it is still of considerable use to the student.

LOVETT, W. J.: "Applied Naval Architecture," Longmans, Green and Company, New York. The application of the principles of naval architecture to practical problems. A good text but has not been revised to cover modern practice. Still of value to the student.

HOVGAARD, WILLIAM: "The Structural Design of Warships," United States Naval Institute, Annapolis, Md. An excellent treatise on the design of warships. Revised 1940.

MANNING and SCHUMACHER: "Principles of Warship Construction and Damage Control," United States Naval Institute, Annapolis, Md. A treatise on the fundamental principles of naval architecture and the control of hull damage. Written for the operating personnel of the United States Navy. "The Design and Methods of Construction of Welded Steel Merchant Vessels." The material in this book is the final report of the board of investigation convened by the Secretary of the Navy to inquire into the failures of welded merchant ships built during the Second World War. The report is complete with photographs, drawings, and tables and gives methods for overcoming the failures. Highly recommended. Published by the Government Printing Office, Washington, D.C.

LEIGH and MANGOLD: "Practical Mechanics and Strength of Materials," McGraw-Hill Book Company, Inc., New York. An excellent book for the beginner. Advanced mathematics not required to follow the reasoning.

TIMOSHENKO and McCULLOUGH: "Elements of Strength of Materials," D. Van Nostrand Company, Inc., New York. More advanced than the preceding text. Well presented. A knowledge of calculus is necessary.

SKENE, N. L.: "Elements of Yacht Design," Kennedy Bros., Inc., New York. A good book for students interested in the design of small boats.

Marine Engineering

"Naval Machinery," United States Naval Institute, Annapolis, Md. Discusses the fundamentals behind the design of the main propelling and auxiliary-machinery units. A good elementary text. Mostly descriptive.

"Marine Engineering," 2 vols., Society of Naval Architects and Marine Engineers, New York. Written by a group of experts. Gives the design principles of marine engines and auxiliaries. Too advanced for the beginner.

OSBOURNE, ALLEN: "Modern Marine Engineer's Manual," 2 vols., Cornell Maritime Press, New York. A good all-round handbook for the operating personnel. Also contains valuable design data.

LABBERTON, J. M.: "Marine Engineering," McGraw-Hill Book Company, Inc., New York. An excellent book for the beginner. Broad coverage of the field, backed up by practical problems.

CHAPMAN, L. B.: "Marine Power Plant," McGraw-Hill Book Company, Inc., New York. Deals primarily with merchant vessels. Good coverage of the engineering developments in foreign ships. Suitable for the beginner.

INDEX